AUDITORIUM

Auditorium International **01**

Editorial Director: Claudio Chianura

Title: *The Sound of the North*
Author: Luca Vitali
English Translation: Melinda Mele
Edited by Fiona Talkington

Printed in Italy

www.auditoriumedizioni.it

THE

Luca Vitali

SOUND
OF THE
NORTH

NORWAY
AND THE
EUROPEAN
JAZZ SCENE

Contents

II - The sound of contemporary jazz in Norway

A guide to the treasures of Norwegian jazz
by Fiona Talkington

It's very difficult to have a quiet cup of coffee or a drink in Norway. It seems that any solitary moment in a bar or café somehow leads to a conversation and, before you get to the bottom of the glass, you're deep in conversation with a writer, film-maker or musician. Before they get to the bottom of their glass they've introduced you to a painter they know, a lighting designer or a choreographer. I know children in Norway can pretty much ski as soon as they can walk, but can they play guitar before they can do a jigsaw puzzle? Where does all this creativity come from? How is it nurtured? And will it continue to be like this? This isn't the book to give all those answers, but, by putting together the colourful mosaic which is the story of jazz in Norway over the last 50 years or so, it goes a long way to understanding the remarkable creative spirit that is Norway.

It never ceases to astonish me that there are now, I'd say, five generations of musicians working effectively, creatively and passionately in Norway. How lucky we are, those of us who live outside Norway, to have been exposed to their music, to have been drawn in to their belief in the individual's search for a voice, to their willingness to listen to others, their technical brilliance, their pride in what they do, and their humility.

Humility is such an important part of this picture. "How can you be interested in us when you come from London?" was the constant refrain when I first started visiting Norway. Norwegian musicians will often give you their friends' CDs to listen to while leaving their own new projects at the bottom of the bag. You have to spend a lot of time listening, establishing understanding and trust, to elicit the news of a new (and undoubtedly brilliant) project from someone.

Humility, trust, the ability to listen, and a belief in the music, are the qualities which Luca Vitali has brought to his quest to uncover the history of Norwegian jazz, to find some of the reasons for its success today and to fill in the gaps for the global audience which has grown to love and admire so many Norwegian musicians through recordings and live performances.

With a gentle yet incisive approach, with a warm humour and a deep admiration for the music and musicians and for all those who work so hard in the music industries, for sound engineers, labels, venues and management, Luca has produced the classic and important history which needed to be written. Fans of Norwegian jazz around the world will welcome this new English translation.

But this is more than a history book, this is a view from abroad, one person's journey of discovery told through his own experiences and his encounters with musicians, writers, journalists, promoters and record labels.

Through this story he steers us through influences from America, traditional music from throughout Norway, and from nature. We learn more about the voice of the marching bands, the growth of conservatoires and the strength of music education, the importance of festivals, church music and clubs. There's the emergence of ECM and the vital exposure the label gave to the rest of the world, the cultural relationship with the rest of Europe, and the confidence of young labels today. He talks about the uncompromising belief in the importance of sound and the growth of the Norwegian sound engineers as world leaders in their field. And, of course, we're asked to consider what jazz is, and where it meets other genres classical or folk, and its place in other art forms.

Luca Vitali has gone to Norway not to intrude or take away its musical treasures, but, with humility and respect, to uncover and reveal the riches which are enduring, the creative and human spirit of a seemingly quiet and reserved nation which, actually, has so much to say and so much to give.

This book tells the story of an important chapter in Norway's history in the way it needed to be told, by exactly the right person.

Reading, UK, May 2015

Fiona Talkington is a BBC Radio presenter, curator and writer with many years working with collaborative projects in Norway.

Dialogue and understanding
by Paolo Fresu

Everybody knows that jazz today is the music of the world. It followed the migration of omnivorous man and took the train from the fields of Louisiana to the great American cities, only to arrive, after World War II, in the European capitals. Not many know, however, that if you wanted to speak about European jazz in those days it wasn't enough to say Paris, London, or Berlin. There were apparently marginal and unsuspected places where this music thrived, toning down the frigid Nordic temperatures with its hybrid sounds of saxophones and trumpets.

Before American musicians ever played in Rome they were performing in Copenhagen, Oslo and Stockholm, where there was a very lively scene, a large audience of jazz enthusiasts, and a scanty (at the time) group of curious and bulimic musicians.

While it's true that there is a rich and legendary literature on European jazz thanks to a few films and to the stories of Chet Baker, Miles Davis and Dexter Gordon, it's also true that Scandinavia was one of the doors that European jazz walked through.

After all Scandinavia is, along with Italy, the place where not only more jazz is produced (and consumed) but also where it fully acquires its original sense as a dynamic music that moves through the planet's crossroads, becoming both a contemporary language and geographically indistinct.

This precious text by Luca Vitali on Norwegian jazz becomes a magnifying lens on the new reality of European jazz, because it illustrates how a relatively small world like Norway can feed on new languages only when it's able to relate to a larger world.

If this has happened and continues to happen, then one can state without the slightest doubt that a European jazz does exist, and a jazz of the world as well. A jazz that stands on its own equal to American jazz, and that is able to give some meaning to the previous century's migrations that opened the doors of continents and tore down the barriers of oceans.

Could it make sense, then, to think of music not only as a tool for redemption but also as one for dialogue and understanding? The answer is yes. It happened in the past between the two coasts at the opposite sides of an immense ocean. In the hope that the new migrations in the Mediterranean will cease being the cause of tragic deaths and become an opportunity for discovery and liberation.

London, November 2013

Champagne and jazz music
by Jan Granlie

It's not a big surprise that Luca Vitali wrote a book about the Norwegian jazz covering the last four or five decades. After all, over the last years he's been a great ambassador for the Norwegian jazz scene and for Norwegian jazz musicians abroad, especially in Italy.

I met Luca for the first time during the showcase JazzNorway in a Nutshell. I think it was in Bergen or Stavanger, some years ago. I realised immediately that he was extremely up to date on what was going on in little Norway. Maybe you think that if you're interested in the new European jazz scene then of course you have to be up to date with what's happening in freezing Norway, with artists like Jan Garbarek, Terje Rypdal, Nils Petter Molvær, Arve Henriksen, Sidsel Endresen and many others who have definitely passed the age of 30 and have been at the forefront of the European jazz scene over the last decades. But it's quite unusual for a simple and ordinary guy from Bologna, who's not working with jazz as a professional, to be so interested, so knowledgeable, and a good friend of so many Norwegian jazz musicians, journalists and festival promoters.

Luca Vitali begins his book talking about the pianist and band leader George Russell, who lived in Sweden during the 1960s, and also visited Norway from time to time. It was at the Molde International Jazz Festival, in 1964 I think, that he met Jan Garbarek during a jam session. Jan Garbarek has told the story that he was playing in a jam session with some Norwegian musicians and that suddenly he felt lifted up by the pianist. And when he turned around he saw that George Russell had been sitting in on the piano.

The book talks about what happened in Oslo at that time. Many jazz clubs opened, and there were a lot of young musicians playing all around town. And a lot of foreign musicians were visiting some of the clubs, especially the Metropol. In mid 1960s Club 7 was established as a centre for jazz, blues and rock music, but also a centre for alternative theatre, film and contemporary art, a club that Luca knows a lot about. Luca also talks about the "Norwegian sound", jazz's connections to folk music, and music education. He's been talking with a lot of jazz musicians, DJs and people who are involved in the Norwegian jazz scene.

Luca Vitali isn't like everybody else. He is one of the few who know more about the Norwegian jazz scene than most Norwegians, and I'm not talking about ordinary Norwegians who are more interested in Idol and other stupid television shows, I'm talking about musicians, journalists and festival promoters.

Over the last ten years or so he's been regularly travelling to Norway to listen to Norwegian jazz and meet the jazz people, going to the festivals and clubs, travelling to Spitsbergen almost at the North Pole, and to the Punkt festival in the south of Norway. He's been to Oslo many times, to Bergen, Voss and Stavanger on the west coast, and to the Ice Festival up in the mountains in the middle of the freezing winter. And everywhere he goes he meets good old friends from his earlier visits. He's also constantly making new friends who are involved in the jazz business, because he's interested and jazz is his passion.

There's only one thing he can't deal with, and that's good and expensive champagne!

Oslo, January 2013
(Jazznytt NO)

I

The Evolution of Jazz in Norway:
from Garbarek to the New Millennium

MAIN CITIES
IN NORWAY
1. Oslo
2. Bergen
3. Stavanger/Sandnes
4. Trondheim
5. Kristiansand
6. Tønsberg
7. Ålesund
8. Haugesund
9. Bodø
10. Tromsø
11. Molde
12. Flekkefjord
13. Geilo
14. Hamar
15. Kongsberg
16. Lillehammer
17. Narvik
18. Skien
19. Sula
20. Voss
21. Svalbard

1
George Russell: influence and inspiration
The importance of Russell's *Lydian Chromatic Concept*
and of folk music in the development of jazz in Norway

"For years Americans have regarded European jazz with the same tolerant smile they reserve for Japanese baseball. But something is stirring in the Old World. A generation of musicians is emerging from Europe's jazz underground, and now they're raising a tolerant smile at the mention of American jazz. Talk to them about the current state of the music, and it's as if an old and dear friend has passed away. They believe American jazz is retreating into the past while Europe is moving the music into the 21st century." [1]

The aim of this book is not to set European or indeed Norwegian jazz against African-American jazz, but rather to shed light on the evolution and importance of the often underrated Norwegian scene, which was sparked by one of the leading figures in contemporary American jazz, George Russell. Until Russell's arrival the Norwegian jazz scene had followed the styles of the legendary American stars, and it now began to enter a period of freedom that - from Jan Garbarek to the present day - transformed it into one of the world's richest and most innovative scenes. Everything began in the 1960s, when Russell moved to Scandinavia and began to create the opening chapters of a story about people, encounters, traditions, culture and so much more.

Russell arrived in Scandinavia in 1964, having just finished touring Europe with his sextet (himself, Barre Phillips, Thad Jones, Joe Farrell, Garnett Brown and Albert "Tootie" Heath). He had been planning to stay in Sweden where, amongst other things, he'd been working at the University of Lund, but later he decided to move to Oslo. There he had a relationship with Marit Jerstad, a member of NyMusikk (the Norwegian branch of ISCM, the International Society of Contemporary Music) and so made an immediate connection with the contemporary music scene. His own influence would soon be felt. Russell's book *Lydian Chromatic Concept of Tonal Organization*[2] had been published in the United States in the early 1950s but his music hadn't had much of a following, and so he arrived in Europe with all his understandable frustrations to find that Scandinavia was a highly receptive place. He was particularly struck by the

George Russell[3] was born in Cincinnati in 1923, the adopted son of a registered nurse and a chef on the B&O Railroad. He began playing drums with the Boy Scouts Drum and Bugle Corps and eventually received a scholarship to Wilberforce University, where he joined the Collegians, whose list of alumni includes Coleman Hawkins, Benny Carter, Fletcher Henderson, Ben Webster, Cootie Williams, Ernie Wilkins and Frank Foster. But his most valuable musical education came in 1941, when, in attempting to enlist in the Marines, he was diagnosed with tuberculosis, spending six months in the hospital where he was taught the fundamentals of harmony from a fellow patient. From the hospital he sold his first work, "New World," to Benny Carter. He joined Benny Carter's Band, but was replaced by Max Roach; after Russell heard Roach, he decided to give up drumming. He moved to New York where he was part of a group of musicians who gathered in the basement apartment of Gil Evans. The circle included Miles Davis, Gerry Mulligan, Max Roach, Johnny Carisi and on occasion, Charlie Parker.

He was commissioned to write a piece for Dizzy Gillespie's orchestra; the result was the seminal "Cubano Be/Cubano Bop," the first fusion of Afro-Cuban rhythms with jazz, premiered at Carnegie Hall in 1947 and featuring Chano Pozo. Two years later his "Bird in Igor's Yard" was recorded by Buddy DeFranco, a piece notable for its fusion of elements from Charlie Parker and Stravinsky. It was a remark made by Miles Davis when George asked him his musical aim which set Russell on the course which has been his life. Miles said he "wanted to learn all the changes". Since Miles obviously knew all the changes, Russell surmised that what he meant was he wanted to learn a new way to relate to chords. This began a quest for Russell, and again hospitalized for 16 months, he began to develop his *Lydian Chromatic Concept of Tonal Organization* [see Box].

[…] Disillusioned by his lack of recognition and the meagre work opportunities in America, he arrived in a wheelchair in Scandinavia in 1964, but returned five years later in spiritual health. In Sweden and Norway he found support for both himself and his music. All his works were recorded by radio and TV, and he was championed by Bosse Broberg, the adventurous director of Swedish Radio, an organization with which Russell maintains a close association and admiration. While there, he heard and recorded a young Jan Garbarek, Terje Rypdal, and Jon Christensen.

In 1969, he returned to the States at the request of his old friend Gunther Schuller to teach at the newly created Jazz Department of the New England Conservatory, where Schuller was president. […] In 1986, he was invited by the Contemporary Music Network of the British Council to tour with an orchestra of American and British musicians, which resulted in The International Living Time Orchestra, which has been touring and performing since that time. Among the soloists of stature are Stanton Davis, Dave Bargeron, Brad Hatfield, Steve Lodder, Tiger Okoshi, and Andy Sheppard. The musicians developed a rare understanding of the music, astonishing audiences with fiery music both complex and challenging, but added to the dynamism and electric power of funk and rock. Russell himself was a tremendously visual leader, dancing and forming architectural structures with his hands. The Living Time Orchestra has toured all over the world.

young saxophonist Jan Garbarek and by the drummer Jon Christensen, and wanted them in his band in Stockholm. They met for the first time at the Molde Festival in 1964, where Garbarek and Christensen had gone to see Russell's sextet. Russell was not the usual bop star who's come to play standards with a local trio, but the leader of a regular band that played original compositions based on a new concept of music organisation. The meeting left an indelible mark on the two Norwegian musicians, especially when George Russell unexpectedly joined their quartet (Garbarek, Christensen, Arild Andersen on double bass and Terje Bjørklund on piano) sitting in for Bjørklund in a thrilling jam session. Russell was volcanic, striking the keyboard with his fists, his elbows and his entire body, feeding an irresistible energy into the group. Garbarek recalls:

"I usually have my eyes closed, we were playing very hard, and free, lots of energy. Suddenly it was like somebody pushed a button and everything went up about fifty notches. There was this tremendous energy, out of this world, and I went for it, and then I looked back and saw our usual piano player wasn't sitting there but it was George who was playing piano. He was playing with his fists, his elbows, using the piano like a drum kit, so we were absolutely out there in a chromatic universe. And afterwards he came to me and he wanted me to join his sextet and go on tour around the world, and that was a very, very crucial moment for me. It was the first time the idea of possibly becoming a musician entered my head."[4]

As the thought of becoming a professional musician crossed his mind, Garbarek was still a 17 year-old school student. Two years before, in 1962, he'd won the prestigious amateur jazz contest Norgesmesterskapet, but because of pressure from his parents decided not to take up the opportunity to join Russell's band. Christensen was a few years older and had been playing regularly since he was 17, becoming a member of Bud Powell's band at 19 and playing at the Metropol, one of Oslo's historical jazz clubs. He was a self-taught drummer and couldn't read music, but in order to play Russell's sextet and big-band music and arrangements bought several of his records and practised the parts: "At that time there were no jazz conservatories, and so we would just listen to the records and play over them".[5]

Russell understood Garbarek's choice, but after some time he insisted, inviting him to some radio and TV recordings in Sweden. He sent him a big parcel with all the saxophone parts and the arrangements for big band and sextet, but Garbarek too, like most Norwegian musicians, was self-taught and couldn't read music. Yet Russell wouldn't give up:

"He said, "You have three months, get it together and then you can come to Stockholm and we'll record this stuff". So that was a very intense three months for me! I went there and I survived, shall I say. I certainly was not great; I still had a problem reading, and I was sitting next to older musicians who were my heroes, basically. The other tenor saxophone player was Berndt Rosengren, the Swedish sax player, who next to Coltrane and Dexter he was the one for me, and there I was next to him! But I learned a lot, and George was trying to teach me." [6]

Garbarek received a copy of *Lydian Chromatic Concept of Tonal Organization* from Russell and went to a few of his seminars, delving into the theoretical aspects of music under the guidance of one of the greatest innovators of the period. In Garbarek's view, Russell's book is a veritable textbook of jazz improvisation. Many years later pianist Gil Goldstein said about Russell's book:

"This concept is based on the idea of tonal gravity, resting the tonal organisation of music firmly upon a tonal centre, inferred by a vertical factor (a chord) or a horizontal factor, the tonic to which a melody or sequence of chords tends to cadence." [7]

These theories had an immediate impact, especially in jazz circles, becoming the direct source for most of the early experimentations by artists such as John Coltrane and Miles Davis, and gradually attracting more and more musicians toward the new "modal" form.

Russell's path was a strange one. He began as a drummer during the be-bop period, and while hospitalized for tuberculosis got into music theory. One of his first compositions is the 1947 "Cubano Be Cubano Bop" for Dizzy Gillespie's orchestra, followed by the fantastic score of "A Bird in Igor's Yard," played by clarinettist Buddy DeFranco's big band, in which Russell made a sort of synthesis between Charlie "Bird" Parker and Igor Stravinsky, bringing together modern jazz and contemporary classical music.

In Norway, George Russell didn't just promote the Lydian Chromatic Concept. He pushed his pupils and sidemen to search for new rhythms and sounds, urging them to dig into the treasure trove of Scandinavian folk music and to blend it with other traditions, to fearlessly and shamelessly integrate into the limited (in his view) language of jazz other colours and rhythms from the most disparate sources. Russell's suggestion attracted a lot of interest, and the purists in the

Lydian Cromatic Concept of Tonal Organization[8] Written in 1953, Russell's text had a profound influence on the evolution of jazz, and on musicians such as Coltrane and works like Miles Davis's *Kind of Blue*, which owes a great deal to Russell's "system". The book presents a chart in which every type of chord is associated with a scale derived from the Lydian mode. The scales or modes offer the improvising musician a wide range of possibilities, opening new horizons for both musicians and composers. In offering sound material, the author's aim is to demonstrate that there is a progressive relationship of consonance/dissonance with the underlying harmony. The first scale presented best embodies the sound and identity of the chord, while a series of alternative scales provide a sort of colour palette - possible ways to change the chord without altering its tonal function. Some results of this approach could already be heard in *George Russell Sextet at the Five Spot* (Decca, 1960), featuring sounds that were highly original though still steeped in a bop context. Composers like Jan Garbarek, Kenny Wheeler and Keith Jarrett developed their own sound taking inspiration from Russell's book, achieving those wide-open ambiences on which a large part of modern European jazz is based. Focusing on specific notes in every scale/mode, these musicians were able to make music without having to rely on the more complex progressions of functional harmony.

world of ethnomusicology began to wonder whether this was in line with the spirit of Norwegian folk music. But to George Russell everything was very clear: "I think music is man's highest language. That's why it's understood the world over [...] You should be able to feel music and learn how to live your life or solve problems".[9]

During his five years in Scandinavia from 1964 to 1969, Russell managed to bring together all the best local jazz musicians, Swedes and Norwegians playing together in a big band ironically led by an American. Something similar had only happened in Scandinavia in 1958, when Quincy Jones directed the Swedish Radio Big Band. Russell's band as it went into the studio for various recording sessions in 1967 included new members Terje Rypdal on guitar, Arild Andersen on bass and Egil "Bop" Johansen (who had worked with Quincy Jones) on percussion. They had joined Garbarek and Christensen as well as the best players on the Swedish jazz scene (including trumpeter Jan Allan and sax players Arne Domnérus, Niels Rosendahl, Lennart Åberg and Bernt Rosengren).

The Norwegian quartet of Garbarek, Rypdal, Andersen and Christensen returned to the studio with Russell and with American trumpeter Stanton Davis in 1970, to record *Trip to Prillarguri*, the only album where one can hear Garbarek play a composition by Ornette Coleman, "Man on the Moon".

Garbarek underwent a real change, shifting from an early bop period in the style of Dexter Gordon towards free jazz, inspired by the musician who had blown him away when he was 14 years old: John Coltrane. From Coltrane he then focused on the freest spirits of the New Thing: Pharoah Sanders, Archie Shepp and especially Albert Ayler. In the next recording session two years later, Garbarek gave a free-jazz rendition of a Norwegian folk melody, bearing witness to Ayler's and Coleman's influence on him, to his rapid parting from be-bop, and to the impact of Russell's mentoring in this return to his Norwegian folk roots. In order to bring in other assorted folk elements, Russell invited as a guest in his band trumpeter Don Cherry, whose music is rich with African and Indian influences. And as Garbarek recalls, Cherry was influential in urging him and many other Norwegian musicians to rediscover their folk music:

> "It was Don who first got us interested in our own folk music, who made us realise how much there was to check out in our own backyard. We were to make a radio broadcast once, and Don asked us if we couldn't perhaps play a Norwegian folk tune. That wasn't exactly what we young Norwegian jazzers were into at the time! But we came to change." [10]

In the late 1960s Cherry was working with Swedish, Turkish and South African musicians.[11] His personality was intense, but he was also very versatile, and at ease with wide-ranging styles and aesthetics. Cherry always had a vocation for collective improvisation that propelled him into free jazz explorations, not just with Ornette Coleman, and the output of these bands showed that the blending of different musical traditions and cultures could widen the language of jazz, offering fresh stimuli through the use of new tone colours, unusual tempos, and much more.

The work of Americans Quincy Jones and George Russell in Sweden was of central importance in the formative years of a Scandinavian jazz tradition - the expression "formative" is carefully used in this context. That the two enjoyed cult status among Scandinavian musicians is not difficult to comprehend. Both had the best credentials, Jones via Lionel Hampton and Russell via Gillespie. The two clearly had something of a charismatic effect on their more reserved Scandinavian colleagues. Jones was at the time an avowed fan of Swedish folk music, a colourful arranger in a bebop-based style who, whilst utilising the whole palette of big band effects, had a keen ear for individual instrumental timbres. Russell, through his Lydian Concept, was more overtly academic in his approach, without sacrificing his sense of humour, and was more of a pedagogue in his attitude than Jones, who was very much a showman in the best sense of the word. Their joint contribution to the emergence of a Scandinavian jazz tradition lies in their intense professionalism, a quality which could be more easily appreciated in Sweden in the 1950s and 1960s than in Norway, where amateurism in music was deeply ingrained in society, and which to this day constitutes a hindrance to the process of raising musical standards in many rural districts. Jones, Russell and Cherry showed the Scandinavians what they could achieve, and all who took part in their jazz "mini-universities" had ample time to find hidden depths in themselves and to acquire confidence and experience before going further in their own countries and abroad to distinguish themselves in improvised music, composition and experimentation. Cherry in particular was in the forefront of the movement soon to be known as "world" music which was to impinge upon certain areas in Norwegian jazz frequented by Russell alumni such as Garbarek, Jon Christensen, Terje Rypdal and Arild Andersen. Already in 1960 Russell had prophesied that many new sounds and rhythms would have to find their way into the language of jazz to help compensate for its then inadequate musical palette, and Garbarek's "open space" aesthetic (the term coined by Garbarek's Norwegian biographer Tor Dybo)[12] follows such a line of development. It is clear that the developments which took place in Norwegian jazz after 1970 did not occur in isolation. The compositional techniques used by Andersen and Garbarek were test-driven in the workshops of Russell in Stockholm and fine tuned in Norway as individual careers developed and opportunity allowed. Ethnic co-operation, often in the shape of immigrant percussionists, helped to broaden the rhythmic palettes of the Norwegian arranger/performers, but Norwegian jazz has never lost contact with its roots, both classical and folk. Norwegian folk music was just one element, albeit a major one, in the unfolding of the history of Norwegian jazz in the 1960s, 1970s and later.[13]

2
Little Oslo
Jazz becomes a new art form: the Munch Museum, the Henie Onstad Art Centre (Svein Finnerud Trio, Arne Nordheim, Jon Christensen, Karin Krog and Garbarek/Andersen/Rypdal's early period)[14]

Contact with the United States was rare until the 1940s, when several Norwegian musicians began to play on the transatlantic ocean liners that sailed between Oslo and New York, and bought records and went to concerts while they were abroad. There hadn't been any opportunities so far to see American musicians performing in Norway, as there had been in the rest of Europe. It was only after World War II that things started to change, with American jazz establishing a firm presence in the late 1950s, when Jazz at the Philharmonic[15] arrived in Oslo. Norman Granz's famous project, comprising concerts and live-recordings and later touring, featured some of the most important and celebrated musicians of the American jazz scene of the time: Roy Eldridge, Ella Fitzgerald, Stan Getz, Dizzy Gillespie and Lionel Hampton, to name just a few.

It was about then that Randi Hultin, a journalist with the Norwegian daily newspaper *Dagbladet* and the wife of Tor Hultin (a jazz pianist working as Josephine Baker's accompanist at the time) began to take an interest in jazz. She had never followed music, preferring the visual arts which she had studied, but her husband Tor "gave me the jazz bacillus" - as she herself wrote in the dedication of her book *Born under the sign of jazz*.[16] Though their marriage fell apart after fourteen years, Randi Hultin's love for jazz only increased, and she went on to become one the most authoritative music critics on the scene. After 1953 her home started becoming a hub for African-American jazz in Oslo. Hultin threw after-concert parties, and in time this house in the Gartnerveien neighbourhood became the favourite hangout for Americans passing through Oslo - the ideal setting, a home away from home, where fully-fledged jam sessions would often take place.[17]

Born in Oslo in 1926, Hultin began to write about jazz in 1956 and continued until shortly before her death on 18 March 2000. After working for several years for *Dagbladet* she moved to another newspaper, *Aftenposten*, and had her own show on Norwegian public radio. She also collaborated with various jazz magazines in Norway, Sweden, Poland, the UK (*Jazz Journal International*) and the United States (*Downbeat*). Randi Hultin didn't just cover American jazz musicians, and relying on her celebrity status in the American jazz world she began acting as an ambassador for young Norwegian talents trying to make it abroad. In 1966 she accompanied Karin Krog and Jan Garbarek's quartet on their first international tour, introducing them to the jazz circles in Czechoslovakia and Poland.

Norwegian jazz in the fifties had been a movement characterized by optimism and progress. Together with the material growth in Norwegian society and the fascination for America, jazz experienced increasing popularity. Not even the entrance of rock in the mid-1950s caused the jazz milieu any lasting harm. In 1960 there were thirty jazz clubs in Norway, more than ever before.

The high level of activity continued, and the number of jazz clubs had settled at around 30 in the period 1960-64. You could listen to jazz six days a week at the Metropol Jazzcenter in Oslo (1960-65) and Hotel Neptun in Bergen (1961-64). Cooperation with Jazzhus Montmartre in Copenhagen (from 1961) and Gyllene Cirkeln in Stockholm (from 1962) made extended visits by famous American jazz musicians possible. There was no dancing at Neptun, Montmartre or Gyllene Cirkeln, and if there was dancing at Metropol, jazz was also here mostly music for listening; at this time jazz was becoming more art than entertainment.[18]

It was in these years that the American giants came to Europe, and could be heard jamming with local musicians in the jazz clubs of most European capitals; the four Scandinavian venues mentioned above started collaborating in 1961, booking overseas artists and projects. The 1950s were characterized by a wide range of styles - from Dixieland and swing, to bop and cool and a fusion of these into the concept of mainstream - but in the years 1958-62 free jazz slowly emerged, along with the names of ground-breaking American musicians John Coltrane, Cecil Taylor, Ornette Coleman, Don Cherry, Eric Dolphy, Archie Shepp and Albert Ayler. Finally, the new wave of more experimental jazz landed in Oslo; some of those concerts were co-produced by the Norwegian Jazz Federation and NyMusikk, and they all went on to transform the jazz scene. In the autumn of 1962 Finn Mortensen[19] praised Cecil Taylor's first concert at the Metropol, and did the same a year and a half later when Don Ellis performed in the same venue.

Yet despite this wave of new music, older swing and mainstream musicians such as Rowland Greenberg (trumpet), Pete Brown (drums), Arvid Gram Paulsen (tenor sax), Scott Lunde (piano), Kristian Bergheim (tenor sax) and

Øystein Ringstad (piano), all born between 1920-1927, continued to be very successful. In addition, there was a younger crowd of be-bop and cool jazz musicians, born in the 1930s, equally worthy of mention: Mikkel Flagstad, Totti Bergh, Harald Bergersen (tenor sax), Einar Iversen, Eivin Sannes, Tore Sandnæs, Kjell Karlsen (piano), Atle Hammer (trumpet), Asmund Bjørken (accordion and alto sax), Erik Amundsen (bass), Karin Krog (voice), Alf Kjellmann (baritone sax), Karl Otto Hoff, Svein-Erik "Atom-Jørgen" Gaardvik and Kjell Johansen (drums), as well as the even younger Bjørn Johansen (tenor sax, b. 1940) and Erik Andresen (alto sax, b. 1941). Many of these artists were regulars with the leading big bands of the period, for example Kjell Karlsen's Orchestra (1959-1964) - Oslo's Penguin Club house band. Others, such as Bjarne Nerem (tenor sax), Andreas Skjold (trombone) and Egil "Bop" Johansen (drums), made a name for themselves abroad, especially in Sweden, whose jazz scene was more cosmopolitan than that of more "remote" Norway.

Norway's most important jazz award, the Buddy Prize (Buddy-prisen), was established by the Norwegian Jazz Federation[20] in 1956 and that first year was presented to the trumpet player Rowland Greenberg. More traditional artists, such as Einar Iversen and Mikkel Flagstad, received the award in the following competitions. The year 1965 marked a turning point, with the award given to Karin Krog and subsequently presented to equally innovative artists such as Jon Christensen, Jan Garbarek, Arild Andersen, Frode Thingnæs and "Calle" Neumann, following a trend that continues today.[21] Meanwhile, in May 1960, the Jazz Federation began publishing the first Norwegian jazz magazine, *Jazznytt*.

The annual amateur jazz contest Norgesmesterskapet, which had been a showcase for young talents (including a 15-year-old Jan Garbarek, in 1962) came to an end in 1964 as jazz became more part of the professional scene. Yet while jazz clubs all over the country were experiencing a golden season, the same wasn't true for record companies, which wouldn't release jazz albums (unlike their counterparts in nearby Sweden). The ice finally broke in November 1963, when Norsk Grammofonkompani recorded eleven Norwegian jazz groups (without paying the musicians) and released the compilation on Harmoni label with the title *Metropol Jazz*. The first LP featuring a single artist was released the following year: Karin Krog's *By myself*, on Philips label. And what about the media?

[*Dagbladet*] had achieved a position as the country's leading jazz newspaper, covering all styles in up-to-date articles on recordings and concerts, as well as portraits of leading jazz musicians including the avant-garde.

The first visits of John Coltrane (1963) and Charles Mingus (1964) were extensively covered by the local press, and Mingus' concert was reviewed in *Dagbladet* by modern composer Arne Nordheim [see Box]. Both of these concerts also made a deep and lasting impression on many younger jazz fans.

The national radio station NRK (until the late 1980s the only radio channel operating in Norway) covered parts of the jazz scene through talks and record presentations, and in 1959 a regular programme "Jazzklubben" (Jazz Club) was introduced, led by veteran trumpeter Thorleif Østereng. Some of the major concerts with foreign musicians and orchestras were also recorded, and NRK soon became a central source of information for jazz fans all across the country. In the early 1960s the issue of forming an NRK jazz orchestra was raised, and pianist Kjell Karlsen's big band became the predecessor to what would eventually become Thorleif Østereng's radio big band.[22]

Between 1964 and 1965 jazz appeared to plunge into a crisis, with over twenty Norwegian jazz clubs permanently closing. In the ensuing debate as to why this was happening some blamed the new music from artists such as Coltrane and Ayler, which many considered to be too difficult for large audiences, while others identified the cause for young people's disinterest in jazz in the lure of rock's electric guitars and the rise of the Beatles, the Rolling Stones and Bob Dylan. Those were the years of race riots in the States, of the escalation of the Vietnam War, of "flower power" and much more.

On the other hand, the crisis came at a time when Norwegian jazz musicians had sufficient recognition, thanks to their visibility at international festivals,[23] to aspire to greater things. So in order to tackle a difficult situation they got together, and taking inspiration from the Swedish example of Emanon,[24] on 10 March 1965 they founded Jazzforum, under Karin Krog's leadership.[25]

Jan Garbarek caught the attention of jazz listeners with new musical forms poised between jazz and art music, also drawing inspiration from the visual arts and stepping out of the jazz clubs to engage the public in venues such as museums and art galleries. In late 1966 there were only a handful of jazz clubs left in Norway: two of them were in Molde and Kongsberg (two of the first European towns to start a festival), along with a few more scattered around the country; only two new ones had opened, in Kristiansund and Ålesund. In Oslo, on the other hand, there was a flourishing of new spaces dedicated not only to music but also to other forms of art and to cultural activities in general. In particular there was the Downtown Key Club (since 1965) and the legendary Club 7 (since 1963), which started hosting jazz music in the early 1970s

Arne Nordheim (1931-2010) is one of the most celebrated figures of Norwegian music. A renowned innovator, he was the contemporary Norwegian composer who received the greatest recognition abroad. He was the recipient of many international honours, among them the Nordic Council Music Prize in 1972, and was made an honorary member of the ISCM (International Society for Contemporary Music) in 1997. Not only a composer but a foremost intellectual and music critic, after World War II Nordheim began to promote cutting-edge international musical trends, at a time when music and the arts in general were still dominated by national romanticism. He transcended and subverted the elitist standards of contemporary classical music and was a free thinker who became a model for many younger people in various musical contexts. Although his output covered all genres, he was essentially an orchestral composer. After an early period focusing on acoustic sounds, since *Solitaire* (1968) he increasingly experimented with electronic music, becoming an inspiration also for artists quite removed from the contemporary classical scene, such as Helge Sten (aka Deathprod), Geir Jenssen (aka Biosphere) and many others. *www.arnenordheim.com*

(discussed in greater detail in Chapter 7).

The Jazzforum too moved away from traditional jazz clubs and started organising concerts in places that weren't even designed for music, turning away from the typical association of jazz with dance music and entertainment. The first Oslo venue chosen for jazz concerts was the Munch Museum, which hosted a dozen Jazzforum concerts between 1965 and 1968. The musicians played for free, with a view to collecting resources for the association's future projects. In the autumn of 1965 the Jazzforum had 45 members, and a few of these were not musicians but simply music lovers wishing to do their part. Among these was, for example, Josh Bergh, one of the founders and the head of the educational section, which organised fully-fledged seminars alongside the concerts. In 1967, in acknowledgement of the good work it had done, the Jazzforum received its first government grant and could start to finance its own projects: workshops with George Russell, the promotion of Garbarek's music, as well as live recordings. The first records to be released were Egil Kapstad's *Syner* (Norsk jazzforum 1967) and *Svein Finnerud Trio* (Norsk jazzforum 1968). Many of the concerts were co-produced with ISCM, and one of these, in 1968, inaugurated what was to become one of Oslo's most important cultural centres: the Henie Onstad Kunstsenter (Art Centre), located in Høvikodden, fifteen kilometres from the capital. The music became increasingly experimental and harder to define, but in their annual report for 1968 the board of Jazzforum could confidently state that their concerts had proved that there was great interest in local jazz, and that the new spaces where one could hear live jazz in the capital four or five times a week were not simply a passing trend.

These were strange years, characterised by the steady decline of mainstream jazz and its famous venues and at the same time by hints of a new golden age that was about to explode, with the arrival in Oslo of Manfred Eicher, the founder of the German label ECM, in September 1970. Eicher had heard Jan Garbarek the previous year, in Bologna, and had been deeply affected, and so he'd decided to come to Oslo to record his album *Afric Pepperbird*. It was the beginning of the rise to international fame of the "Norwegian generation".

Oslo was swept by a flurry of cultural activity. The Henie Onstad Art Centre filled the void left by the closing jazz clubs with contemporary art events inspired by Dada and Fluxus, a movement brought to life by experimenters in various creative fields, working together towards a concept of total art that celebrated music, dance, poetry, theatre, and performance art.

The Henie Onstad was one of the first important private ventures. Oslo certainly had its art galleries, but it didn't have a space that could host experimental events in music, film and novel arts. As Lars Mørch Finborud [see Box] recalls:

"It was the first time that I'd come across such an impressive privately owned art gallery. The strangest thing was that is had been founded by Sonja Henie, the famous three-time Olympic figure skating champion (1928, 1932 and 1936) who later became an actress in Hollywood, in roles that showcased her skating. After making quite a lot of money and marrying the Norwegian shipping-magnate Niels Onstad, in the early 1960s Sonja Henie decided to put her money into a contemporary art museum. She died in 1969, just a year after the museum was opened. The Henie Onstad Art Centre was a revolutionary place, the only one to embrace all contemporary and experimental art. The museum director at the time was pianist and art-music composer Ole Henrik Moe, a very important figure who insisted on also building an auditorium and a recording studio." [26]

During that period Jan Garbarek, the Svein Finnerud Trio, Jan Erik Vold, Terje Rypdal and other musicians were doing a great deal of performing and recording. All this material is still available on tape (mostly as radio recordings at NRK archives) and has never been released, with the exception of what was more recently published by Lars Mørch Finborud's Plastic Strip Press. The so-called "ECM generation" model emerged as one that could be exported, thanks to the German label's international profile, and yet the groundbreaking scene in those years was extremely rich and not limited to Garbarek, Andersen, Christensen and Rypdal. Pianist Egil Kapstad, for example, who had been studying with guitarist and contemporary composer Bjørn Fongaard, shifted increasingly from the mainstream toward experimentation, so much so that in a 1967 interview he stated: "The jazz pianist in me is most likely on his way out of the picture".[28] The trio of talented pianist Svein Finnerud, with Bjørnar Andresen on bass and Espen Rud on drums, playing avant-garde jazz and clearly inspired by Canadian Paul Bley, came on to the scene in 1967 and immediately caught the public's attention, featuring that same year as one of the headliners in the events organised by the Jazzforum at the Kongsberg Jazzfestival. In 1968 Finnerud was the organiser of a psychedelic musical happening at the Munch Museum and performed improvisations to a graphic score at the Molde Festival. He went on to explore many other forms of experimentation between jazz and contemporary music until 1970, when Sonet Records released his *Plastic Sun*, a small masterpiece that crowned him as one of the leading figures of this modernist wave in Norwegian jazz. Through Kapstad and Finnerud the cooperation between jazz and contemporary art musicians got increasingly more intense, and in 1969 a group of composers including Arne Nordheim, Kåre Kolberg and Gunnar Sønstevold, joined forces with Karin Krog, Jan Garbarek, Terje Rypdal, Arild Andersen and a host of other musicians to record the album *Popofoni*,[29] a statement against the vapid artistic content of pop productions and of the Eurovision Song Contest.

Popofoni was recorded in 1970 and thus came after George Russell's masterpiece *Electronic Sonata for Souls Loved by Nature*,[30] which blended improvisation, electronics and ensemble passages, and on which Garbarek and friends had played. As a precursor to *Popofoni*, *Electronic Sonata* also had a profound impact on the young Terje Rypdal, who began to take an interest in compositional and orchestral aspects of contemporary symphonic music, on the trail of Polish composer Krzysztof Penderecki. The Henie Onstad Art Centre hosted the first ECM recording ever to be released, *Afric Pepperbird*, later re-recorded in the studio because Manfred Eicher apparently disliked the hall's excessive natural reverb. Many other musicians gravitated towards this creative factory, for example Carl Magnus "Calle" Neumann (alto sax), who was a stereotype of the musician with a hard and tormented life. He played both jazz and blues, and could never come to terms with the life of an international musician, taking care of bookings, public relations and promotion. Neumann was a steady sideman to Ben Webster during the year the American sax player stayed in Norway, and was a member of all the most interesting groups on the

---

Lars Mørch Finborud An important collector of all kinds of records, Lars Mørch Finborud is one of the founders of Oslo Nerd Army (*www.oslonerdarmy.no*), a blog that since the 1990s has made available to researchers, jazz lovers and collectors a large quantity of contents, musical extracts, record cover art and much more. With the income he made by selling half of his vinyl collection to a Japanese dealer (several thousand euros), in 2007 he founded Plastic Strip Press, a unique record label that publishes real gems from the period we are talking about: electronic music from the NRK archives, experimental music from the Henie Onstad Art Centre archives and from those of producer Arne Bendiksen, new hip-hop and various types of avant-garde Norwegian music. "Every record is released at a loss" - Mørch Finborud says - "this is absolutely true, but I find it simply fantastic that with the sale of my vinyl records I was able to publish and document much unreleased material from the early jazz scene, as well as some NRK sessions and various other experimentations. There so much more that I'd like to release, but I also want to try to document new contemporary projects".[27]

---

circuit. He was an extremely talented musician who never managed to make a name for himself outside of Norway, where he would most often be heard in the company of pianist Christian Reim.

To sum up, there was no scarcity of talented musicians around and yet, just a week after the official opening, it was already clear that the real stars of the Art Centre's musical scene were going to be Jan Garbarek and Svein Finnerud. In the following years they played there with Fred Nøddelund, Eberhard Weber, Sheila Jordan, Maurice Weddington, Jack Reilly, Jan Erik Vold, as well as with their respective trios, quartets and quintets. And a highlight came with the memorable concert/happening *Samklang!* (Unison!)[31] of February 1971, when Garbarek's quintet and Finnerud's trio played together for over seven hours: it was to remain the only true performance of the two pioneering bandleaders together, an event in true hippie style, complete with exercise bikes on stage and final shower of peas on the audience...

Oslo's Henie Onstad Art Centre became a hub for all new artistic trends in the capital, hosting cinema, literature, dance and music events, and especially new music bringing together the jazz and contemporary traditions. This unique venue showcased screenings, action painting, light design, readings from John Cage's writings and echoed the jazz notes of the Svein Finnerud Trio. It was there and in those precise years that the hybrid, unfettered scene that was coming took shape. A scene in which the question "is this jazz?" began to lose all relevance.

3
Norwegian jazz makes an impact abroad
Karin Krog. From Dexter Gordon's African-American roots to Don Ellis's research, to the electronics of the Oberheim modulator

Until the 1960s Norway had little impact on the international jazz scene. Although during the previous decade several American players had settled in Denmark, finding a kind of paradise there,[32] those same musicians only spent as much time as necessary in Norway: they arrived, played their gigs, and left. A case in point was Dexter Gordon, who collaborated for a long time with Karin Krog and who lived in Europe for about fifteen years, mostly in Paris and Copenhagen, but never in Oslo. For this same reason, before the arrival of ECM, Norwegian musicians would often move to Sweden, where most of the jazz being played was American influenced. While Norway was home to the first Scandinavian jazz festival (Molde, 1961) and to many jazz clubs, the fact that the clubs had concerts only once or twice a week and were not easy to travel to obviously made the country less attractive than Sweden and Denmark, and American jazz musicians, who generally relied on local rhythm sections, would often bring to Stockholm the best Norwegian musicians as well.

At the time Norway had a population of less than three million, one of the smallest populations in Europe, despite being the sixth largest country.[33] Because of its geography, travelling within the country was costly and difficult, as it mostly still is today. The roads in the north were narrow and crossed rough terrain between fjords and mountains. with snow, ice and darkness for a good part of the year. Direct flights from the rest of Europe were rare and stop-overs in Oslo were necessary; travelling between two important cities such as Trondheim and Molde - both on the western coast, 200 km apart - took four hours by car or two flights (Trondheim-Oslo and Oslo-Molde). Most of what happened in Norway happened in Oslo, and if a jazz club elsewhere managed to get an audience of sixty or seventy the evening was considered a success. This was the case for example with one of the best and most renowned Norwegian jazz clubs, the one in Molde, which gave plenty of space to entertainment and dancing in the early days and which came to have six-hundred members - something akin to Club 7 but with less of an international profile. Jazz lovers and clubs were scattered all around the country, but except during festival periods international jazz could only be heard in Oslo and to a much lesser degree in Bergen and Stavanger, on the south-western coast. Molde, for example, didn't have an airport at the time, and it was quite difficult to get international artists there by car or ferry, as happened at Club 7. So, between the late 1950s and the early 1960s the scene outside of Oslo was almost exclusively made up of local musicians; at Oslo's Metropol and Penguin the first artist who began to make a name for herself outside the country's borders was Karin Krog, being at the forefront of a scene that would take shape only later, toward the end of the 1960s, with Garbarek and the ECM generation.

Karin Krog was born in 1937 into a family of musicians. Her father played drums in a local Dixieland band while her great-grandfather, Anders Heyerdahl,[34] was an accomplished violinist and composer. Krog took an interest in jazz from an early age, and as soon as she was old enough she started taking part in the Penguin Club's jam sessions, where the house orchestra's director Kjell Karlsen soon noticed her.

"Every day there would be a great discovery. At that time the musicians had to work hard to get people to dance in the restaurants, but for us [who were jamming at the Penguin] it was different: we could explore. We were in a transition between swing and be-bop and for me it was still just a hobby. It was only in 1962 that I started taking individual lessons from the American classical singer Anne Brown: she'd sung in the original *Porgy & Bess* and lived in Oslo at the time [...] I started becoming familiar with the technique and began to have a good control of my voice. I studied with her for six years. Back then the conservatory only taught Italian opera, and I wasn't interested in that." [35]

A few years older than Garbarek, Krog was the first musician to receive recognition abroad. She immediately captured the essence of the changing times and of the public's growing interest in new forms of expression, at first veering more and more towards be-bop and later towards free jazz, and exploring them with curiosity. After the release of *By myself* [36] in 1964, her reputation grew both in Norway and in the rest of Europe, leading to her first contact with the American trumpeter and bandleader Don Ellis, who invited her to record with his big band in the United States. This was in 1967, a time when Ellis was recording with the cream of jazz - Charles Mingus, Eric Dolphy, George Russell - and drawing attention for his experimental approach. "We were looking for new things and were trying to develop them, we didn't want to just play standards over and over. All those new ideas... It was a very exciting period. Today Don has been almost forgotten, but back then he was definitely daring." [37] Krog was especially taken by the electronic effects that Ellis used in his compositions. She began using an Echoplex (a tape delay effect) to get vocal reverb, and later, in the 1970s, she bought an Oberheim modulator that she used to further modify her voice, although without losing sight of her original musical roots: "I was doing experimental things, but I always stayed with the song [...] a straight, simple line. The more I can strip off the better and just get to the message".[38] At the same time, Krog began long-term collaborations with Dexter Gordon, Archie Shepp, Warne Marsh, Toots Thielemans, Bengt Hallberg, Red Mitchell, Kenny Drew, Nils Lindberg, playing music that explored the African-American jazz tradition. What is most surprising is how in those years she managed to tread two quite different paths of artistic exploration, exemplified by the mainstream work with Dexter Gordon (well documented by the 1970 album *Some Other Spring* on Arne Bendiksen's Sonet Records, which won a Grammy in Japan), and the prolific experimental work with Don Ellis, which she then continued in Germany with the exploration of electronic music. For several years Krog regularly went to Baden Baden for an annual week-long workshop with MPS Records producer Joachim-Ernst Berendt, which Krog called "free jazz meeting" in the liner notes to *Different Days, Different Ways*. It was Ellis who set her on that path while in Los Angeles, introducing her to the young Tom Oberheim (builder of the modulator she was using, who a few years later invented the first polyphonic synthesizer) and suggesting that she explore new roads with electronics, as he himself was doing with the trumpet before Miles Davis and many others ever did.

"At that time jazz was more traditional and American-style, and I tried to break free of that. It wasn't easy. People would tell me "What the hell are you doing?" It wasn't easy then, and it's still not easy now. The only singer whom I'd heard do something different at that time was Sheila Jordan." [39]

Krog was a deeply innovative artist with a strong personality, on the frontline at the Munch Museum and the Henie Onstad Art Centre, and was chosen as representative by the musicians who founded the Jazzforum in order to tackle the closure of Norwegian jazz clubs. A free and independent creative spirit, she didn't sign the contract Ellis offered her while in Los Angeles[40] and also didn't consider the possibility of a contract with ECM, as did Garbarek and Rypdal and, with some reservation, Andersen and Christensen as well. In 1987 Karin Krog founded her own label Meantime, and began to buy back ownership of her works, re-releasing them when possible (for example her pioneering work *Joy*) or licensing them out, as was the case in 2004 to Japan's Muzak Inc. for the album *Different Days, Different Ways* - "A work that was too difficult for the Norwegian market back then". [41]

4
The "ECM generation"
Manfred Eicher meets Jan Garbarek in Bologna and begins a partnership
that was to have a remarkable effect on the Scandinavian scene

The 1967 readers' poll in *Jazznytt* magazine[42] showed a lot of support for the
younger generation of jazz musicians who chose their favourites such as pianist
Einar Iversen, guitarist Jan Erik Kongshaug, bassist Arild Andersen, drummer
Jon Christensen, trumpeter Ditleff Ekhoff, trombonist Frode Thingnaes, alto sax
player Calle Neumann, singers Karin Krog and Arild Wickstrøm. And let's not
forget a young tenor sax player by the name of Jan Garbarek.[43] The singer Karin
Krog had received good reviews for her first album *By Myself* (1964) including
the Swedish *Orkesterjournalen* and America's *Downbeat* magazine and that
attention began to establish her international reputation: Don Ellis invited her to
Los Angeles to record with his Big Band. Jon Christensen was the most in-
demand drummer and was working with George Russell's projects (Russell was
living in Stockholm at the time). But the Norwegian artist receiving the most
attention for critics and public alike was the young Garbarek who, after
appearing in the famous jam sessions in Molde, was playing regularly with his
quartet at Club 7 and at the Henie Onstad Centre, and was invited to the Warsaw
Festival with Karin Krog in 1966. Arild Andersen and Jon Christensen then
became regular members of Garbarek's trio, which at this time was still highly
influenced by free jazz, Russell's modal jazz and John Coltrane. In 1969
guitarist Terje Rypdal, despite being busy with the rock group Dream, joined the
trio, and the resulting quartet was active for several years. It was at this time that
George Russell, having moved to Oslo, decided to take his sextet and big band
on tour, recruiting Garbarek and Christensen, who were already regular
members of both ensembles, as well as Andersen and Rypdal. In early October
1969 the sextet arrived in Bologna for the International Jazz Festival, and it was
there that Manfred Eicher was struck by the sound of Jan Garbarek. At the time
Garbarek was working on material that would later be released, by George
Russell, on Flying Dutchman Records with the title *The Esoteric Circle*. Eicher
wanted to launch a label and suggested to Garbarek that he and his group be the
first to be recorded.

In the spring of 1970 Stan Getz played in Oslo accompanied by British musicians. After this, Getz was going to play a five week engagement in Johannesburg, South Africa, but the English trio were both unable and unwilling to go, among other things because of the international boycott of South Africa. Several American jazz musicians had already been put on the international boycott list[44] for having played there. Arild Andersen and Jon Christensen agreed to join Getz for the engagement, a decision that caused a great deal of surprise and consternation. The leader of the Norwegian Artists' Guild criticized their decision, referring to the boycott decision, which, admittedly, the Norwegian Musicians' Union had not signed. Talking to *Dagbladet* after the engagement, Andersen reported that they had also played for black audiences and had been very well received.[45]

Fortunately the incident didn't have any long-term consequences for Andersen and Christensen, and in September 1970 Eicher contacted Garbarek to organise the recording in Oslo. Eicher made a two-day train journey to Oslo from Munich via Copenhagen. Oslo seemed like a small, dark city, isolated from the rest of Europe and quite different from the capital it is today, and yet it was fascinating: a city which appeared to come from another era, and where East and West seemed to meet, creating a unique atmosphere.

At the time Garbarek was playing quite often with his quartet at the Henie Onstad Art Centre, so it was decided that the recording would take place there. Eicher hired Bjørnar Andresen, the bassist of the Svein Finnerud Trio with a reputation as an excellent sound engineer. Eicher wasn't happy, however, with the results of that first session of *Afric Pepperbird*, there was too much reverb for his taste, and he scheduled another at the Arne Bendiksen Studio, a small studio which did mostly pop music. The room was tiny, but everyone was welcoming and helpful, and the atmosphere was perfect. Andresen wasn't available this time, but this gave the opportunity for another key figure to make an entry: Jan Erik Kongshaug, not as technically experienced then as Andresen, but he was very much in tune with the sound Eicher was after. The experience at the Arne Bendiksen Studio marked the beginning of a long and prolific relationship between Kongshaug and ECM, which continued at the bigger Talent Studio and later at the first Rainbow Studio. Together they developed new ideas and brought in a piano. Eicher began looking ahead and would book a lot of studio time, sometimes even a year or two in advance, just to make sure there was availability for his growing number of projects. He made a large number of recordings, bringing to Oslo artists such as Keith Jarrett, Charlie Haden, Egberto Gismonti, John Abercrombie and many others. All these musicians came to the city to record, play and take part in memorable jam sessions at Club 7. There were still difficulties: both financial, because of the high cost of intercontinental flights, and logistical, because small Fornebu airport was often closed due to snow, forcing travellers to get as far as Copenhagen by train and then take the boat to Norway from there.[46]

Whatever the difficulties, thanks to ECM Oslo became a centre for international jazz. The city received a massive boost to its creativity from the presence of artists of the calibre of Chick Corea, Dave Holland, Sam Rivers, Ralph Towner, and Miroslav Vitouš, and in exchange offered to these musicians a unique atmosphere alongside experiences quite unlike those of the usual international tours where the guest star played with local musicians.

In the autumn of 1972 Garbarek appeared at the Warsaw festival with a new quartet that over the next 3-4 years was to become one of the most remarkable units of his career, including Swedish pianist Bobo Stenson and bassist Palle Danielsson alongside Christensen. *Witchi-Tai-To* was recorded in the autumn of 1973, and this quartet was a sure breadwinner for Norwegian jazz clubs.[47]

Around the same time, Garbarek began a long collaboration with the American pianist Keith Jarrett, joining him along with Danielsson and Christensen in what came to be known as Jarrett's Nordic Quartet. The group went into the studio in 1974 to record *Belonging* and in 1977 to record *My Song*. This golden age in Garbarek's and Jarrett's career was recently given a new lease of life by ECM with the release of the box-set *Dansere*[48] and of the almost forgotten gem *Sleeper*,[49] recorded live in Tokyo on 16 April 1979 and previously unreleased.

With both Jarrett and Stenson, Garbarek's repertoire included folk tunes. In as early as 1970, he'd done a TV recording with an Indian sitar player. In 1969 the Garbarek Quartet had made a quite special recording *Briskeby Blues* where the distinguished Norwegian poet Jan Erik Vold[50] recited his own poems.[51]

Rypdal and Andersen soon chose their own musical paths as well.

After studying musicology at Oslo University and composition with Finn Mortensen, by the early 1970s Terje Rypdal had embarked on a parallel career as composer of contemporary music, initially inspired by Mahler, Ligeti and Penderecki, and then slowly developing his own style. He debuted with *Eternal Circulation* (1971), performed with the Garbarek Quartet and the Oslo Philharmonic Orchestra. Among his most important works are *Symphony No. 1* (1975), commissioned by Norwegian television, *Orfeo Turns Around and Watches Eurydice*, which premiered at the Henie Onstad Art Centre in 1972,

Concerto per Violbasso e Orchestra (1973) for American bassist Barre Phillips, and *Undisonus* (which was awarded "work of the year" by the Society of Norwegian Composers). Rypdal's jazz music was strongly influenced by rock, as is well documented in the album *Min Bul* (1970), with Bjørnar Andresen and Espen Rud. Later in the 1970s he began a long collaboration with Danish trumpeter Palle Mikkelborg.

Arild Andersen formed his own quartet with Knut Riisnæs on tenor sax, the 18 year-old Jon Balke on piano, and Pål Thowsen on drums, recording *Clouds In My Head* for ECM in 1975 (later rereleased in the box set *Green in Blue*).

Jon Christensen established himself as a drummer with his own distinctive sound and technique and a unique *rubato*,[52] playing with various groups in Norway and abroad.

The meeting between these and other musicians and ECM Records gave rise to a distinctive European style,[53] with which this new jazz freed itself from the African-American tradition without losing sight of its roots. It is a style that has fuelled a lively debate between both its supporters and its opponents, one that has never really died down since the start of ECM.

Even its fiercest opponents can't deny that Manferd Eicher helped a large number of talented musicians to emerge. If they had worked with less important record companies, most of them would have probably taken off in other creative directions, but these wouldn't have had worldwide distribution. Examples of such musicians in Italy are Enrico Rava, Stefano Bollani and Gianluigi Trovesi: the humorous, swaggering spirit of their early records with Label Bleu, Egea, and Enja, is a distant memory compared to the flawless sound of their ECM records today. And I know for a fact that the same is true for Henriksen, Eilertsen, Seim and other Norwegian musicians, who locally produced works that were less perfect but highly creative and experimental, and that were never heard in Italy because of the lack of distribution. It is well known that ECM's owner has never renounced his role as producer, still going into the studio, making sure that all the recordings maintain the sound and identity of the label. For all its limits, I believe ECM's role has been a remarkably positive one, making possible projects that would never have seen the light of day otherwise, giving all music lovers the pleasure of hearing Egberto Gismonti, Arve Henriksen, Nils Petter Molvær, Arvo Pärt, Gavin Bryars, Keith Jarrett, Jan Garbarek, Marcin Wasilewski, Tomasz Sta_ko, Iro Haarla, Tigran Mansurian, Anouar Brahem, John Surman... to mention just a few of the names featured in over a thousand productions over a 40-year history.[54]

5
Norwegian traditions:
marching bands and Church music

The Brazz Brothers. The church as a music venue in a largely rural country
& Erik Hillestad's Kirkelig Kulturverksted - a jazz voice in the city

"Our father directed the school band in Sula. There was not much music on the
island back then, but fortunately the owner of the local Devold textiles factory,
inspired by a similar story in a mining town in the United Kingdom, decided to buy
a whole lot of musical instruments for his workers. And they got these good brass
instruments and became excellent musicians." [55]

The island of Sula, just south of the city of Ålesund on the west coast, is the
setting for this particular story. It is where, in the early 1930s, the famous
Norwegian marching band tradition was born, a tradition which went on to play
a significant role in the history of Norwegian jazz.[56] It was there, on this small
island, that one of the most important brass ensembles in Scandinavia came into
being: a quintet of the three Førde brothers (Jarle, Jan Magne and Helge) and two
Tafjord brothers (Runar and Stein Erik), in other words, the Brazz Brothers.
When the instruments arrived it was like a gift from heaven and they opened up
unexpected possibilities for the townspeople, who began listening to some of the
recorded milestones of that era, from Armstrong to Ellington. The jazz
phenomenon took hold, and grew and grew until 1976, when the Ytre Suløens
Jassensemble (the local Dixieland brass band) was invited to the Jazz & Heritage
Festival in New Orleans. It was the first time a Norwegian band had been invited,
and for the musicians that brought great excitement as well as a huge sense of
responsibility. This ensemble had been founded by Jens Arne Molvær (father of
the now famous trumpeter Nils Petter Molvær), the 20 year old trumpeter Jarle
Førde and other members of the Brazz Brothers. When they were in New Orleans
they came into contact with some of the legendary figures of Dixieland jazz, most
of them in their eighties, an inspirational experience that reached a peak when
they were invited to play at the funeral of the owner of one of New Orleans's most
important clubs, the Preservation Hall Jazz Club. They were deeply touched by
the opportunity of experiencing jazz in its historical cradle alongside the players
who had put this music on the map.

The situation waiting for them on their return to Sula was quite different: places where you could play and hear jazz were still quite rare, although the wheels were in motion. There were still no jazz studies courses in the Norwegian conservatories, but very soon the one in Trondheim would open its doors to the new music, and the passion for brass music helped to spread the interest in jazz. The Brazz Brothers became a regular ensemble and started expanding quite freely into improvisation, stepping increasingly away from the classical world and exploring jazz harmonies. It is interesting to note here that Nils Petter Molvær had studied with Jan Magne Førde since he was 10 and the young Arve Henriksen came from nearby Stryn to study with Jarle Førde. The marching band tradition spread from Sula to the whole of Norway and today is represented by about thirty professional musicians, who come from the island (most of them enjoyed a reunion when Nils Petter Molvær was Artist in Residence at the 2010 Molde Festival, including Lena Nymark, Hild Sofie Tafjord, Kåre Nymark, David Gald, Jan Inge Melsæter, and the five Brazz Brothers). It is because of this brass tradition that, in Norway, it seems quite normal to find a voice and tuba duo such as Silucian Town (Lena Nymark and Martin Taxt) or a trio with singer, tuba and drums like Pelbo. Summer workshops for jazz take place where the young aspiring musicians take part in the street parades and have the opportunity to study with the best players and teachers around.

Norway is well known too for its church music tradition. In a country with such a small population and with a landscape that offers so many challenges to the traveller, especially in the north, people living in small towns have had to learn to be self-sufficient and create a life independent of the cities. If you look at a list of Norwegian musicians, you discover that many of them started their musical career in church: Tord Gustavsen, Solveig Slettahjell, Torun Eriksen, Kristin Asbjørnsen, Nikolai Eilertsen, David, Susanna and Christian Wallumrød, just to cite a few, started playing and practising in church because only churches (of all denominations) offered space and instruments. Churches almost always had a good organ, or perhaps a piano, and possessed perfect acoustics for this kind of music: As Tord Gustavsen explained, "Over the years I played a lot in the churches and with choirs. Then when I began to discover jazz, the switch came very naturally".[57] There are many musicians in their forties today that were born and grew up away from the cities, and when you say outside of the cities in Norway you're talking about something very small: Gustavsen comes from a town of 7,000 people, the same town that Jarle Vespestad and Martin Revheim come from. Revheim recalls:

> Jarle was my hero. He is five or six years older than me and was without a doubt the best musician around. Everybody talked about him, about how he'd never stop

practising. He could play any style, say like Stewart Copeland and then play with brushes with Kenny Clarke's technique. He just studied and studied. He'd never stop.[58]

Similarly, Christian Wallumrød came from Kongsberg, a town of around 25,000 people where it also wasn't easy to find places where one could play and practise every day.

Of course the church is more than just a physical place, it is a spiritual one that has a significant relationship with the world of culture, art and music. The Church of Norway professes the Lutheran Christian faith and was established as the country's official Church in the 16th century, with the King at its head. There are, however, many other Christian denominations, for example the particularly lively Pentecostal movement, worth mentioning not only because the parents of one of the central figures of Oslo's scene, Bjørnar Andresen, belonged to it, but also because it is one of the largest religious movements and is characterised by a musical culture not dissimilar to that of the Roma people. Bearing witness to the importance of the religious musical scene in Norway was the birth in the late 1960s of the Christian youth programme Ten Sing (Teenage Singing), which encouraged young people's expression through music and the performing arts. In 1967 the inspirer of Ten Sing, the priest Olaf Hillestad (1923-74), founded Forum Experimentale, whose premises were used as both a chapel and a youth club, where worship rubbed shoulders with poetry, theatre, concerts and workshops.

The second half of the 1960s was a period of major change for churches in Norway, which went out of their way to involve young people in their activities. Prayers became imbued with rock 'n' roll, beat, jazz and protest songs, over a few short years collectives, festivals, fan clubs and record labels were born.[59] The music began to play an active role in the spread of the Gospel, and the Christian music industry became almost as powerful as the secular one. Moved by their desire to bring the new forms of cultural expression into the church, young Norwegian Christians produced a catalogue of albums poised between jazz, psychedelia, beat, funk and folk music, all of it duly incorporating the Christian message. This was a very important part of the Norwegian scene that had been almost forgotten until the invaluable research of Lars Mørch Finborud brought it back to light in 2011 with the release of *Lukk Opp Kirkens Dører* [Close the Church Doors]. *A Selection of Norwegian Christian Jazz, Psych, Funk & Folk 1970-1980:*[60] "a hidden and fantastic catalogue of progressive and experimental Christian music", as Finborud himself states in the liner notes.

The record company Kirkelig Kulturverksted (KKV), mentioned in footnote 4, deserves a few more words. With a happy-go-lucky spirit and without worrying

Ketil Bjørnstad (b. 1952) is a unique figure in the Norwegian music scene. A key ECM artist as performer and composer his work encompasses the jazz and classical worlds. He has worked with musicians ranging from Terje Rypdal and Jon Christensen, to singers such as Anneli Drecker, Kristin Asbjørnsen and Randi Stene, as well as choirs, orchestras and chamber ensembles. Bjørnstad is also one of Norway's most prolific writers of poetry, novels and essays. His passion for the paintings of Edvard Munch has found voice in his "documentary novel" *The Story of Edvard Munch* (1993) as well as in his music (for example *Sunrise: a cantata on the texts of Edvard Munch*, ECM, 2014). His novel *To Music* (*Til Musikken*) was published in English to great acclaim, nominated for the 2010 Independent Foreign Fiction prize, and winner of the prestigious French Prix des Lecteurs. Part of a trilogy, the novel opens up the reader to a world familiar to the young Bjørnstad growing up in Oslo as a classical pianist: "a story of music written by a master in the field". [*The Independent*] Bjørnstad trained as a classical pianist and proved his talent very early by winning the Youth Piano Master award in 1966 and 1968, and by appearing as soloist at the age of 16 with the Oslo Philharmonic Orchestra in Bartok's *Piano Concerto No 3*. His first contact with the jazz scene dates back to 1971, when he played with the avant-garde group Svein Finnerud Trio and with Ole Paus. He performed frequently with jazz and rock musicians, and in 1973 released his first album *Åpning*, featuring Jon Eberson on guitar, Arild Andersen on bass, and Jon Christensen on drums. One of the great communicators on the touring circuit, Bjørnstad has a great affinity with audiences as a speaker and as an improviser who can lead his listeners on an effortless and inspiring journey from jazz to Schubert. *http://www.ketilbjornstad.com*

much about religion, since its founding in 1974 it has released almost 400 albums, including the 1989 masterpiece *Rosenfole* by Agnes Buen Garnås and Jan Garbarek, re-released some time later by ECM, as well as Arild Andersen's *Sagn* (1990) and *Arv* (1994), two other masterpieces inspired by folk music. When he founded the label, Erik Hillestad was director of a youth choir and had a musical background as a drummer. He began working in an attic in Oslo, and not having access to a church where he could record he had to hire one for each project, which led to frequent arguments with people who weren't exactly on his wavelength. The first album published by KKV was a sort of compilation of choir music and folk singing entitled *Open the Church*, while the first famous artist to enter their catalogue was Bjørn Eidsvåg in 1976.

What happened on the jazz scene between the late 1960s and early 1970s really inspired us. After the great pop experiment of the Beatles, the time had come for Norwegian jazz. It was such an interesting period, so sophisticated and so experimental... We tried to build a bridge between jazz, pop, folk and classical church music, without ever being conservative. Our composers invented a new style of church music. Egil Hovland and Knut Nysfeldt, for example, they wrote choir and organ music that was way ahead of its time.[61]

More recently KKV has also released several works by the pianist Ketil Bjørnstad and by some of the big names in Norwegian jazz, as well as all the music by Kari Bremnes, a singer who is something of a household name in Norway, and with whom Audun Kleive (a drummer who will be talked about in greater detail later) and his keyboard player brother Iver started their career.

Erik Hillestad finally found a location for his KKV in 2000 after experimenting with the acoustics of some of Oslo's best churches (Sofienberg, Uranienborg, Ris, Gamle Aker and Jar). When he rented a Steinway to make a few recordings and brought it into the church of St. Jakob, close to the lively area around Hausmanns Gate, he knew right away that the acoustics of this church were absolutely perfect. Hillestad established the headquarters of KKV in this space, perfect for electric-acoustic jazz, and also began to put on jazz concerts. Soon the church transformed into one of Oslo's most active concert venues, especially during the month of August, when it becomes one of the venues of the Oslo Jazz Festival.

6
The importance of festivals and commissions
Molde, the first Norwegian jazz festival
and one of the oldest in Europe (1961).
Vossajazz, a legacy of landmark commissions
(Il Cenone, Labyrinter)

"If you come to Norway as a tourist in the first half of July and, from pure curiosity, start to leaf through a section of the larger Norwegian newspapers, you might erroneously believe you have landed in a nation of jazz-lovers."[62]

Strangely enough, according to the renowned Norwegian jazz critic Terje Mosnes his fellow countrymen are not jazz lovers, although the impressive number of festivals in a country of just five million would make you think otherwise. You could say it all began on 20 February 1960, when in a Danish-Norwegian jazz magazine the actor, musician and writer Rolv Wesenlund asked the provocative question "Which city is the Newport of Northern Europe?" [63]

At that time the city of Molde had a very active jazz club, Storyville (1953). Known as "the city of jazz and roses," Molde is set in breathtaking countryside on the Romsdal fjord, along the west coast, surrounded by mountains. Not far from Molde, near the town of Åndalsnes, the famous Trollstigen ("troll's ladder") climbs up through its eleven hairpin bends to the 858 metres of Stigrøra, and the Atlantic Road almost seems to imitate the trajectory of a pebble bouncing on the surface of the water, connecting various islands in the archipelago. For anyone who's seen Molde in good weather, it's hard to forget its outstanding beauty. When Wesenlund's article came out, his provocative question caught the eye of two members of Storyville's management, Per-Inge Hansen and Otto Christian Sættem Jr. (better known as Pingen and Kikkan), who took up the challenge, as they had already been toying around with the idea of a festival. The first Molde Jazz Festival took place in August 1961, with a three-day programme featuring many Norwegian artists, including Karin Krog, Laila Dalseth and Kjell Karlsen. The bill also featured American trumpeter Benny Bailey, giving it an international touch, since the organisers' intent was clear from the start, to make the Molde festival an international one, one of the first in Europe.

The second festival offered a broader programme and also featured jam sessions, providing great opportunities for all the musicians. The media began to take the festival seriously, and the journalist Solve Kern made a 35-minute documentary that was broadcast the Saturday of the festival (18 August 1962). It was a great showcase for the town, which thanks to the festival began to see the opportunities for tourism and beyond.[64] Despite a few problems (typical festival complaints related to alcohol and noise), the response of the press was consistently positive. Among the many music lovers who were crammed into Molde in that August of 1962 were two young artists from a Oslo: pianist Morten Lassem and saxophonist Jan Garbarek. Interviewed by a local journalist, they said they had been looking forward to the event, reserving a place to stay and buying tickets well in advance, and they just couldn't wait! Organising the festival took resources away from the jazz club, but the day after the second festival was over, the article in the local section of the newspaper *Sunnmørsposten* concluded with these words: "It seems clear that the loss of Molde's Storyville Jazz Club is a small thing compared to the great festival that just came to an end".[65]

Over time the organisation of the club and festival was separated, becoming two distinct entities that continued to collaborate through the years, without ever competing with each other. The Molde International Jazz Festival has a long history filled with dreams and musical adventures that continues today, although it took several years for residents to drop their initial scepticism towards the visitors that invade their town,[66] and to learn to accept and support the event with pride. The festival continued to grow:

> Six hundred volunteers annually work 30,000 unpaid hours at the festival, which is Norway's biggest annual cultural event (after the Bergen International Festival) with an estimated turnover in 1998 of some USD 1.76 million.[67]

American artists began to play an increasingly significant role in the festival, some appearing when they were still young and largely unknown (Keith Jarrett, Herbie Hancock, Pat Metheny, John Scofield, Bill Frisell and Ralph Towner), and some when they were already celebrated stars, for example Dexter Gordon, Sonny Stitt, Freddie Hubbard, Wayne Shorter, Stan Getz, Elvin Jones, Art Blakey, Tony Williams, Eubie Blake, Bill Evans, Oscar Peterson and Miles Davis.

When Garbarek, Andersen and Christensen met George Russell for the first time,[68] Molde was a real launchpad for the young and emerging Norwegian scene. A few years later, between the late 1960s and the early 1970s, the festival had become a very special place. Much smaller than it is today and still featuring a line-up of mostly Scandinavian artists, it provided the ideal setting where they could meet and interact with the selected foreign musicians who were playing there as well. It was in Molde that Keith Jarrett, before recording

Belonging, started studying Garbarek's phrasing and figured out what melodies to write for him.

In 2010 Moldejazz celebrated its 50th festival and took the opportunity to look back at its high points and achievements, as well as its financial and organisational challenges (the latter usually due to the unpredictability of the Norwegian weather!). Major concerts take place outdoors and when it rains constantly, as it did in 2010 and 2012, the festival's success is naturally compromised.[69] The fifty years of this historical event are well documented in two books by Terje Mosnes, one written for the festival's twentieth anniversary, the other for the fiftieth.[70]

After Molde, a festival was established in Kongsberg in 1964. Ten years later, in 1974, Nattjazz was born in Bergen taking place at exactly the same time as Festispillene, Bergen's classical music and arts festival. Even the small mountain town of Voss formed its own jazz festival - Vossajazz - in 1973, one which was to prove vital for the unfolding Norwegian jazz history. After these pioneering jazz festivals, many others followed, including Dølajazz in Lillehammer, the Varanger Festival north of the Arctic Circle, the Sandvika Big Band Festival, Sildajazz in Haugesund, the Oslo Jazz Festival, and Maijazz in Stavanger.

Well, sure, when in Kongsberg they started thinking about it and came to tell us that they wanted to start another festival in competition with us, we weren't happy... but we soon realized that the presence of so many festivals strewn across our rugged land and held in different periods of the year meant that more and more people would be exposed to jazz and interested in this music. This is why we started a kind of virtual competition, which actually led to a very active collaboration. I think it's really great and important that we have so many festivals in Norway today - about 25, all over the country![71]

Over the years all of these festivals that contributed to the development of Norwegian jazz and nurtured young talent have been coordinated by the Jazzforum, which sets guidelines so that each festival can thrive and develop its own identity.

When I was directing the Kongsberg festival I was closely in touch with the other festivals, which often were a source of inspiration for me. We discussed extensively about programmes, about how much to pay artists, and ideas for the future. I mean, we were in competition with each other, but the whole situation was quite open and transparent. Each one of us wanted to present the best music, sell the most tickets, and come out as the best festival, but at the same time there was a lot of sharing, just like the title of Bugge's [Wesseltoft] album *Sharing*. This probably all came about thanks to the musicians and the music. You know, Bugge is developing his music according to who he meets and who he plays with. His music is elastic. He's not one specific, defined, type of musician. He started with dance music, he played in a band for entertainment, then started playing funk and stuff, then suddenly he was developing the piano and then doing folk music like Arild Andersen's *Sagn* and *Arv* - very divergent projects. He is always developing. Just like Arild Andersen, who is also a great source of inspiration for me. They make me think of how I'd like to be when I'm 65 years old![72]

Like the musicians, the festivals also worked hard to establish their own identity, thus improving the standards of a scene that gave artists constant challenges and opportunities for growth. Each festival found its own niche: Molde has the reputation for being the most "international", Kongsberg is known for its free jazz and avant-garde, Vossajazz for its folk and traditional music heritage, and Nattjazz for its nurturing of young talent and young audiences. But even more than that, each festival became a sort of laboratory, going out of its way to come up with formulas (endowments, competitions, artist residences and more) that would give the more talented musicians an opportunity to grow and develop.

Vossajazz in particular is notable for having given so many important works to the jazz world through its annual commission, important not only for the Norwegian scene but, through the recordings and touring of these pieces, to the international scene. In 1992, for example, the festival commissioned the pianist Jon Balke. His project *Il Cenone* became the turning point in his career. This opportunity to compose for large ensembles set Balke on a new path that through the Magnetic North Orchestra, and then Batagraf and Siwan led to excursions into "world music" with compositions for string and percussion ensembles, and went on to define a new musical universe for this musician. Although often underrated (a point that will be explored more in detail later), Balke is actually a key figure in Norwegian music, who started from improvisation and then explored African folk music,[73] Baroque music, the Arab-Andalusian tradition, and composition. Vossajazz was also responsible for the birth of Nils Petter Molvær's memorable *Khmer*, a work commissioned by the festival in 1996 and originally entitled *Labyrinter*, which was released as *Khmer* on ECM and became one of the label's best-selling albums. With such a history, it's easy to understand what an honour it is to be asked to produce a work for Vossajazz. The commission includes preparation and rehearsal time in Voss, so the musicians can go up into this town in the mountains and work far away from the distractions of the city.

7

Club 7

The beginnings: Jon Balke, the meeting with Momodou "Miki" N'Doye,
the band E'Olen and the birth of Oslo 13, the first open collective
in Norway

Jazz in Norway enjoyed a golden period between 1961 and 1962,[74] when about forty jazz clubs and numerous jazz bands were active throughout the country, and NRK's live concert broadcasts attracted a great deal of interest. After this, and quite unexpectedly in the spring of 1964,[75] the number of clubs drastically fell as the younger generation that should have taken over the running of the clubs seemed to have lost interest in jazz, drawn instead to the new names like the Beatles, the Rolling Stones, Joan Baez and Bob Dylan. There was also something of an anti-American feeling because of the embargo against Cuba and the Vietnam War.[76]

Here is where Attila "the Hun" Horvath comes in, a key figure in the history of the Oslo jazz scene and Norwegian jazz as a whole. An amateur actor and theatre enthusiast, he fled his native Hungary after the 1956 uprising, finally settling in Oslo in 1959. Writer Jon Rognlien described the city in those years as one where "the cultural scene was quite limited, with very little going on: one television channel, one radio station, and not much more. The luckiest received the Swedish TV channels, or London's Radio Luxembourg. Back then Norway was a bit like Albania today".[77] The cultural movements sweeping through America and Europe seemed to bypass Norway. Staying in Oslo you'd never know this was the period of the Beat generation, for example. Horvath soon got tired of the city's dreariness and lack of cultural activity and decided to do something about it. It wasn't easy to get an alcohol licence, and jazz clubs were among the few establishments that could be granted one, so he decided to form an organisation and in 1963 founded what was to become a legendary establishment for jazz in Norway: Club 7.

The idea was to create a space for all forms of artistic expression - music, theatre, visual arts, cinema, literature - and for people to meet in a friendly, respectful atmosphere. Horvath had given it a go before, in Vienna, opening a club in a city basement. For all its drabness, Oslo in the early 1960s offered fertile ground for the movement that was about to explode in the United States and spread all over Europe, since the Metropol was the only place where one could hear jazz and the Munch Museum had just started hosting avant-garde events and concerts.[78] Club 7 opened as a cultural centre in 1963 at the Kafé René in Lilletorget, taking its name from the play on words by the poet Kate Næss, *Mer enn sex* ("more than six/sex").[79]

After a trial period at the Kafé René, by 1965 the club had moved into the tiny basement of the Cavaletto, then to the cabaret theatre Edderkoppen, to the Kongen Restaurant during 1966-71, and finally moved in 1971 to what was the lower floor of today's Oslo Konserthus, the legendary premises where it remained until it went bankrupt in 1985.

In the early years Club 7 became a centre of attraction for young people looking for new culture and the latest trends from abroad. The move to its final and historic location took place a few months after ECM's release of Jan Garbarek's *Afric Pepperbird*,[80] at a time when important things were happening in Oslo. The Henie Onstad Art Center [81] was becoming a real hub for the avant-garde, where jazz started taking different directions next to other forms of art, and where the major figures of Norwegian contemporary music (Arne Nordheim, Kåre Kolberg, Bjørn Fongaard) mingled with the younger jazz scene represented by Karin Krog and the emerging ECM generation. Performances by international artists who had come to Oslo to record with Manfred Eicher became more and more frequent at Club 7, which in those years was the only venue in the capital where music could be heard five or six days a week. The programming was quite varied, sometimes with a lot of Norwegian artists and at other times showcasing international musicians, but the club's atmosphere was consistently special, so much so that even in the early 1980s Miles Davis refused to play anywhere else in Oslo, creating serious difficulties for the organisers who had do try to cover his high fee with just 700 seats.

During the early 1970s Club 7's programme included modern jazz as well as rhythm and blues, and regularly featured Carl Magnus Neumann, Christian Reim, Espen Rud and other increasingly popular younger artists such as the brothers Erik and Jon Balke (respectively alto sax and piano), saxophonists Vidar Johansen and Arne Frang, and guitarist Jon Eberson. In the mid 1970s, a period of profound change in Oslo and Norway, Club 7 launched the singer Radka Toneff, who was to become one of Norway's most famous voices, and a new generation of local musicians that emerged on the heels of the ECM generation's rise to international fame. Oslo was coming into its own, offering a jazz scene that was veering away from those of nearby Copenhagen and Stockholm, freeing itself from African-American roots and exploring its own roots in folk music and, for example, the sound of the Hardanger fiddle. These roots turned out to be strong, growing into a style of music whose connection with jazz was simply a departure point.

In Oslo, and in the rest of Norway, these years saw many musicians who were popular during the 1950s and 1960s continuing to be very active on the music scene.[82] It was a period when many big bands were formed. Norwegian Radio gave birth to what became known since 1970 as Østereng Thorleif/Helge Hurum big band, and other bands included the Bodega Band led by pianist Per Husby and bassist Jan Tro from Trondheim, the Sandvika and Guttormsen/Ekholt Big Bands, and finally the Big Band of Oslo University, which experienced its greatest popularity between 1969 and 1977. Enjoying continued success were trumpeter Rowland Greenberg, alongside musicians such as pianist Øystein Ringstad, clarinettist Terje Larsen, drummer Per Nyhaug and saxophonists Kristian Bergheim and Totti Bergh. In addition, there were various neo-bop and mainstream musicians like bassists Terje Venaas and Sture Janson, pianists Egil Kapstad, Ivar Antonsen and Terje Björklund, trombonist Frode Thingnæs, singer Laila Dalseth, sax players Bjørn Johansen, Knut Riisnæs and Harald Bergersen, drummers Ole Jacob Hansen and Svein Christiansen, and trumpeter Ditlef Eckhoff.

Because of the challenging geography of the country and the often adverse weather conditions, which frequently meant that, for example, musicians from Tromsø or Bodø couldn't play in Oslo, the music scenes around Norway became "localized". In Trondheim, saxophonist Asmund Bjørken was impressed by the qualities of bassist Bjørn Alterhaug and formed a new band with him along with Ove Stokstad on sax, Kjell Johansen on drums, and Lars Martin Thomassen on trumpet; more to the south, Bergen saw the rise of the young talented pianist Dag Arnesen, who was destined for great things in later years; to the north the emerging figure was Kjell Bartholdsen, along with guitarist Thorgeir Stubø who was living in his native Narvik, where he collaborated with trombonist Viggo Hansen; in Tromsø there were the pianist Tage Lof and drummer and bassist Kjell Svendsen Rønne; sax player Guttorm Guttormsen moved from the north to the southern town of Skien, where he teamed up with another up-and-coming musician of the time, bassist Bjørn Kjellemyr.

After the crisis of the early 1960s jazz clubs began to thrive again reaching a total number of 40 by the end of the following decade. This new boom and the rise of jazz festivals made it possible for many musicians to make a living playing just jazz.

Oslo, which had always been the centre of Norwegian jazz, began to get international attention thanks to Club 7 and ECM, transforming into a flourishing cultural capital. Eicher arrived in Oslo in September 1970 for the first in a long series of recordings many of which became milestones in contemporary jazz, bringing with him some of the best jazz players on the circuit. The first non-Norwegian to come with Eicher was Chick Corea, who recorded *Piano Improvisations Vol. 1* in April 1971. The following November, Keith Jarrett recorded his first piano solo album, *Facing You*, in Oslo. By now Oslo was hosting many of the greatest names in contemporary jazz, including Bobo Stenson, Paul Bley, Gary Burton, Bennie Maupin, John Abercrombie, Bill Connors, Ralph Towner, Jack DeJohnette, Steve Kuhn and many others. Many of the artists passing through performed in memorable concerts and jam sessions at Club 7, whose reputation grew and drew to Oslo an increasing number of internationally renowned musicians, especially from the United States. The economics of the club got an important boost from organising rock concerts with Keith Emerson, Spirit, Deep Purple, at the same time emerging as one of Europe's major jazz clubs. The young sound engineer Sven Persson, a pupil of Jan Erik Kongshaug, came to the club in the mid 1970s. While Kongshaug had developed an affinity with Eicher in his search for a realistic and transparent acoustic sound,[83] Persson immediately appeared extremely gifted in the eyes of Terje Rypdal, and began to work on new types of amplification closer to the world of rock, taking the first steps in the club's exploration of the so-called "Nordic sound" of the coming years. There are countless anecdotes about this period of great excitement and creativity:

> During the second half of the 1970s there were some amazing things going on, there were regular acts like Miki N'Doye's band E'Olen, the Balke brothers, the young Radka Toneff… it's hard to sum up in a few words! […] Once, while Betty Carter was performing, a very particular voice was heard coming from the backstage. It was a Norwegian folk singer. Betty was not bothered at all, in fact she said "Wow! Who's that?" and insisted that the singer join her on stage. It was Agnes Buen Garnås.[84] That's not something that happens often, it was a really touching moment.[85]

In this period Arild Andersen, having just returned from New York, formed his own band with the 18 year-old pianist Jon Balke, saxophonist Knut Riisnæs and drummer Pål Thowsen, releasing *Cloud in My Head* in 1975. Although he was young, Jon Balke was very active along with his brother Erik, and was a member along with Arild Andersen and Jon Christensen, of the band led by Radka Toneff, who won a Norwegian Grammy (Spellemann Prize) in 1977 for best voice. Despite being self-taught, Jon Balke soon took an interest in composing for large ensembles, and eventually founded the first truly open collective in Norway, called Oslo 13.

It was around this time that the Norwegian percussionist Helge Linnaae went to Africa and, after meeting percussionist Momodou "Miki" N'Doye while in Gambia, insisted that he come to Oslo to form a band with him. Miki N'Doye arrived in Oslo in 1976, "after a hair-raising 11-day journey on West-African roads and finally a flight on a small plane that took me to the Norwegian capital".[86] N'Doye, who had become popular with his band in Gambia from his youth, had never thought of living abroad, but has now spent over 30 years of his 50-year career as a percussionist in Norway. In Oslo he was immediately integrated into the local scene, starting the band E'Olen with the two Balke brothers, plus Pablo Guanio (trumpet), Sveinung Hovensjø (bass), Carl Magnus Neumann (sax), Finn Sletten (drums) and, naturally, his friend "Zakhir" Helge Linnaae. As well as that he was always in great demand for the jam sessions at Club 7, and soon became the club's resident drummer: "It seemed inconceivable, but at a certain point I was playing there every day of the week".[87] Every Norwegian improviser who wanted to connect jazz with African music turned to him, and later he also played with foreign musicians of the calibre of drummer Ed Blackwell and trumpeter Don Cherry (who had moved to Scandinavia), who joined his band Tamma for concerts in Oslo and Molde.[88]

E'Olen, founded by Jon Balke and Miki N'Doye, brought to Oslo a wave of novelty with its African jazz rhythms, releasing its first album in 1979.[89] Working with N'Doye in this project was what inspired Joh Balke to compose for large ensembles and start Oslo 13, a collective that, under his leadership, saw the collaboration of Audun Kleive, Nils Petter Molvær, and Jon Christensen, followed by many other leading names in Norwegian jazz.

8
Jan Erik Kongshaug and Sven Persson
The importance of sound. A generation of outstanding sound engineers opens up a new world

"You brain's been fucked up!! You can't even recognise real sounds anymore because they've been feeding you fake, inflated sounds, full of reverb, and ECM is the one who's most responsible for this horror. It's like putting MSG all over your food, you get used to it and then everything else tastes insipid."[90]

I came across this rather colourful post one day in an online forum of hi-fi enthusiasts. They were hitting out at the amount of reverb which is typical of many ECM productions (in that specific case, the topic was Enrico Rava's album *Easy Living*). Some of the people on the forum railed against ECM, saying for example how Rava's trumpet sounded *grande* [91] (big) and unreal compared with Chet Baker's "real" trumpet (in *The Touch of Your Lips*, Steeplechase), and similar comments. The post was provocative, but brought attention back to a debate that has been going on for over 40 years between fans and critics of the so-called "Nordic sound", also known as the "ECM sound", in other words the result of the collaboration between Manfred Eicher and Jan Erik Kongshaug from 1970 until today.

All too often you hear people talking about the Norwegian scene as one that is interesting because it is "exotic"; it is the scene of the "Nordic tone", evoking fjords, snow and mountains, and it is also that of ECM and its "slick" sound. Yet this image doesn't tell us anything about the inherent quality of the music; it's like saying about a person that they are "nice". It's an approach that doesn't do justice to the artistic qualities of the musicians of the Norwegian scene. There are really too many clichés about Norway and the Nordic Tone. Undoubtedly this sound played a crucial role in Norwegian jazz and especially in Oslo's scene, as we said before referring to the recording of *Afric Pepperbird*,[92] and the impact this album had on the early Club 7. This doesn't mean, however, that Norwegian music can be boiled down to a single aesthetic or sound.

It was Kongshaug and Eicher who started it all, when they began exploring uncharted territories through the pioneering use of reverberation and of Lexicon's model 960L. The result was that trademark sound we already mentioned,[93] a sound of pristine clarity conveying an unimaginable sense of space. But more importantly, what Kongshaug and Eicher did was to initiate a tradition of audio engineers who profoundly influenced the music scene's development, and who a few years later would veer towards a powerful and even wider rock sound, which had a great impact on future Norwegian music.

Born in Trondheim in the mid-1940s to musical parents (his father was a guitarist and his mother a singer), Jan Erik Kongshaug started playing at an early age. After dabbling with the accordion he wanted to switch to the piano, but since it wasn't easy at the time to find one he opted for the guitar. It was with a guitar that he played on board a ship sailing between Oslo and New York, playing on board for an entire year, an experience that was quite common among aspiring jazz musicians of that era. Back in Oslo he enrolled at the University for a degree in Electronics, and there he had his first contact with the field that defined his future. A few years later he became a staff member at NRK, and after graduating from university in 1967, he began to play with Kjell Karlsen's band at the Eurovision Song Contest. As music was becoming more of a profession for him, Kjell Karlsen introduced him to Arne Bendiksen, at whose recording studio he subsequently started his career as an audio engineer.

When I came to Oslo in 1967 and started working in the studio I had no experience of recording. In the early days the studio was very simple, a valve mixing console with six channels, three on the right and three on the left, without panorama. And we had two 2-track recorders. So we recorded the band in stereo on two tracks, and then we copied that tape onto another 2-track tape, and you could repeat the process but the rhythm section got washy, and you couldn't change the balance anymore. And we did the editing with a razor blade... In 1969 we got an 8-track recorder, so then we could record each instrument on a separate track and still have the possibility to control the balance when we did overdubs. And we also got a new Neve console, a fantastic mixing desk, still considered one of the best brands today.[94]

At the time Bendiksen's studio was in the eastern part of Oslo, in the former biscuit factory Sætre Kjeksfabrikk. It was a small studio, but when Eicher arrived there it was fortunately equipped with a brand-new console and EMT reverb. Kongshaug was playing gigs at parties with the Beef Eaters, but his work as a sound engineer slowly began to take over. The owner Arne Bendiksen was a singer, composer and producer later known as "the father of Norwegian pop", and his studio focussed mostly on pop productions. Working with him along with Kongshaug was Hallvard Kvåle, who had been interested in folk music for some time.[95] On the fateful day of the first ECM recording[96] Kongshaug and Eicher were both beginners, but had clear ideas and came out satisfied. It was the first in a long series of recordings that worked brilliantly, at least until *Belonging*.[97] Over time, the studio's live room proved to be too small and unsuitable for what they wanted to do, so Kongshaug started looking for another recording studio, a decision than turned out to be crucial. Back then in Oslo it wasn't easy to find an alternative, but chance had it that Hallvard Kvåle introduced Kongshaug to Arve Sigvaldsen, a producer who made his name with folk music and who had plans to establish a label and a recording studio, called Talent Produksion. While Kongshaug was freelancing for this new studio he also started playing again, this time acoustic bass with Frode Thingnæs's quintet, and began experimenting with direct to disc recording.[98]

> Arve and I worked first at building up the studio and then, from 1974 to 1979, we did a whole lot of great recordings, for example we did the mix of the live recordings in Tokyo of *Personal Mountains* [99] - actually those took years and we finished them at the first Rainbow Studio. Yes, we recorded a lot of albums… It was the ECM years![100]

Kongshaug recorded a lot with Eicher during his five years at Talent Produksion, also working at the legendary Power Station studios in New York with Kenny Wheeler and many others. When Sigvaldsen's label and studio business started faltering, Kongshaug, who while freelancing was living in Trondheim, decided to move with his family to Oslo where, after Talent closed in 1984, he finally opened his own studio: the first Rainbow Studio. It was a real turning point in his life and the beginning of 20 years (1984-2004) of hard work full of risks as well as of gratifications, in his own studio helped by two freelance engineers. The studio in the area of Grünerløkka was beautiful, with a lot of wood, filled with light and quite large for those days (about 150 sq m). It was an ideal place for Manfred Eicher, who spent a great deal of time there. Eicher was always a hands-on producer for ECM recordings, which accounted for almost half of Rainbow's studio time. Although Kongshaug recorded all kinds of music, including classical, pop and folk, about 60% of his studio's time was dedicated to jazz projects, including all the ECM recordings as well as recordings for Blue Note and other labels and self-producing artists from Germany, the UK, Brazil, and elsewhere. The work done by Kongshaug and Rainbow Studio during these years included albums by Paul Bley, Masqualero, Charles Lloyd, Pat Metheny on the Geffen label, Sidsel Endresen's ECM debut album *So I Write*, and Ornette Coleman's *Song X*. Then, in 2004, a restaurant under the studio began to host live music and made recording impossible. Kongshaug was forced to move, and set up in a new studio, larger and better equipped than the previous one, that had good natural reverb and could also hold large ensembles. The reputation earned by Kongshaug and his second Rainbow Studio make him highly sought after by many Norwegian and international musicians in the jazz field. Some of these are artists who have worked with ECM in the past and have switched to other labels in search of more creative freedom, while others come to the Rainbow precisely in search of that famous ECM sound.

In the early 1970s Jan Erik Kongshaug was the link connecting ECM and Oslo, the referent for all those who arrived in the city to record with Manfred Eicher and his record company. It was a real turning point for the Norwegian scene, as many international musicians came and took part in memorable concerts and jam sessions at Club 7. Kongshaug, however, wasn't at ease working in these live events. It was a different job, and he much preferred the recording studio.

> I did a few live recordings, like George Russell's *Listen to the Silence* at the Kongsberg Festival, in a church with the vocal chorus and Garbarek; and then I did a few at Club 7. Really great recordings, for example Webster Lewis with Jimmy Hopps on drums, and then Hallvard Kvåle, and Inger Lise Rypdal (Terje's then wife), but I didn't like it. It was too hard to get a good sound with all that amplification on stage.[101]

So it was another sound engineer, the young Sven Persson, who got his chance to emerge at Club 7. In 1973 Persson was one of the members of Rufus, a Norwegian fusion band that was the supporting act for Terje Rypdal. The band wasn't doing so well, so he began to explore with Rypdal the problems of sound and amplifying systems. He spent many days as an apprentice in the studio with Kongshaug, observing during the recording sessions and learning the fundamentals, which were the same as those of live recording. Persson seemed to be a perfect complement to Kongshaug: "I wasn't particularly interested in studio recording. What I was really interested in was what happened on stage, I was excited by what happens in that hour and a half in which you have to do your very best otherwise someone else might be negatively affected..." [102] He began doing short tours, then in 1974, by a stroke of luck, he was hired as a sound technician at Club 7. He immediately started working with the amplification system, which in his view was what could really revolutionise the playing of jazz musicians, giving them the big, high-quality sound they never had. Among the regulars at Club 7 at that time was the noted Terje Rypdal, as well as Arild Andersen and the younger singer Radka Toneff. After trying out various amplifications, initially working with Rypdal himself, Persson developed his own system, and American artists passing through were struck by the unique quality of the sound in that basement club in the heart of Oslo. Jack DeJohnette was among the first to expressly ask for it, followed by Jon Balke and many more. After arguing with him during the sound-check, Carla Bley regularly called Persson in as sound technician for 12 years.

All those recordings happening in the city gave a great boost to the club scene. During the recording sessions I was always spending time with Eicher, I would buy him a newspaper and sit down with him and listen. Yes, it was a great period. The important thing for me was to become familiar with the instruments' sounds so that I could later improve them through amplification and reverb. The first to make good use of reverb was Jan Garbarek. I remember exactly when he took it out at Club 7. And I also remember very well when Pat Metheny came a few years later, with the Pat Metheny Group (Lyle Mays, Dan Gottlieb and Mark Egan). I did three shows with them, in Oslo, Molde and near Molde. They had a really impressive setup, with a Lexicon reverb. That device changed my life, to me it was a totally new way of treating sound. Pat was unique, he'd been able to get a completely new sound from the drums... it was real cutting-edge.[103]

During his time with Carla Bley, Persson moved to New York for a year and worked with many American musicians. When his experience with Carla Bley was over, back in Oslo where Club 7 was about to close down, Persson had enough of the jazz milieu and wanted a change. He moved to London to work with indie rock band The Adventures on the British pop scene, but that didn't last long. After touring with Lou Reed and Chaka Khan, Persson began working with the leading Norwegian pop group A-Ha, putting his previous London experience to work. An important result from Persson's work came in the second half of the 1980s, with the trio The Chaser (Terje Rypdal, Audun Kleive and Bjørn Kjellemyr), an act for which sound quality, intensity and control were key. Persson worked a lot on the length of the reverb, trying to obtain what he describes as a "cloud", or as the "Kompet Går" sound, named after a track from the trio's second album (*Blue*) that was used for a long time by hi-fi stores to demonstrate their audio systems.

With his way of being on stage like the other musicians Persson set himself apart, and his intention of bringing a Pink Floyd sound to jazz made him a unique sound engineer that left a big mark. Persson was undoubtedly a pioneer who with his early work at Club 7 helped put Oslo at the centre of international jazz, catching the attention of artists such as Jack DeJohnette, Carla Bley and Pat Metheny, and at the same time opened the way for a younger generation (Audun Kleive, Nils Petter Molvær, Bugge Wesseltoft) that a few years later would come to so-called "nu jazz". In the late 1990s Persson himself returned to jazz, next to a host of excellent sound engineers, Asle Karstad being perhaps the brightest star.

The school of sound engineers that emerged in Norway and that is represented today by many brilliant sound technicians[104] developed an extraordinary sound for live performances that has nothing to do with the "typical" ECM sound of the Rainbow Studio. It is a sound that unites highly transparent and realistic acoustic quality with previously unthinkable intensity and space, much closer to that of Pink Floyd than to the one of jazz.

9
The connection between jazz and folk music
Through a form of genre-crossing improvisation
Norwegian jazz comes into its own. Østerdalsmusikk, E'Olen,
the Frode Fjellheim Jazz Joik Ensemble and Utla

In November 1972 Jan Garbarek went into the studio in Oslo with the Finnish percussionist Edward Vesala, bassist Arild Andersen, and Jan Erik Kongshaug as sound engineer, to record an album that, like the previous *Afric Pepperbird*, had a great immediate impact, but also left a lasting mark: *Tryptykon*. Although largely influenced by free jazz, the album included two tracks inspired by folk music, "Selje" and "Bruremarsj". The first evokes the atmospheres of the fjords, and in it Garbarek plays the wooden flute, while the second is a wedding march based on a melody for violin by Olav Holø,[105] a tune that's very familiar to Norwegian folk musicians and that was originally transcribed by Ole Mørk Sandvik,[106] one of the major figures in the resurgence of Norwegian folk music. Garbarek's interpretation of Holø's version, one of the many variants in circulation, is charged with an energy very different from the traditional folk music.

Tryptykon represents the first true contact between Sandvik's research and the world of jazz. It's hard to say how much this album influenced other jazz musicians, but its historical value is undisputable, even just for the fact that it was the first time that Garbarek put into practice George Russell's teaching, by using a Norwegian folk tune as the basis for improvisation.[107] What's more, it was not released on an obscure local label but on Germany's ECM.

Soon afterwards, in August 1975, Garbarek returned to the studio to participate in one of the most representative projects of Sandvik's work, and specifically his collection *Østerdalsmusikken*. The project was led by Torgrim Sollid, who had been the drummer in Garbarek's first quartet[108] between 1962 and 1963. Originally from eastern Norway, the Østerdal region near the Swedish border, Sollid took an interest in the transcriptions Sandvik had made of the traditional music of that region, and started the project with Alf Kjellman and Erling Aksdal. Sollid had never had close contacts with folk music until he heard the Hardanger fiddle (*hardingfele*) played by the great Martinus Helgesen (1849-1926).[109] So in 1973 he embarked on this project, which he described as "really complex", and which culminated in the release of the album *Østerdalsmusikk*.[110] No musicians in Oslo except Garbarek had done work of this kind, and after a few concerts with

Alf Kjellmann and Erling Aksdal, Sollid started engaging other musicians for the project. The first was trumpeter Lars Martin Thomassen, who at the time was making a living as an architect and seemed to be the one of the few interested in a less "American", softer sound. Next he recruited his old friend Knut Riisnæs, and finally he asked Jan Garbarek, who had recently come out with *Tryptikon*, and whose unique sound seemed ideal for bringing Sandvik's transcriptions back to life. Garbarek accepted, on the condition that he play the role of simple session musician. As Sollid recalls, however, "it was clear that Jan had been studying Norwegian folk traditions and *Østerdalsmusikken* for a while, because when we got together he immediately started suggesting what to play and how to play it. And it was enlightening. I never asked him directly, but I'm sure of this".[111] It's true that there was the precedent of Jan Johansson, who in 1964 released an album based on Swedish folk songs, *Jazz på svenska*,[112] one of the best selling albums in the history of European jazz, but Johansson used typical jazz harmonies, while Sollid's group, despite their jazz background, went in the opposite direction, creating arrangements that tried to capture the feeling of the song and the context or taking them directly from Sandvik's book:

> [...] because the oral tradition was gone. Sure, we also made errors, but later we corrected them. I worked hard, I relied on theories and hypotheses, I tried to imagine and to identify how much there was of the more popular French song, how much of wedding marches, and as I went on I discovered many of them that I didn't know but were still played in various areas. I'd never been interested in the past and in traditional music before, it was like a great black hole. I still don't know how I really got started on it, but I know for sure that a lot of people hopped on that train after that.[113]

Ole Mørk Sandvik had done an excellent job, but had run into difficulties when he had to interpret the rhythms and keys of the dances. These doubts found a totally unexpected solution in the 1970s, when some phonograph cylinders[114] recorded by Sandvik with Martinus Helgesen were found by chance in a barn near Østerdalen. These were not the only recordings that Sandvik made with some of the best violinists of the time,[115] but they are among the few that came to light, and to Sollid they represented a priceless treasure. Decades after the recordings were made, Sollid was able to listen to them and, through a great deal of hard work, to transcribe the complex and sophisticated rhythms of folk music and find solutions to many of the problems that Sandvik wasn't able to resolve. Once Sollid could rely on Helgesen's interpretative clues he was able to start recording the album, inviting guest players and choosing a Polska dance from his native town, children songs, lullabies and mountain tunes, all from the *Østerdalsmusikken* collection. Curiously the label that released the record was the Communist MAI Records, which subjected Sollid and Knut Riisnæs to a sort of interrogation, requiring them to declare their political orientation. It was the 1970s, and chance had it that Sollid had taken an interest in the Black Panther Party active in the United States at that time, and was able to answer the questions: "that was probably the only reason why they let us record the album...", he recalled.[116] With *Østerdalsmusikk* Sollid took the direction advocated by George Russell, and a few years later, when he had the opportunity to talk to him about the album, he found out that Russell knew about it and was interested in what scales and keys were used (and was surprised to learn that most of the songs were baaed on the Dorian and Lydian scales).

Sollid's project somehow went in a direction opposite to that of the American swing or be-bop traditions, which started from their African-American roots and then moved away from them. By substituting New Orleans funeral marches with the wedding marches of Østerdalen, the Norwegian scene increasingly set itself apart from the rest of the world.

Aside from Garbarek, Sollid was the person who drove Norwegian music the most in this direction, and this impulse, along with George Russell's earlier contribution and ECM's influence in the early 1970s, combined to bring a profound change to Norwegian jazz, which until that point had been closely tied to the African-American tradition like the Danish and Swedish jazz scenes. It was a process that was further confirmed and energized at the end of the decade with the birth of the Trondheim Conservatory.

This evolution was succinctly summed up by the musicologist Tor Dybo,[117] who divided musicians into two categories: those who use the background of improvisation and the American tradition to explore new forms of expression (Norwegians), and those who continue to consider the American tradition of jazz as a living tradition (Americans, Danes and many others). To support his thesis he drew on the examples of Jan Garbarek and *Østerdalsmusikk*, the Frode Fjellheim Jazz Joik Ensemble's *Saajve Dans*[118] (a project based on the Sami music collection *Die lappische Volksmusik*)[119], and finally the trio Utla,[120] which blends folk music, free jazz and rock elements using unusual instruments such as goat horns, Hardanger fiddles and very unusual percussion. A fourth example could have been E'Olen (and actually Dybo mentioned this band on other occasions),[121] a band that mixed Norwegian improvisation with rhythmic and drumming elements from Gambia.[122]

Through all these different experiences musicians, including musicians coming from jazz, appropriated and renewed other traditions, thus moving away in many directions from the American jazz tradition, and giving birth to new forms of intercultural expression. This is a point emphasized by Dybo, who also points out how jazz in Norway is constantly evolving, compared with musicians in the United States who adopt the American tradition as their musical identity. In other words, you could say that Norwegians have learned from the tradition (American, Norwegian, African, or whatever else it might be), making it their own and making it relevant for the times, while Americans have learned the tradition and tend to constantly go back to it. These two approaches correspond to two distinct educational strategies, represented by the Trondheim Jazz Conservatory on one hand and the historical Berklee College of Music on the other, which will be explored in more detail in the next chapter.

10
Music education
The Trondheim Conservatory of Music opens its doors to jazz, followed by the conservatories of Oslo, Tromsø, Stavanger and Kristiansand

The first State music faculty at university-level in Norway was the Norwegian Academy of Music (Norges musikkhøgskole) in Oslo, established in 1973. It was, however, dedicated entirely to classical music, and any aspiring jazz musicians, once they had finished their studies there, often went on to the Berklee College of Music, the famous American music school founded in 1945 in Boston.

Terje Bjørklund[123] was among the first to obtain a Masters Degree in Musicology (1971) there when it was still a private conservatory, going on to study composition with Finn Mortensen for the following two years. He continued to work as a musician, unable to find work in academia, until the Trondheim Conservatory finally offered him a position of professor (he still teaches music theory and composition there today). In 1979, after a few years teaching classical music, Bjørklund and his friend and colleague John Pål Inderberg established the first jazz course. Soon after the course began, Bjørklund stopped working as a pianist and wrote the book *Moderne jazzimprovisasjon*,[124] which earned him Jazzforum's highest award Buddyprisen. The educational model he proposed was in stark contrast with the one followed at Berklee, mixing traditional musical training and the study of improvisation and focusing primarily on nurturing the students' personalities, rather than on skill and technique as was done in Boston.

The jazz course gained popularity, and selecting the students wasn't easy, as so many wanted to enrol. In the first year only six students were admitted, and the organisers tried to select a varied group that could play together and could provide an initial core of players: piano, drums, bass, guitar and horns. Some of the students that attended were already making a living playing music, so it wasn't easy to manage them. For example Tore Brunborg and Nils Petter Molvær, who joined the course the following year, were already very busy playing professionally, and in the end didn't even complete the course. These two were extremely talented players who soon went on to join Arild Andersen, Jon Christensen and Jon Balke to form the legendary band Masqualero. Initially the course lasted three years but soon was extended to four, with two foundation years leading into two years of intensive course. The course grew slowly but steadily, and by the late 1990s it had expanded dramatically.

When Arve Henriksen arrived in Trondheim in 1987 there was only one class for each year, and his class included the drummer Sverre Kjetil Gjørvad from Hammerfest (in the northern region of Finnmark), and the bassist/pianist of the local pop band Tre Små Kinesere,[125] Baard Slagsvold. Among the students in the years above them in the course were the guitarist Nils-Olav Johansen, the percussionist Helge Norbakken and a few others, ten students altogether. According to Bjørklund, keeping the numbers low was a deliberate choice, as the organisers preferred maintaining an almost one-to-one student-teacher ratio. Joining the course the following year were the keyboardist Ståle Storløkken and the drummer Jarle Vespestad, who with Henriksen started one of the most representative bands of the Trondheim conservatory's "revolution": Veslefrekk. During the same period, saxophonist Petter Wettre, born in 1967 and a year older than Henriksen, moved to Boston to attend the Berklee School of Music, from which he graduated in 1992. Wettre and Henriksen represent musicians who took opposite roads, developed different outlooks, and had quite differing careers.

In the early phase, Trondheim's students had great freedom, often choosing the direction they wanted to explore on their own, with professors setting guidelines but not imposing any model, pattern or form. This freedom had its risks, because it was up to the students to decide how much to practise and how much to study. Today things have changed, and Trondheim too has a much more structured course of study. Following the conservatory's success, the number of students has vastly increased and it's no longer possible for teachers to follow them individually: in 2012 the jazz department had 16 professors (8 full-time and 8 part-time) and admitted 35 students per year. The original philosophy, however, is still the same, aiming to foster and develop the aspiring musicians' identities and personalities. The Trondheim educational model, quite unlike the one followed in the United States, was a source of inspiration for all the conservatories that were established afterwards, which all contributed to freeing the Norwegian jazz scene from the influence of the American tradition.

In the early 1980s, after the *Østerdalsmusikk* project, Torgrim Sollid[126] moved to Trondheim to teach at the Conservatory and adopted its model. In 1983, when he went to New York for six months to play with his friend Warne Marion Marsh,[127] he went up to Berklee to meet a pianist friend, coming into contact with that prestigious school for the first time. He was struck by the difference in philosophy and method:

It was like a factory. It was directed by musicians my age or a few years older, who were terrified by the idea that be-bop could vanish. While going out of their way to save it, and to save the jazz tradition with it, they were destroying all the rest. Everybody was focused on how to listen, learn and interpret that music, how to play those licks as fast as possible. It was a constant running up and down the scales, all the students were playing the same exact phrases. It was the exact opposite of what we were trying to do! Yes, because we thought it was more important that in the phrasing the musician's personality come through.[128]

While most of the world was studying exclusively the African-American jazz tradition, the Norwegian scene took a different direction, influenced perhaps by its folk music, so open to highly individual traits and so rich in originality. One could argue that it was precisely this that sparked a different idea of schooling, which today is a fully-fledged educational method. "You can't imagine how much work we do, with the number of students we have today at the Conservatory, to put this method into practice and to keep their personalities alive"[129] Sollid says, referring to the jazz department of Oslo's Norwegian Academy of Music, where he currently teaches.

Today in Norway there are at least six jazz conservatories of equal excellence (Oslo, Bergen, Stavanger, Tromsø, Kristiansand and Trondheim), as is evidenced by the fact that the more recent winners of JazzIntro, a competition dedicated to young jazz musicians, are no longer only students from Trondheim but also from Oslo or Stavanger (i.e. Monkey Plot, In the Country).

The early years of Trondheim's jazz department, however, are seared in the memory of many. The third-largest city in Norway (with a population of about 170,000), Trondheim became a magical place, the ideal breeding ground for musicians of all kinds, who immediately felt at home and were easily integrated into city life. With its beautiful historical centre and set in a mostly agricultural countryside, the city became an open-air workshop, and in the evening there would be music everywhere: in the characteristic red round building of the Studentersamfundet, in Albert's cafe (the local jazz club) and in many other smaller venues. It was an extremely lively atmosphere that got even better when the jazz department moved to the centre of town[130] in 1995. Many of the students worked at the jazz club or were involved in other music-related activities, holding seminars and teaching improvisation to musicians coming from the local rock groups and marching bands. Trondheim didn't offer many other distractions, and with so many musicians around, holding seminars during the day and playing at night, often with their own students, jazz became the heart of the city's life.

Arriving in the city in the early 1990s were several students destined to become some of the key musicians on the contemporary scene: Helge Norbakken, the already mentioned Ståle Storløkken, Jarle Vespestad and Arve Henriksen (Veslefrekk trio), Christian Wallumrød, Trygve Seim, Johannes Eick and Per Oddvar Johansen (Airamero quartet), as well as Nils-Olav Johansen and Stian Carstensen, who a few years later would form Farmers Market. It was an entire generation that emerged in Trondheim in those years and that now, 20 years later, still works in close contact with the school and with the same enthusiasm. A few of them - Tor Haugerud, Trond Kopperud, Vigleik Storaas - even decided to stay on in Trondheim, touched by their experiences as students there. The only other scene that could compare to that of Trondheim with its special atmosphere is that of Bergen which, towards the turn of the millennium, became peopled of highly innovative artists, such as Bjørn Torske and Röyksopp, who'll be discussed in more detail in the chapter on DJs.

Martinus Helgesen in 1890 © Christian Eggen (family archive)

George Russell directs his big band (Bernt Rosengren soloist with Jan Garbarek), Club 7, Oslo 31 August 1967

George Russell with Jan Garbarek, Jon Christensen and Per Løberg at the Bikuben, Oslo 1967 © Randi Hultin

The Metropol jazz club, Oslo © Per Rønnevig

Karin Krog and Dexter Gordon in Molde, 1965 © Randi Hultin

Karin Krog and Laila Dalseth © Per Rønnevig

Don Ellis and Finn Mortensen at the Metropol jazz club, Oslo 1963 © Randi Hultin

Don Ellis (trumpet), Arild Wikstrøm (piano), Per Løberg (double bass), Bjørn Johansen
Bjørn Johansen (tenor sax) and Ole Jacob Hansen (drums) © Per Rønnevig

From the left: Jan Garbarek, Jon Christensen, Arild Andersen and Frank Phipps -
Oslo, 1967 © Arthur Sand

Don Cherry, Jon Christensen and Jan Garbarek © Arne Schanche Andresen

Terje Bjørklund receives the Buddy Prize at Club 7 (Espen Rud, Knut Kristiansen, Rolf Grundesen and Terje Bjørklund), Oslo 1983 © Arthur Sand

Jan Garbarek and, in the opposite page, Jon Christensen © Arthur Sand

Randi Hultin at the Metropol jazz club, Oslo 1964 © Per Rønnevig

Rune Klakegg © Per Husby

Don Cherry, Jacques Thollot, Al Heath, John Hendricks and Kjell Johansen in Hjertøya, Molde 1968 © Arthur Sand

E'Olen reunion (Helge Linnaae/Demba/Miki N'Doye) in Molde, 1985 © Per Husby

Egil Kapstad, Sheila Jordan, and Bjørn Johansen during the rehearsal of *Bill Evans in Memoriam*, 1983 Vossajazz © Per Husby

Jan Garbarek and L. Subramaniam in Molde © Per Husby

Svein Finnerud Trio with Kåre Kolberg during the rehearsals for the perfomance *Jaba*, Molde, 1968 © Roger Engvik

Jan Berger (guitar) and Erik Amundsen (double bass) at the Munch Museum, Oslo © Randi Hultin

Svein Finnerud trio at the Henie Onstad Art Centre, Oslo © Arthur Sand

Arild Andersen © Per Husby

Radka Toneff © Per Husby

The Brazz Brothers

George Russell Sextet (Bjørnar Andresen,
Terje Rypdal, Arild Andersen and Bertil Lövgren)
in the square of Bologna's train station, 1969

Svein Finnerud Trio with Svein Christiansen on drums (replacing Espen Rud) and Carl
Magnus Neumann on alto sax, Henie Onstad Art Centre, Oslo © Svein Christiansen

Afric Pepperbird's quartet (from the left: Terje Rypdal, Jon Christensen, Arild Andersen and Jan Garbarek) in Molde, 1969 © Roger Engvik

Jazzpønkensembleet (Tore Brunborg and Erik Balke) at Vossajazz © Per Husby

Jan Garbarek and Keith Jarrett (the day before recording *Belonging*) at NRK TV
Studio,Oslo 1974 © Terje Mosnes

Keith Jarrett's European quartet (the day before recording *Belonging*) at NRK TV
Studio, Oslo 1974 © Terje Mosnes

From the left: Terje Mosnes, Manfred Eicher and Jan Erik Kongshaug
at the Rainbow Studio, Oslo

Keith Jarrett and Manfred Eicher at the Rainbow Studio, Oslo © Randi Hultin

Jon Eberson Group (Atle Bakken, Geir Holmsen, Sidsel Endresen, Jon Eberson and Bjørn Jensen) © Pål Rødahl

E'Olen © Randi Hultin

Torgrim Sollid

Bjørnar Andresen, Jan Garbarek, Arild Andersen, Espen Rud and Terje Rypdal during the concert/happening Samklang! at the Henie Onstad Art Centre, Oslo © Arthur Sand

Jaga Jazzist at club Blå, Oslo © Robin Ottersen

Radka Toneff and Steve Dobrogosz at the Amalienborg Jazz Club (Malla), Oslo 1980 © Terje Mosnes and, on the right, Dag Arnesen © Per Husby

Farmers Market © Anne Lise Flavik

Christian Eggen © Svein Christiansen

UTLA (Håkon Høgemo, Terje Isungset and Karl Seglem) © Kaare Thomsen

Martin Revheim in front of club Blå, Oslo, 2002 © Gustav P. Jensen (*Dagsavisen*)

Veslefrekk (Jarle Vespestad, Ståle Storløkken and Arve Henriksen) © CF-Wesenberg

Jaga Jazzist at the Molde Jazz Festival, 1999 © Gustav P. Jensen (*Dagsavisen*)

Jøkleba (Per Jørgensen, Jon Balke e Audun Kleive) © CF-Wesenberg

Bendik Hofseth © Per Husby

Lars Mørch Finborud and Arne Bendiksen © Arne Ove Bergo (*Dagsavisen*)

Masqualero (standing: Nils Petter Molvær, Jon Balke and Arild Andersen, crouching: Tore Brunborg and Jon Christensen) © Annette Jackbo

Element (Paal Nilssen-Love, Ingebrigt Håker Flaten, Gisle Røen Johansen and Håvard Wiik © Helmly production

Airamero (Trygve Seim, Christian Wallumrød, Per Oddvar Johansen and Johannes Eick © Andrzej Tyszko

Jan Garbarek © Knut Strand

Nils Petter Molvær © Per Husby

Jon Balke and Bjørn Kjellemyr, Jazzpønkensemblet at Vossajazz © Per Husby

Terje Rypdal © Per Husby

11
From Oslo 13 to Jøkleba, via Masqualero
Three generations of musicians and the importance of the collective

The late 1970s were Club 7's golden period, when soul, funk and especially pop started mixing with jazz, adding to the broad palette of jazz that had already seen influences from folk, rock and contemporary music. A new wave of younger musicians was emerging, and while Jan Garbarek's flourishing international career with ECM had set him apart from the Norwegian scene, the same wasn't true for others in his generation. Among these, Arild Andersen was the one to engage younger musicians and give them the most prominence. He did this with Jon Balke and Pål Thowsen in *Clouds In My Head*[131] and continued with Radka Toneff and Terje Rypdal, helping a new generation emerge. More importantly, what began to happen was something unusual for the jazz world, in the sense that the more famous musicians didn't seem interested in forming groups that followed the standard jazz practice, preferring a more collective and democratic idea, perhaps something more characteristic of rock music. It mirrored the Norwegian culture and politics of the time which, as early as before World War II, had provided a model for left wing policies in Western democracies.

Jon Balke, who had debuted on ECM with Andersen's quartet and had been in the limelight at Club 7 with Miki N'Doye's band E'Olen[132] and with Radka Toneff's group,[133] joined Oslo 13, a sort of new jazz orchestra. The 13-member band, founded by trumpeter Bror Hagemann in 1981, had started out performing Hagemann's compositions, strongly influenced by Gil Evans's music and arrangements. One year after the orchestra had come into being, Balke's arrival radically changed everything. Playing drums at that point was the very young Audun Kleive, who had moved to Oslo from his native Skien in the south of Norway. Balke, who replaced Rune Klakegg on piano, immediately exerted a strong influence, to the point that Hagemann left the ensemble:

Balke attended a few rehearsals and then came into the project, and we found each other immediately. He was extremely influential for the whole development of rhythmic structures and focus on rhythmic stuff, he knew a lot about beat [...][134] It started out with Hagemann writing everything, and then it became a sort of collective experiment, with everybody bringing in their music and trying to explore new ground. Then after a few years of sharing all the material, we found out that we had to concentrate on some part, and that was for the most part the stuff the Jon Balke wrote.[135]

So Balke, who was younger than Finnerud and Garbarek but older than Kleive, began to compose in earnest. His gifts as a composer and leader made him the central figure of the collective, which turned professional: in 1983 Oslo 13 went into the studio as an 11-piece band to record their first album *Anti-Therapy* for Odin, Jazzforum's label.[136] They were all excellent musicians, but two of them stood: trumpeter Nils Petter Molvær and drummer Audun Kleive, two young lions that were destined to write many pages in the chapter of Norwegian jazz's history. As Kleive recalls:

> The bass, drums and piano were in focus all the time, so more than a big band it was a trio with a large horn section. It was kind of spectacular when we played live, we always had the trio front-stage and all the other guys in the back. It raised a lot of eyebrows, because it was completely new and it went against the jazz tradition. But it reflected our thought that the three of us were driving the whole thing, because we were playing very interactive music all the time, even my drumming was very soloistic.[137]

Oslo 13 was an extraordinary ensemble, which saw the comings and goings of some of the best young musicians on the circuit: trumpeters Nils Petter Molvær, Jens Petter Antonsen and Staffan Svensson, and saxophonists Morten Halle, Tore Brunborg, Odd Riisnæs, Erik Balke and Trygve Seim. In 1988 Oslo 13 released, always for Odin, *Off-Balance*, an album that won the Spellemann Prize and marked one of the peaks of the ensemble's creativity and popularity. It then returned to the studio in September 1990 to record *Nonsentration* for ECM,[138] and when the album was released it was credited to both Jon Balke and Oslo 13, underlying the difference in mentality between the Norwegian scene and the international one. The communal spirit that animated the world of music in Norway was reflected not only in the groups' music, which was often the result of a truly collective interaction, but also in their band names, unlikely to go by the name of this or that member. It was a typically Norwegian characteristic that musicians sharing ideas joined under abstract, extraordinary names, resulting in such bands as Masqualero, Airamero, Supersilent, Farmers Market, Close Erase, Jaga Jazzist and many more. Oslo 13's golden period ended in 1992 with the release of *Live*, recorded live at Oslo's Cosmopolite for the Norwegian label Curling Legs.

Club 7 was the hothouse where all this emerged, even though different generations didn't always mix. As Kleive recalls, "I've never played with Svein Finnerud, Christian Reim, Calle Neumann, and so on. I knew them, and I heard them play at Club 7, but the opportunity of playing together never came".[139] Oslo 13 was one of the first acts to emerge out of the exceptional period of Club 7, in the late 1970s and early 1980s. Another was Chipahua, a sort of soul-jazz orchestra that often gigged at the club and shared some members with Oslo 13 (Morten Halle, Nils Petter Molvær and Torbjørn Sunde), and also included orchestra leader and guitarist Jon Eberson, singer Inger Lise Rypdal (then wife of Terje Rypdal) and the young and talented vocalist Sidsel Endresen, who had returned from the UK after living there a few years. Still in her twenties, Endresen was truly a star: fresh on the scene, she was also singing with the Jon Eberson Group, whose album *Jive Talking*[140] sold more than a quarter million copies and was an unprecedented hit in Norway. Chipahua was formed in 1979 and in 1984 released its one and only LP, *The Soul Survivors*,[141] the recording of their many live performances at Club 7. In this moment of particular creative fervour, these were all acts that gravitated around Club 7 and the University communities, and had a local or at best national impact. While Oslo 13 veered away from the jazz tradition into a more "art-music" territory, Chipahua instead took in pop and soul influences, not concerned with fitting into a specific music genre or context. They represented of a new generation that mixed jazz experiences and pop/rock collaborations, widening their background to new elements that informed the emergence, in the 1990s, of what Bugge Wesseltoft defined as "nu jazz". This period also saw the first use of electronics, especially by the pioneering Atle Bakken,[142] who emerged first as a musician and then as a producer.

Bakken was the keyboardist for the Jon Eberson Group, and played a big role in the production of *Jive Talking*. He brought a wave of novelty into the world frequented by Radka Toneff, Arild Andersen, Jon Eberson and Terje Rypdal, even though his career later took a radically different direction, as a producer for Sony Music and then touring with Stevie Wonder, Sting, Diana Ross and Andy Summers.

Atle Bakken was an amazing guy. I remember his ideas and instrumentations, they were so far ahead. I remember that we went on tour and he had a Lexicon reverb. I think in Oslo only Jan Erik Kongshaug had another one of those: it cost what the average Norwegian made in two years' salaries! Well he had one on tour and we got a sound that I'd never heard before, at least in jazz.[143]

Nils Petter Molvær and Tore Brunborg arrived in Oslo just out of the Trondheim conservatory in the early 1980s, eager to be in a band. As Jon Christensen said to *Jazznytt* journalist Johan Hauknes, "Tore Brunborg had just gotten off the train from Trondheim carrying two plastic bags, and before he even found a place in Oslo said 'Yes! I'm in!'".[144] As Jon Christensen went on to explain, this was the beginning of one the bands that best represented Norwegian jazz in the world: Masqualero.

Tore and Nils Petter came from Trondheim and settled in the city. They were very good and so Arild, Jon Balke and I decided to form a group. In the beginning the idea was to put together a quintet in Arild's name, but when we released our first album *Masqualero*, taking inspiration from Wayne Shorter's composition for Miles Davis's band, we decided to take that name as well. Unfortunately when we went to play in Sweden, Denmark, the UK or the United States we had to go by another name, because people would identify Masqualero with the Latin American dance. So we would go as a quintet in Arild's name and mine, since at that time we were better known than the others.[145]

The quintet was formed in 1982 and in the following year released its first eponymous album for Odin, which won the annual Spellemann Prize. When the group toured abroad, billing themselves as the Arild Andersen/Jon Christensen Quintet in order to get gigs at festivals, people had the idea that they were a traditional jazz quintet, but Nils Petter Molvær (trumpet), Tore Brunborg (sax), Jon Balke (piano), Arild Andersen (bass) and Jon Christensen (drums) were more of a rock band, which developed its own very original identity. Masqualero was a great example of three different generations of musicians coming together, the two veterans Andersen and Christensen taking under their wing the young talents Molvær and Brunborg, as well as the slightly older Jon Balke, who displayed an exceptional artistic maturity. If the first album *Masqualero* surprised and impressed, the following *Bande à Part*[146] only confirmed the band's success, winning a 1986 Spelleman Prize, and featuring brilliant compositions and a more meditative music. Andersen's very spacious sound and Christensen's artistry provided a solid ground in which the other musicians made constant forays, able to express at the same time joy and pain. And space.

Not content with having reached the top of the Norwegian charts, Masqualero aimed to make their mark in the United States, and went on to do precisely that on a widely acclaimed tour that included concerts in New York and the West Coast. This was a super-group, which put all its members' ideas in play, with excellent results in terms of both quality and creativity. Andersen flexed muscle more than usual, always delivering his rich double bass sound, while opening new spaces for all the others to move into. As Jon Christensen recalled:

After releasing the first record with Odin we started recording for ECM. And then came the point when Jon Balke decided to leave the band. So we tried out a few guitarists, and we went to America, and it was a great period, full of excitement. It was a milestone for me. After meeting Jan Garbarek and Manfred Eicher I started working with ECM: Bobo Stenson, Pålle Danielsson, Keith Jarrett. Forming an all-Norwegian band that worked with ECM was one of the most important steps in my career. I remember it as a thrilling period: during the time we worked together it was fantastic to see young and talented musicians like Tore and Nils Petter grow day after day.[147]

In the following years the band released *Aero*,[148] the first album without Balke and featuring Frode Alnæs on guitar, and *Re-Enter*[149] as a quartet, which earned them their third Spelleman Prize in 1991. The story of Masqualero was an intense one, that saw two legends of Norwegian jazz, Arild Andersen and Jon Christensen, and their ideal accomplice Jon Balke, form a band with two of the most talented emerging musicians of the time. After all, since we are talking about the legacy of Miles's quintet, how could you not notice that young Tore Brunborg on sax, and that equally young Nils Petter Molvær on trumpet?

After leaving Masqualero, Jon Balke began collaborating with drummer Audun Kleive and trumpeter Per Jørgensen, in what would turn out to be another historical band: the trio Jøkleba.[150] Balke and Kleive had already found themselves very much along the same wavelength playing together in Oslo 13, the project that at that time was winding down. Per Jørgensen, the singer, guitarist and leader of the Bergen Blues Band, had recently acquired a reputation through his work with Dag Arnesen and with *Ny Bris*'s band,[151] two projects that had been going on in his native city of Bergen.

The trio Jøkleba was formed in 1991 and became an extremely popular live band, recording three albums in its ten years of activity.[152] Over this period, the band explored free improvisation that propelled them into new, vast territories of ecstatic liberation, accompanied by increasingly ambitious inner expectations. Jon Balke summed it up:

Beginning in 1991, based on the vague structural idea of musical microstructures and maximum freedom, we moved through a many-year-long peak of joyful playing with our own and our audience's expectations, and then on to a period of ever-rising internal ambitions, finally leading to the decision to stop. During all this the trio developed into a tight musical and social unit that demanded a devotion unparalleled in any other musical venture I have experienced.

I came fresh out of groups like Oslo 13 and Masqualero, and felt that some of the ideas that were researched there needed a smaller format. The concept of playing trio without bass was clearly inspired by an experience in Poland, where, after playing a gig, I managed to catch the last set of Edward Vesala, Adam Macowicz, and Tomasz Stanko - an experience I still recall vividly. A trio of masters moving completely organically in streams of wonderfully rich sound. What struck me as ingenious was that the trumpet tones could be harmonized in an unlimited variety of ways by not being rooted by a bass tone. But I wanted to explore the outer limits of composition, so I felt like organising the freedom in a different manner, reducing the compositions to bits that could be inserted freely to give the improvised flow a new direction, when needed. [...] I already felt completely in sync with Audun Kleive's fantastic playing from Oslo 13 and had always wanted to work with Per Jørgensen, so the choice of players came naturally.[153]

It all began thanks to Balke. A rising star in the 1980s, he really came into the limelight in the 1990s, but was a humble and generous musician, shunning fame and on a constant quest for ideas and companions to create new projects. Initially, Jøkleba's popularity was confined to Norway, with the trio recording their first album with the label Odin. Then came an unexpected break. Balke was touring in Europe when he received a call from Bjørn Nessjø, a producer renowned for the commercial success of some of his pop-rock productions. Nessjø wanted to bring Jøkleba into the recording studio, and while surprised at first, Balke realised he was serious. They started recording in 1992, and Nessjø gave them total freedom, at one condition only: that after they do a take they would decide whether they liked it or not, and if they didn't they would erase it. There was not a trace of alternate takes left, a practice quite opposite to what happened in jazz recordings. As Balke recalled:

> It all seemed a bit dogmatic and totalitarian at first, but we soon realised that it was a very stimulating way to work. It was a bit like a painter when he paints: we just recorded an improvisation, and would just listen to it and decide. And later we would work on the details, a bass line here, some high frequencies in the background, etc.[154]

The trio recorded in the studio for two weeks, which was another novelty, being used to working as fast as possible to keep the costs down. Between recording and post-production, the whole thing lasted five weeks: "It was really an extraordinary event for us. We were staying in a hotel suite in Trondheim, where

Bjørn had his studio, treated like pop star. Incredible!".[155] The resulting album *Jøkleba!*[156] was really successful in Norway and in the whole of Scandinavia, soon becoming a cult record. After a year it sold out, but Bjørn Nessjø's label Norsk Plateproduksjon was bought by BMG, which didn't seem interested in a reissue.

When the trio went back into the studio some years later to record another album with Bjørn Nessjø, they chose to cover a selection of well-known pop tunes - something currently quite in vogue among jazz trios such as Bad Plus, Rusconi trio, Doctor3, etc. In their brilliant reinterpretation of the famous melodies they transformed them with their unmistakable sound - the trumpet in the centre, over landscapes of percussion and electronics. But towards the end of the 20th century, independent labels were facing growing difficulties, with a shrinking market and the competition of Napster, iTunes, and Spotify. Constantly going against the grain, the band developed a quality of music that was too far ahead of its time. Nobody seemed interested in releasing the trio's new work, and after a few attempts they gave up:

> Jøkleba faced a kind of double block: we had arrived at a point where our own expectations and demands were exceeding our abilities, and the music business was not responding to what we created. We stopped playing live, and we all moved on to different projects. But the recordings remained as a volcanic force, boiling in the vault, waiting for the eruption. So it was inevitable.[157]

Indeed, that volcanic force was able to explode only in 2011 thanks to Universal Music Norway, with the release of *Nu Jøk?* as a box set that also contained *Jøkleba!*, the record that sold out in less than a year in 1993. The magical trio that in the 1990s had thrilled the whole of Scandinavia and offered unforgettable performances,[158] came back after a 10-year break, and not only on record: when bassist Dave Holland had to pull out of his performance at Vossajazz 2011, the festival organisers approached Jøkleba to see if they would fill in. The trio accepted, and their performance, according to the Norwegian press, was one of the best live shows of 2011.

12
Jon Balke
The musician's evolution from Oslo 13, Masqualero and Jøkleba,
to the period of Nonsentration, the Magnetic North Orchestra,
Batagraf and Siwan, up to today's current Magnetic Book

I started playing various instruments when I was five years old. My father wasn't a professional musician, he was a teacher, but he should've been, and I had the luck of growing up in a home full of music. I never decided to become a musician, it was just the most natural thing that I could do. I started studying music, but not at a conservatory, it was a sort of secondary school that had a music department, it was the Folkehøgskole in Hamar.[159]

Born in 1955 in Hamar, Jon Balke left school in 1971 and worked for a few years at a record company, until he was able to buy his first Fender Rhodes electric piano. Like many in the previous generation (Garbarek, Andersen, etc.) he was self-taught,[160] having learned the fundamentals of music at the Folkehøgskole, and then immediately starting to play in amateur bands. His career started in earnest when he met Arild Andersen, who had just returned to Oslo from a period in New York. At just over 18 years old, Balke debuted Andersen's first quartet, which included saxophonist Knut Riisnæs and the young drummer Pål Thowsen. In 1975 the quartet's members recorded Andersen's first album for ECM, *Clouds In My Head*, which was Balke's first contact with Manfred Eicher and his label. Balke played with Andersen's quartet for three years, as well as in Radka Toneff's quintet, at a time when Toneff and Andersen were partners. After some disagreements with Radka Toneff, Balke then decided to leave the band and began to play at Club 7, then at the height of its popularity, with his brother Erik, Miki N'Doye, Helge Linnaae and the band E'Olen. Taking an increasing interest in ethnic music (or in what a few years later would be called "world music"), after the release of E'Olen's first album[161] Balke went on tour in northern Norway with brother Erik and violinist Lakshminarayanan Subramaniam. The trio's name was Surdu, and it caught the attention of Eicher who asked Jon Balke to come to the studio to record. Balke went with Tomasz Stańko, the Indian percussionist Ramesh Shotham and Jon Christensen, but it didn't work out: there were complications with the session and nothing was ever released. Balke continued to collaborate with L.

Subramaniam, playing with him at Vossajazz in 1982, and with his brother Erik he created the ethno-funk show *Pålmevinsdrankeren* for the 1984 Kongsberg festival. The turning point in Balke's creative experience, however, came with Oslo 13, as he delved into new approaches to composition and orchestration:

> I didn't have any formal training, so at a certain point I felt the need to approach music theory. This is how I got in touch with Olav Anton Thommessen,[162] a composer who was teaching at the Conservatory in Oslo. He told me that I could attend his classes even though I hadn't done the admissions test, that I couldn't have done the exams but that nobody could stop me from coming to orchestration classes [...] I followed several of these classes. He was very kind, he'd invite me to his home where we would drink wine and listen to Mahler. Besides teaching he'd also worked a lot in radio, and he had a real gift for transmitting music theory and the history of music. It was an extremely stimulating period of my life, thanks to him I learned about Stockhausen and the whole range of 20th-century music. That's how I got involved in composition and contemporary music, moving away from jazz.[163]

The early 1980s was a period of intense activity and growth for Balke, not only with Oslo 13 but also with Masqualero, and and in 1984 he won Norway's most illustrious jazz award, the Buddy Prize. Balke had come into his own and moved to Paris for a few years. He would develop his projects, complete them, and only then present them to Eicher. Unlike his predecessors (Garbarek, Andersen and Rypdal), he decided not to tie himself to ECM, something unusual for that time, when all the major companies (not only ECM, but also Polygram, CBS and many others) would want artists put under contract. Balke left Masqualero in 1988, began writing music for dance and the theatre,[164] continued to explore composition for large ensembles, and formed the new trio Jøkleba. Around this time he also received a commission for a work from Jan Ole Otnæs,[165] the director of Bodø's jazz club, which had just been elected jazz club of the year in 1987 by the Foreningen Norske Jazzmusikere (Norwegian jazz musicians' association). Accepting enthusiastically, Balke put together a band with a large brass section and seven percussionists, three playing Western percussion and three playing African percussion, with Miki N'Doye sitting at the centre. The project was called Ø, and marked the beginning of a new phase of composing for large ensembles that continues today, and that shortly afterwards led to *Nonsentration*[166] and a few years later to the Magnetic North Orchestra.

In 1992 Balke received another commission from Vossajazz, and welcomed the opportunity to continue the type of work he had done in Bodø composing *Il*

Cenone. As Balke himself admitted, he wasn't happy with the orchestration. He had become used to working with powerful players such as Marilyn Mazur and Audun Kleive, and it was simply too much. The strings required over-amplification and he never got the ensemble result he had been looking for. Greater balance in orchestration was achieved with his Magnetic North Orchestra, with which in 1993 he released *Further*. The album was on ECM, but Balke felt that Eicher wasn't giving him the support he needed, taking three years to release it. Through Sten Nilsen, co-founder with Bugge Wesseltoft of Jazzland Recordings, Balke came into contact with the Norwegian label EmArcy, and when another Magnetic North Orchestra project was ready he went with them, retrieving some of what had been recorded with Kongshaug at the Rainbow Studio and completing the recording in Skien in Audun Kleive's studio. As soon as the cover art was done, the new album, *Solarized*,[167] was in the stores. EmArcy, however, had a dreadful distribution network and, in a short time, the record disappeared as though it had never been released. But Balke's work was good, so Eicher contacted him, and the two finally agreed on an informal deal that would allow them to collaborate once again, with Eicher guaranteeing that he would release Balke's current work and not live recordings of music he had done years before. Following this agreement, Balke returned to the studio to record *Kyanos* (meaning "blue" in Greek) for ECM, with a selection of players from his "orchestra", a sextet of some of the best Scandinavian soloists around. *Kyanos* is a dark, throbbing and intense album, "an album with gloomy atmospheres, because we recorded it a few weeks after 9/11",[168] as cellist Svante Henryson recalled, and as can be seen in the documentary *Magnetic Music* on the making of the album, directed by Audun Aagre and broadcast on NRK. This work is the result of a long process, and in it each element of the group skilfully adapts to the composer's orchestral texture.

The ensemble later grew to become the Grand Magnetic with a 16-string section, after Jon Balke had met the Baroque violinist Bjarte Eike in Copenhagen. This meeting was an important turning point, bringing a wave of novelty and change to the group; they dropped Audun Kleive and adopted a new focus on strings, while the two trumpets, Per Jørgensen and Arve Henriksen, were freer to move and had more room for improvisation.

The next project, in 2003, was Batagraf. Balke revisited his passion for percussion and, instead of planning a tour as he would have done before, stayed in Oslo and created a sort of laboratory where a number of percussionists joined him to explore new horizons, playing and recording a tremendous amount of material, which they regularly listened to and shared insights about. Rather than focusing on technique and performance, the intent was to start from a purely percussive project and try to establish a link between languages and percussion, between language and rhythm, "a sort of research that explored the connection between our way of speaking and our way of perceiving rhythm and time".[169]

At a time when technology had helped make the rhythmic aspect of jazz so ordered, efficient and organised, Balke returned with Batagraf to an organic, tactile approach, leaving behind that drums and bass microcosm called swing and entering the field of ethnic music, which is much less metronomical and filled instead with rhythmic variety stemming from personal chemistries. It was a freer way of interpreting percussion independently of mathematical subdivision, much closer to the Norwegian folk music tradition and yet in a context that looked to "other worlds" for inspiration. Batagraf was strongly influenced by four percussionists: Kenneth Ekornes, Harald Skullerud, Helge Andreas Norbakken and Ingar Zach, the first three having an ethnic music background (having played with Mari Boine, Niko Valkeapää and Solo Cissokho), and the fourth coming from both improvisational jazz and contemporary art music. Although the project didn't exactly fit the typical ECM catalogue, in 2003 Eicher decided to release the album *Statements*, and part of the ideas contained in this record flowed into the 2004 release *Diverted Travels* recorded by the Magnetic North Orchestra with a Baroque string section and percussion.

Balke could have settled into becoming a successful European jazz pianist on contract with ECM, recording a piano solo or group album every two years, along the lines of, for example, Bobo Stenson. But as an artist with a deep and complex personality he has always needed a challenge, always wanting to go further and deeper. That's what he did in 2006, when the noted promoter of world music in Norway and Moroccan director of Oslo's Cosmopolite, Miloud Guiderk, proposed that he do a series of concerts with Amina Alaoui to celebrate the club's 15th anniversary. Balke thought about it and realised that by exploring Al-Andalus (the period of Muslim domination of the Iberian Peninsula) he could not only make some valid world music but also initiate a very interesting project, one that would be informed by the history of music, by philosophy and politics. It was the birth of a complex and challenging work that became a record, *Siwan*, in 2007. The leader of the Baroque ensemble Barokksolistene, the violinist Bjarte Eike, who was part of the project, said that:

> Working on the *Siwan* project was a real eye-opener for a lot of people! Everybody involved - the composer, the musicians, the record producer, audiences and critics

- experienced something unexpected, profound, real, and new, and yet with lots of references to and respect for the traditions. It touched both musicians and audiences alike and has a real sense of hope to it.[170]

Eike speaks of hope because this work evokes the respect and tolerance between Arabs, Catholics and Jews in 13th-century Andalusia through three different musical traditions and the voice of three great performers: Balke for jazz, Moroccan singer Amina Alaoui for world music and violinist Bjarte Eike for Baroque music. Once again, it was a project that went well beyond "world music".

The long journey that Balke began in Bodø in 1988 led him to the recent Magnetic Book, a project that is not so much an orchestra as a collection of scores written for flexible performance situations with string ensemble and improvisers. Evolving directly out of Balke's earlier projects, Magnetic Book reflect his brilliant work not only as a composer but also as a talent scout, who is now mentoring some of the most promising musicians on the current music scene in Norway.

13
The folk roots of Norwegian jazz
The Sami people and Mari Boine; Agnes Buen Garnås

It's almost impossible to speak of the evolution of Norwegian jazz without considering the influence of Sami culture. This music tradition of course cannot be connected to any one country in particular, as it is widespread over the whole northern latitudes, linking the European Nordic countries. But as we are talking about Norway, the effect of this culture and of its music tradition on Norwegian folk music and jazz cannot be ignored.

When the Sami people began to fight for their civil and political rights, and first and foremost for the official recognition of the Sami languages and for their introduction in schools, the socio-political conditions of the individual Nordic countries were quite different. The powerful protest movement of the Sami, who are known particularly for their nomadic life and their livelihood based on reindeer herding, had different consequences in the countries involved. While Finland was the first to grant its approximately 5,000 Sami people their rights, the 60-100,000 Sami present in Norway achieved political weight when the country recognised their self-governing council (*Sameting*), while a similar self-governing body was denied in 1993 to the 15-20,000 Swedish Sami.[171]

The cultural, demographic, social as well as cultural context of these countries in turn affected the music of the Sami. In Norway, a deeply nationalistic country with a small Sami minority, this music represented mostly by the joik or yoik tradition became rather well-known in jazz circles thanks to a few important figures in that scene, such as Jan Garberek, as well as other artists not affiliated with jazz as closely, such as Mari Boine and Frode Fjellheim. If it weren't for the pioneering work undertaken by Garbarek in the late 1980s, this music's strong tie with the jazz world would certainly not be as strong and wouldn't have achieved the same results, even though Garbarek was not the first to develop an interest in the Sami tradition. In the early 1980s, in fact, Norwegian composers such as Ketil Vea and Folke Stromholm used joik as a source of inspiration, but Garbarek had a different influence, and obtained unprecedented results in terms of quality and visibility.

Interest in the Sami tradition was not exclusive to jazz: well before Garbarek's involvement, during the 1980 Eurovision Song Contest, Norwegian singer Sverre Kjelsberg and the Sami Mattis Hætta interpreted together the track "Sámiid Ædnan" ("Lapland") - Kjelsberg singing in Norwegian and Mattis Hætta using joik. The song took inspiration from the movement for autonomy of the Norwegian Sami, and it was a first tentative sign of their emerging claims.

When Garbarek became interested in the joik tradition, however, a great deal more attention was brought to it by virtue of his stature as an artist. Garbarek's interest in joik was in line with his constant process of elaboration and assimilation of musical traditions from other cultures. At the same time, however, it was probably also the result of his work since 1973 with Finnish musicians such as Edward Vesala (in the album *Tryptikon*), and of Arild Andersen's work with another Finn, the saxophonist Juhani Aaltonen. It was in Finland, in fact, that the connection between jazz and joik was first made.

The first signs of Garbarek's interest in the Sami musical tradition came in 1988 with *Legend of the Seven Dreams*, followed by the 1990 album *I Took Up the Runes*, which marked a turning point in his career and displayed a fully-fledged use of this tradition as a source of inspiration for a jazz album. The core of this record is the five-movement suite "Molde Canticle", commissioned that same year by the Molde Jazz Festival. The album's opener, however, was perhaps not surprisingly the track "Gula Gula", from the album by the same name[172] with which Mari Boine Person - an important representative of the Sami tradition - had won so much acclaim the previous year. In this respect the record was a sign too of the outcome of his collaboration with her. As Mari Boine Person recalled:

> Before recording *Gula Gula* I was looking for a producer for my second album, and I asked Jan Garbarek if he was interested. Unfortunately he didn't have time at that moment and told me he couldn't, but also asked me to join his group. So I toured with him in Norway and abroad. It was an intense period of great development for me, it was 1990. I'd heard Garbarek for the first time in 1988, at a festival. I'd never been interested in jazz but I was really struck by him, and I realised that thanks to him you could do music with much more freedom than you could in the pop world. I'd never had any contact with the world of jazz before I heard Radka Toneff's *Fairy Tales*, and I fell in love with that record so much that I included the cover of one of its tracks, "The Moon Is a Harsh Mistress", in my first album.[173]

Garbarek's album is a masterful integration of joik in a jazz context: the melody is drawn from the pentatonic scale, while the rhythm is quite free and, as is typical in jazz, never mathematically precise. The interest in the joik tradition continued in Garbarek's following album *Twelve Moons* (1993), which connected the Norwegian folk tradition of the Telemark region of Agnes Buen Garnås (the singer with whom Garbarek had recorded *Rosensfole*) and the Sami tradition of Mari Boine.

These three Garbarek albums are extremely significant, especially when they are considered within the musical context they belong to and in terms of the influence they had on the evolution of the music of that period.

The work of Frode Fjellheim and his Jazz Joik Ensemble of Trondheim was different. In 1994 he recorded *Saajve Dans*,[174] featuring his takes of songs and tunes from the joik tradition transcribed by Swedish collector Karl Tiréns and published in *Die lappische Volksmusik*.[175] The arrangements were mostly the result of a collective effort on the part of the band's six members, who used vocals, percussion and wind instruments, and even a Bulgarian bagpipe.[176] This was a collective work that didn't put a single instrument at the forefront as Garbarek did with his sax, and in which the frequent changes in instrumental tone colour gave great variety. Overall, the ensemble brought a fresh and original contribution to the Norwegian jazz scene, yet it struggled to find gigs south of Trondheim. Ultimately it was the record that gave the project the most visibility.

The Sami singer Mari Boine Persen is undoubtedly a true superstar. Born in 1954 in Karasjok, in Norwegian Lapland, she was first involved in rock music, gaining acclaim with her first 1985 LP *Jaskatvuoda maŋŋá?/Etter stillheten/After the Silence* (Sami/Norwegian/English). The album was very well received despite the fact that some of its tracks voiced an open criticism towards Norway's attitude towards the Sami people. It was in 1989 that she really made a name for herself, with the release of *Gula Gula* ("listen all, listen all!"), an album that includes the track by the same name reinterpreted by Garbarek, which we mentioned earlier. The lyrics seemed rather ideological, but the music changed dramatically: a melting pot which also saw the collaboration of Swedish musician Ale Möller and the Peruvian Carlos Zamata Quispe. This was one of the first world music albums to combine rhythms from East Africa and rock influences, with a unique voice and an extremely original singing technique towering over a mix of African drums, mbira, bouzouki, electric guitars, and percussion. Thanks to this work's success, Mari Boine's celebrity was no longer just limited to Scandinavia: on a Scandinavian Airlines magazine of 1991, the former Genesis member and leader of the label Real World, Peter Gabriel, declared his interest for *Gula Gula*, which he went on to release, giving it worldwide distribution.[177]

After the first album and before *Gula Gula* I started working with my band and with the guitarist Roger Ludvigsen, who was not really a jazz musician but had been involved in that scene for some time. That's how I started working with Helge Andreas Norbakken and Gjermund Silset: it was my first active contact with the jazz world.[178]

Boine began to collaborate regularly with Ludvigsen, Norbakken and Silset, an exchange between jazz and Sami tradition with excursions into African music and more, a mixture of styles and genres that made a real mark in the jazz world of the early 1990s. Mari Boine herself was struck by the interest and openness displayed by jazz festivals, which began inviting her. Roger Ludvigsen, the most celebrated Sami guitarist of all time, was extremely important in her development, and their artistic relationship continues strongly today. His role was especially important in inspiring and prompting her to delve into a quest for the shamanic soul of the Sami people. Helge Norbakken, on his part, moved increasingly away from jazz towards world music, exploring all kinds of percussion, and achieving extraordinary results thanks to the contribution of two exceptional sound engineers: Asle Karstad (mentioned in Chapter 8) and, a few years later, Geir Østensjø.

In this period jazz and joik helped each other to develop. Mari Boine's reputation grew as she became the world's best known artist of the Sami tradition; she also began to collaborate with Bugge Wesseltoft, while Ludvigsen instead took part in Nils Petter Molvær's *Khmer* - artists and albums that constantly emerge when speaking of the development of Norwegian contemporary music history.

The Sami tradition, which saw moments of glory and prominence in Norway since the early 1990s with Mari Boine and Frode Fjellheim, also gained some visibility in Finland, first with Nils-Aslak Valkeapää and then with Wimme Saari, both male singers. The exploration and the exchange with the jazz world were constant and reciprocal, with these two worlds displaying great openness and a total lack of dogmatism. In more recent times other riveting joik singers have emerged, treading in Mari Boine's footsteps, always in close contact with jazz musicians. Particularly interesting among these is Torgeir Vassvik, who after the album *Saivu* featuring Arve Henriksen released *Sápmi*, in which he brought in contemporary music players, as well as singer Inga Juuso, who recently released *Skáidi*, in duo with jazz bassist Steinar Raknes.

14
Nature as an inspiration
Terje Isungset: water, ice and wood. Karl Seglem and NORCD.
Music and extreme sports. Polar Jazz in Svalbard

"The connection with nature is really strong here" says Terje Isungset, the creator of Geilo's Ice Festival, "it is nature that decides the weather, the quality of the ice, the sound, the temperature, if it'll be windy or it'll rain... and it's because of this that we decided to connect the beginning of the festival with an important natural event such as the full moon".[179] I was lucky enough to go to this incredible festival in 2008, and moved by great curiosity and the desire to have a deeper understanding of an element as fascinating and intriguing as ice, I interviewed Isungset. I asked him if he had ever used glacial ice:

Yes, from the Svartisen glacier, in the north of Norway. I feel honoured to be able to play on ice, the fruit of the world's most important resource, water, and to have been able to use 2,500 year old ice is an even greater honour, but most importantly it helps me find my right place as a human being before nature: infinitely small in space and time.[180]

Although many consider Terje Isungset's idea to work with natural elements such as ice rather exotic and sensational, he certainly doesn't, nor do Norwegians in general. The connection with nature for a country of just 5 million people, scattered over such a vast land so rich in natural beauty, is very strong, a concept that is quite clear to Isungset, who is always listening carefully to nature in its every nuance and to what it teaches him. "The intent is always to improve, both as a musician and as a human being, and ice music has taught me a great deal. Most of all, it has taught me to be small."[181]

It all began in 1999, when the Winter Games Festival in Lillehammer (the city that hosted the 1994 Winter Olympics), asked Isungset, along with the Danish trumpeter Palle Mikkelborg and Swedish singer Lena Willemark to produce a work for the Frozen Waterfall Concert of 2000. This event was, by then, a tradition, having been held for a number of years each February. Artists appearing ranged from Geir Jenssen aka Biosphere (1999) to Nils Petter Molvær (2004), via Anneli Drecker with the band Bel Canto. At the same time Isungset received a commission from the Molde Jazz Festival, a project using industrial sounds with the musicians interacting with various sound samples. Isungset also began to explore the use of natural materials such as stone, birchwood and other types of wood, delving deeper and deeper into these ancient and primordial materials to discover what sounds could be drawn from them. Isungset found himself at a crossroads, facing the choice of working "with" or "against" nature; like a good Norwegian, he decided to work "with" or rather, as it turned out, from deep "within" nature. Not content with having found a source of inspiration and working with sampled sounds, during the summer he went to the waterfall to gather stones and wood and he started to use them to build instruments. When he returned in the winter he found only a lot of ice... and that is how he began experimenting with this truly unusual musical "material", and developed a passion for it. By pure chance (or perhaps by a twist of fate), just around that time he was invited to the Ice Hotel in Jukkasjärvi, in Finnish Lapland, to create music with ice during the celebrations for the new millennium, along with ice sculptor Bengt Carling. Isungset made his first percussion instruments and on that very special New Year's Eve concert, which was broadcast on Swedish television, began to show his work to the whole world.

What interests me is not transforming ice into common instruments, but taking a piece of ice and hearing its sound, making it "sing". It's not a sound that I create but one that already exists in the ice itself. There's nothing you can plan for or decide in advance, all you can do is be open to what will come, be ready to listen.[182]

This set him on a path of deeper and deeper discovery of natural materials, with which he worked for many years. With Isungset it's not just about ice: for many years his drum set has lost all the appearance of a conventional set by including elements made of stone, wood and other materials. The set is assembled in a very natural way without any special effects, allowing him to continue his search for truly unusual timbres and colours.

His search took a new turn in 2010. Working on an idea for the celebrations of Tallinn 2011 European Capital of Culture with the journalist and producer Madli-Liis Parts, Isungset took on the challenge of working with glass. With the help of Estonian glass artists and craftsmen he started a project that culminated in a series of performances with Arve Henriksen, for the closing of the celebrations on 20 December 2011. The result was once again something exceptional: "World of Glass",[183] featuring 30 unique instruments, which Isungset had created using his experience of working with ice.

Terje Isungset has always been a percussionist, but he also experimented with other types of instruments, for example the goat horn, playing with his friend and saxophonist Karl Seglem.[184] It was around the time when Isungset performed in the Frozen Waterfall Concert in Lillehammer that he and Seglem decided to explore sounds that were more in keeping with the Norwegian folk tradition, such as the Hardanger fiddle, although they didn't try to transform the horn into a conventional, tempered instrument.

Seglem went on to make a name for himself as an excellent sax player and continued this line of exploration on his own, finding a different yet equally interesting sound in the antelope horn. He also became one of the leading figures of the Norwegian jazz-folk scene, founding his own label NORCD in 1991, and winning the Buddy Prize in 2010.

Initially strongly influenced by Garbarek, over the years Seglem broke free and found his own path drawing inspiration from folk music and nature. Like Isungset, he became passionate about this research, and in early 2000 created a festival for improvised music, installations, video-art, literature, music and "land art" in Måren, an enchanting place north of Sognefjord - one of the deepest and most beautiful fjords of the entire Norwegian west coast. The location was truly magical, almost unreal, and could be reached only by ferry disembarking at Sylvarnes. There, in an old school owned by Seglem, he and the organic farmer Ivar Orvedal organised a three-day event featuring some of the leading figures of the international contemporary scene. The festival has been held occasionally in following years under the direction of Ivar Orvedal, resembling a small Scandinavian-style Woodstock where the audience bring their own tents, sleeping bags and food.

Similar events are also organised in nearby Sweden and Finland. It is not unusual for Scandinavian musicians to put on small festivals in their own homes or in their neighbourhood, as did Joel Grip in Dala-Floda with Hagenfest, or Jon Balke with Madstun in Fall, where he lived in the middle of the forest, an hour's drive away from Oslo. It was in 2010 when Jon Balke,[185] after many years of living in Oslo, decided that he needed a place where he could give more space to his ideas. So he moved with his family to Madstun, a location of rare beauty near Fall, a hilltop with a breathtaking view of the lake below. His home is made with compressed wood panels, without any plastic or synthetic material, and heated with pellets, wood chips and solar energy. In his home Balke kept some space for a studio, where he recorded a few tracks with the ensemble Batagraf, which were included in his last album *Say and Pray*, released towards the end of 2011.

As well as being a musician and composer, for several years now Jon Balke has also been a fan of paragliding, one of the many extreme sports that are very much at home in Norway. He started paragliding in Voss, which is a centre for these kinds of sports as well as being the location of Vossajazz. For years, Balke nurtured the idea of mixing music with paragliding, two arts that in his view have a lot in common:

> Both as a musician and as a paraglider you find yourself having to make choices, and perhaps getting to a point of no return. [...] You look for interaction, in the first case with nature and in the second case with the musicians you're playing with. What hang gliding teaches you most of all is how to deal with forces much greater than you that are totally unpredictable, which is exactly what you need to do when you climb on stage.[186]

Exploring the affinities between these two different forms of adrenaline rush, Balke started working with the festival and with Even Rokne of the local extreme sports club (Ekstremut Vikling), creating Ekstremjazz. In the first year of Ekstremjazz, the sound and the parachute were still separate elements, but by 2010 music and flight were more directly connected. The final result was a unique "multimedia" event, a performance that had to compete with something truly impressive - nature!

> There's something deeply natural about playing percussion in the open air, in the middle of nature, and from the very start it seemed ideal for this project: a mix of electronic and acoustic percussion with phrases and themes played in unison, in order to give the whole thing more power. Because when you're out in the open, you need a lot of power to fill up the space.[187]

For three consecutive years Balke organised a unique event, involving an "extreme" situation: on the slopes of the mountain above Voss, the audience arrived by cable car wearing ski clothes, and the musicians interacted with the paragliders circling above them, trying to find a point of contact. On the first year of Ekstremjazz, in 2008, Balke was accompanied on the stage of compacted snow by his percussion ensemble Batagraf and the Dutch vocalist Jaap Blonk. The following year, Batagraf interacted instead with the Wee Dance Company of Italian choreographer Francesco Scavetta (who had moved to Oslo a few years earlier) and their *Salto - Goodbye, have a safe journey and follow your heart.* In 2010, the last year of Balke's directorship, the musicians featured were

Snorre Bjerck and Helge Norbakken of Batagraf, Per Jørgensen on trumpet and Petter Vågan on guitar. In 2011 Balke handed over to Karl Seglem, and returned to play in 2013 with the trio Jøkleba.

Norway is filled with extraordinary natural spots that become locations for very unlikely festivals. One example is Polarjazz, probably the most northerly festival in the world, held in Longyearbyen, in the Svalbard archipelago. Here in February 2010 the Nordnorsk Jazzsenter invited the composer Brynjar Rasmussen and the photographer Werner Anderson to produce the project *Arctic Mood*. The Jazzsenter's aim was to publicise the Svalbard Islands, which in the 1920s served as a base camp and departure point for the North Pole expedition of the Italian Umberto Nobile and the Norwegians Roald Amundsen and Fridtjof Nansen.

The Norwegian soul is deeply connected to nature, it respects it and is always open to learn from it. Nature is a life teacher, even in small everyday things. In Norway the theme of nature permeates not only music but all of the arts, including, of course, poetry. Olav H. Hauge (1908-94) is one of the country's most representative literary figures, a poet and gardener who wrote some of the most significant pages in Norwegian literature. His poetry is deeply inspired by the countryside of Ulvik, an agricultural village where he spent his entire life, located in Vestland on the Hardangerfjord (the fjord that gave its name to the national instrument of Norway, the Hardanger fiddle). This region plays a key role not only in the work of Hauge but also in all of Norwegian literature and art, as can be seen in the painting *Bridal Procession on the Hardangerfjord*,[188] which has become a sort of national icon. Hauge's relationship with nature was similar to the one he maintained with the local folk culture and poetry, and with the literary tradition of Europe and of the rest of the world, all the way to Japanese haiku. In his poems, the depiction of a natural phenomenon such as an avalanche is often the starting point for sometimes concrete and sometimes universal reflections on the condition of man.

Artists draw inspiration from nature and find their special place in it: just as Måren was ideal for Seglem, and Lillehammer stimulating for Isungset, Pulpit Rock, the sheer rock on Lysefjorden, was thrilling for Nils Petter Molvær,[189] because it conveyed the spirit of the dauntless Vikings. In doing all this these artists are never motivated by the wish to cause a sensation or to merely "show off" Nordic exoticism; they are simply acting like the Italian who hums an opera aria under the shower, or the Japanese who applies Zen while raking his garden. Of course!

15
Conductor Christian Eggen
From *Popofoni* (Nordheim, Kolberg, Finnerud) to the new period
of collaboration between contemporary ensembles and jazz musicians
such as Jøkleba, Borealis, and the Oslo Sinfonietta

The pianist and orchestra director Christian Eggen emerged on the contemporary scene a decade after George Russell's workshops and the experience of *Popofoni*,[190] a project that brought together the cream of Norwegian jazz and contemporary music. Born in 1957 in Drøbak, just south of Oslo, by the age of 11 Eggen was already a soloist with the Bergen Philharmonic Orchestra directed by Karsten Andersen, and at 16 made his debut in a solo piano recital at Oslo University. Yet his extremely precocious talent as a concert pianist wasn't his only gift, as just a few months after his debut he released *Ufuge*,[191] an album of original compositions that he wrote for fun when he was 13-14 years old. The album's music is not exactly jazz, but in many ways recalls *Jazz på svenska*[192] by the Swedish composer and pianist Jan Johansson, although with fewer references to folk music.

After his early success as concert pianist and composer, Eggen came to a turning point in his career when he became interested in conducting. He studied in Oslo, then went to Salzburg and Vienna and, a few years later, to New York and Paris. His first challenge came in 1980, when he was appointed music director of the NyMusikk Ensemble, the contemporary music orchestra that later became the Oslo Sinfonietta.

Given this opportunity, he abandoned his career as a pianist and concentrated on conducting and composing, and did so with a rather unconventional goal. By directing a contemporary ensemble, he aimed to become thoroughly familiar with the instruments and develop as a composer: "To me it was much better than studying theory: I understood what worked in the orchestra and what didn't, and this was how I got into the world of orchestra conducting, just learning to compose".[193] By preferring the practical to the theoretical despite his classical music background, Eggen actually expressed a rather Norwegian attitude. It is really quite special for a talented pianist and academically trained composer to take on the opportunity to direct an ensemble of that calibre just to study other composers' scores and to become one himself. During this seven year experience he performed all over the world, improving every day and going on to become the star of the Norwegian contemporary music scene, in demand by orchestras at home and abroad all of which, however, took time away from composing. In the meantime he developed a fruitful collaboration with the Oslo Philharmonic Orchestra, giving him a further opportunity to develop the idea of an orchestra open to all musical genres. Eggen conducted works of classical music as well as contemporary art music, jazz, and crossover, becoming particularly known for his solid sense of rhythm and timing - something fundamental that classical music conductors don't always possess! Eggen's technique appeared particularly suited to contemporary music, and he became the preferred choice whenever a complex score needed to be performed, while the occasions in which he would conduct Mozart or Mahler became less and less frequent. It was in these years that Eggen laid the foundations for his future work, and did so with two of the most prestigious Norwegian ensembles, Cikada and Oslo Sinfonietta, of which he became artistic director.

During that time NRK was commissioning many projects, and Terje Rypdal was frequently invited to compose works for large orchestra, which Christian Eggen directed. Between the 1950s and the 1970s NRK made major investments in its symphony orchestra (apparently allocating 5-10 million Norwegian Kroner annually), which guaranteed three to four weeks of new music per year. These weren't just simple concerts, but fully-fledged radio productions, with Rypdal and Eggen recording entire symphonies. Occasionally Garbarek featured as composer or performer, but the key figure here was Rypdal, who had been composing for some time, studying with the likes of Finn Mortensen and Kryzstof Penderecki.[194] Thanks to NRK the collaboration between musicians coming from jazz and from contemporary art music became more common, and in 1986 put Vinko Globokar[195] at the centre of a very important and innovative project called *Hello, do you hear me?* It was a work for orchestra, choir and jazz quintet, which saw the simultaneous performance of the Finnish Radio Symphony Orchestra from Helsinki, the Swedish Radio Choir directed by Eric Ericson from Stockholm, and the quintet Masqualero from Oslo. The orchestra, choir and quintet might have come from three different places, but they played as one on the radio, and in juxtaposing three such diverse ensembles, the work had a very contemporary orchestration.

A few years later, in 1991, Rypdal and Eggen recorded *Q.E.D.*, released in 1993 on ECM,[196] the first real documentation on record of their work. This composition for electric guitar and chamber ensemble by Rypdal was performed for the first time at the 1992 Molde Festival, featuring Rypdal, Eggen conducting, and the Borealis Ensemble (gathering the first instrumentalists of each section of the Oslo Philharmonic Orchestra), as well as extra strings and woodwinds. As Eggen recalled, Rypdal's "compositions were filled with suggestions but he didn't write exactly what we should play. He would write three notes and then give indications, for example 'continue with strange harmonic sounds on the instrument's bridge', or things of that sort..."[197] and so each musician had a creative role shaping the piece according to those instructions. Rypdal was the composer, but the development, the sounds and textures were up to the musicians, a practice that was quite common in jazz (although jazz improvisation tended to be tonal and chord-based) and not entirely new for contemporary music, but light years away from many of the common practices in classical music. It must have been interesting to see how these classical musicians responded to this kind of "playing in the moment". Rypdal developed this experience further by forming a new ensemble with classical and jazz musicians, whose first concert saw David Darling on cello, Palle Mikkelborg on trumpet, the Oslo Philharmonic's first violin Terje Tønnesen, Paolo Vinaccia and Jon Christensen on drums, Rypdal himself on guitar, and Eggen as conductor and pianist. It was the line up for *Skywards*,[198] also released on ECM.

Before the sessions for *Q.E.D.*, Terje Rypdal introduced Eggen to Manfred Eicher, who immediately realised his talent and his importance for Norwegian music. In the beginning Eggen was very influenced by new music and later by the contemporary music of Kurtág, who came to admire Eggen's work so much that he later collaborated with him. Whenever a conductor was needed who could interact with jazz improvisers, Eggen was top of everyone's list. That's how he built himself a great reputation over the years.

Among Eggen's many projects involving jazz musicians was the one that saw his Oslo Sinfonietta play with the trio Jøkleba in the mid-1990s. Eggen chose a piece by the French composer Philippe Hurel, and broke it down into small parts which he distributed to the wind and string sections, transforming it into a sort of puzzle that served as a starting point for a new way of improvising while conducting. Much like John Zorn in the live version of *Cobra*, Eggen had pieces of paper with numbers on that he showed to the musicians, each number corresponding to an extract of the score they had to perform. The Sinfonietta and Eggen began by playing the entire original piece. Jøkleba continued, responding to what they heard, then the Sinfonietta started coming back and responding to them. Even the Sinfonietta were improvising, with the improvisations based on the original material. Eggen applied this approach again at the 1999 Kongsberg Festival reinterpreting Rolf Wallin's *Boyl* (1995) in what he recalled as a fantastic experience. Thanks to Eggen, the two separate music scenes mingled more and more.

Among contemporary composers, Rolf Wallin was very influential in the jazz world. Eggen's contemporary and born in Oslo, Wallin took his first steps in the context of classical music but matured as a musician and composer within the ensemble Oslo 13.[199] As a young man, while studying at Oslo's Music Academy with Finn Mortensen and Olav Anton Thommessen, he was also involved in the rock scene, playing with different groups and, when 18, joining Holy Toy, a well-known rock band. That was a brief experience that led Wallin to end his career as musician and to dedicate himself whole-heartedly to composing, concentrating exclusively on contemporary art music. In the mid 1980s he moved to San Diego to study with Joji Yuasa and Roger Reynolds at UCSD, where he was particularly impressed by the work of Vinko Globokar, who was Artist in Residence there for three months. His debut as composer came in 1988, thanks to a Molde Jazz Festival commission. Wallin put together three jazz groups and two contemporary music ensembles, which had their own repertoires, and Wallin directed the whole event. The music was mostly inspired by that of the German composer Karlheinz Stockhausen. The audience was made to sit at the centre of the hall in four sections facing the middle, while the musicians were in a circle, surrounding the audience. The event took its name from the sort of intersection created between the four sections of the audience: *Crossroads*. Wallin also participated actively in the event, playing a plastic tube along with two trumpeters, Per Jørgensen and Torgrim Sollid. "It was three of us and we were playing like a single trumpet, and then there were some audio clips that I'd modified of a guy who was the Oslo police chief, and who had said some very strange things on the radio during a demonstration against Margaret Thatcher." [200] According to Wallin it was a very positive experience, especially for the great respect that musicians from different backgrounds showed each other. Wallin and Eggen seem to agree:

> Jazz musicians admire the ease with which classical musicians read music, and in turn classical musicians admire the ability of jazz musicians to play by ear, to create on the spur of the moment without reading a single note. It's funny to see how they can come to the same result from opposite directions. The only difference is that the jazz musician can't repeat himself exactly while the classical musician can, but only with a score.[201]

Wallin's interest in the interaction between jazz and contemporary music grew, and through his large orchestra arrangements for Nils Petter Molvær and other jazz artists, became one of the pivotal figures of the contemporary jazz scene in Norway.

These works were quite diverse. For example *Lautleben*, a 25-minute radio work for female voice and 4-track tape made in 1999 with Sidsel Endresen for NRK, was an important collaboration that brought Wallin back into the world of jazz and improvisation:

> I could choose a singer and an orchestra, and I said to myself, I want Sidsel, and I want my studio to make soundscapes with electronics. It was a long piece that was already structured, within which she was left free to improvise, trying to keep in mind that it was 25 minutes long.[202]

Wallin recorded Endresen's voice and then worked on it in the studio, trying to get a sort of symphonic string orchestra with vocal improvisations. While he had initially thought of a work composed in all the smallest details he changed his mind, realising that Endresen deserved more room for her improvisations. The outcome was, inevitably, a work of which they shared authorship. The intense and satisfying experience of commissioned radio works continued with *Too much of a good thing*: six rock guitarists, including Jon Eberson, and three contemporary music percussionists, with Wallin conducting the triple trio (each trio consisting of two guitarists and one percussionist). Over the years, Wallin rose as one of the most important contemporary music composers in Norway and was often involved in the jazz scene, mostly as an arranger of jazz works for large orchestra or of new compositions, in projects that Eggen was conducting.

Further examples of Eggen's important contributions include directing Nils Petter Molvær and his band with the Stavanger Symphony Orchestra, and the quartet Come Shine[203] with the Norwegian Radio Orchestra, in works rearranged and orchestrated by Erlend Skomsvoll, a pianist and composer not very well known abroad but highly respected at home. The two works were quite different, as was the outcome of their performance. The first didn't work out as Molvær and the band started playing very loudly. Although Skomsvoll had rewritten a great deal of material for the orchestra, the band's sound was so dense, compressed and loud that it overpowered the orchestra. Skomsvoll's idea seemed good, but the band should have thought more about its role. This didn't happen, and with very little time to rehearse everybody ended up playing as loudly as they were used to.

On the other hand the work involving Come Shine (of which Skomsvoll is a founding member) was quite successful. It was based on jazz standards that the quartet had played hundreds of times in clubs, and that Erlend decided to rearrange for quartet and orchestra. The impeccably arranged material gave way to a high-quality performance, which was recorded and released on Curling Legs in 2003, with success.[204]

All the ideas illustrated here became part of the jazz scene and went on to strengthen the process that had begun in the late 1960s with George Russell, and had continued later with Finn Mortensen, Arne Nordheim and other key figures of Norwegian contemporary music. Thanks to this evolution, contemporary classical music became a source as rich as folk music from which Norwegian jazz musicians could draw on.

16
Nu jazz
Bugge Wesseltoft, the New Conception of Jazz, Eivind Aarset,
Wibutee, and more

"Talk to them about the current state of the music, and it's as if an old and dear friend has passed away. They believe American jazz is retreating into the past while Europe is moving the music into the 21st century. The highly praised Norwegian pianist Bugge Wesseltoft spoke for many recently when he said: "I think American jazz somehow has really stopped, maybe in the late 70's, early 80's. I haven't heard one interesting American record in the last 20 years. It's like a museum, presenting stuff that's already been done…" [205]

In the same article quoted at the beginning of this book, Nicholson observed how, for a long time, European musicians had been treading in the wake of American productions, considered to be the natural evolution of ragtime. In the late 1990s, however, the situation appeared to change, as a small group of musicians (particularly French and Scandinavian) started to follow a new creative path, making original music that was rooted in jazz but at the same time abandoning some characteristic elements of this music that had never been called into question before. In other words, they freed themselves from the shackles of repetitive and anecdotal music which so often makes jazz seem "museum music". It was a sort of cry of liberation with which they returned to the original function of jazz as music for entertainment and dancing, although the music was miles away from classic New Orleans swing. They drew generously on jazz as well as techno, house music, drum and bass, and jungle music, re-establishing a contact between jazz and popular culture.

This wave of novelty was embodied, in the late 1990s, by the musical movement identified by the pianist Bugge Wesseltoft as "nu jazz".

This movement was not confined to Norway: in France it gave way to a real sensation with Ludovic Navarre's project St. Germain, whose album *Tourist* (Blue Note, 2000) sold over 600,000 copies in one year. A sort of mutation was under way: a new genre began to appear in record stores and in jazz festivals, where it was met by the inevitable scepticism. The unusual mix of traditional acoustic instruments and electronics prompted the question that has been a recurring leitmotiv since the 1990s: is this jazz? Becoming a subject of argument and discussion, this new music crossed different music scenes, exploring sometimes familiar and sometimes vastly distant territories, while always maintaining improvisation as its supporting element and rhythmic and timbral inventions as its bonding elements. In the process it moved away from the typical jazz clubs, but unlike the new music that emerged during the Jazzforum era it didn't invade the contemporary museums[206] but the disco clubs and the more modern dance floors.

One could take as case in point the trumpeter Nils Petter Molvær:[207] his music combines the styles from his native country with the rhythms of North Africa and of techno, in a mix of divergent traditions that produces truly original and unexpected results. All too often Molvær's work is compared to the electric Miles, or to Jan Garbarek's Norwegian folk, when, instead, his way of telling stories[208] is light-years away from that of musicians who preceded him. In his trademark style, a strong European template is grafted on to the music of Africa and the Maghreb with all its distinctive metres (7/8 and 9/16), which thanks to electronic delays become rhythms that seem to fluctuate in their surrounding soundscape.

Almost 20 years after the rise of Nordic jazz with Jan Garbarek and other ECM artists, this period of transition brought Oslo and the Norwegian scene back to the centre of Europe, especially thanks to Jens Christian Bugge Wesseltoft and a host of musicians in their twenties. It was a post-modern movement that injected new life and adrenaline into the world of European jazz and into the Norwegian scene which, after breaking free of the African-American model, seemed to have become stuck in the stereotype of ECM, the only record company through which Norwegian jazz had gained international prominence.

It all started in the mid-1980s, when Wesseltoft, born in 1964 in Porsgrunn and raised in the nearby city of Skien, about 100 kilometres south-west of Oslo, began to take an interest in electronic music (having grown up listening to jazz with his musician father Erik). As a self-taught jazz musician he had already made great progress and was playing with the best musicians on the scene, but his growing passion for electronic music led to a shift in direction. He had an old computer and a few synthesizers, and with this equipment he started to experiment, and got the musicians he was playing with listen to some of his work. Nobody seemed interested, however, until Wesseltoft met the trumpeter Nils Petter Molvær, the drummer Audun Kleive (also from Skien) and the double bass player Bjørn Kjellemyr and formed a quartet with them.

The quartet combined jazz and electronics, and didn't have a particular leader, with all the members bringing in their material and ideas. The quartet then went on tour, and Wesseltoft remembers it as a great time of his life: "the period between 1989 and 1991 was a truly fantastic for me!"[209] In those years he also played frequently with Arild Andersen, Jan Garbarek, and Terje Rypdal, and was increasingly in demand in the jazz world, which was great except that it distracted him from what he really wanted to do. So in the summer of 1993, he started working on his first album.

> I stopped listening to American jazz in the late 1980s, because it just became boring. It didn't really have any development, it wasn't evolving. Those were the years of fusion, and I found that music stupid, I didn't like it at all. Emerging in those years were also several well-dressed young African-American musicians who were playing traditional jazz 1960s style: they were also boring and didn't bring anything new. It really seemed like every form of research and experimentation had stopped, and the same was unfortunately true for Scandinavian jazz [...] I came from there, and I'd loved the music of Jan Garbarek, Arild Andersen etc., but the time had come to do something new, something different. That music didn't speak to me anymore.[210]

Over the years Wesseltoft developed various ideas, mostly based on the blending of techno rhythms and jazz elements. The first recording session for his album started in January 1994, and the project was finished two years later, in 1996, released in October on his new label Jazzland. Provocative even in its title, *New Conception of Jazz* combined jazz, house, techno, ambient, noise and free improvisation. On it Wesseltoft played acoustic and electric piano, other keyboards, and percussion, and did sampling and vocal effects, calling into the studio some of the best Norwegian musicians on the circuit to play the acoustic instruments: Ingebrigt Håker Flaten (double bass), Anders Engen (drums), Vidar Johansen (saxophones), Eivind Aarset (guitar), Bjørn Kjellemyr (bass), Rune Arnesen (drums), Nils Petter Molvær and Jens Petter Antonsen (trumpets). Wesseltoft's music had a strong component of collective improvisation, in line with the project's basic concept of revolving around a collective of improvisers, both in the studio and in live performances.

The project's first concert was in May 1996 at Bergen's Nattjazz Festival. The line-up was very similar to the one in the studio, with Wesseltoft and Ingebrigt Håker Flaten, Anders Engen, Eivind Aarset, Erlend Gjerde (on trumpet) and Vidar Johansen: this was the band that accompanied him for two years of very intense touring, and then returned to the studio, with the only addition of maverick Jan Bang, to record the second album Sharing in 1998.

Jan Bang, a musician and producer from the southern city of Kristiansand, is another key figure in Norwegian jazz. He met Bugge right after the release of *New Conception of Jazz*, and introduced him to other protagonists of the world of techno music such as Olle Abstract, encouraged him to work with deejays and finally became a member of his band. In the 1990s Bang worked intensively at Oslo's Disclab studio, producing pop music and many remixes mostly for clubs and coming into contact with figures of the Tromsø electronic music scene such as DJ Strangefruit, as well as musicians of the jazz-improvisation scene, and starting to collaborate with Molvær, Endresen, and Kleive. Ultimately Jan Bang became a pivotal figure, the point of contact between quite different scenes, initiating a very interesting phase by dramatically widening the scope of Bugge Wesseltoft's original project. As Wesseltoft recalls:

The 1990s were a wonderful time. I had the chance to do a great deal of experimenting with people from different scenes and musical backgrounds because you could mix elements of jazz and electronics and open to new audiences. We started playing in the disco clubs, and it was a lot of fun. Then, between the late 1990s and early 2000s, there was a shift to a new style, an important change for our generation.[211]

Bugge Wesseltoft is convinced, and it's hard not to agree with him, that each generation tells its own story and that it doesn't make sense to try and recreate what went on decades before. What is most important for an artist is to be able to convey his own vision.

If you're a musician, you've got to use your environment, you have to bring into your music the impulses that come from your own generation. This is why each generation - especially in Norway, and I'm really proud of this - tries to find its own spirit and do its own music. And this is why there'll always be something new coming out, something intimate that the artist finds within himself, with no need to imitate anybody else.[212]

Perhaps the results won't always be excellent, but they will be original and, most of all, they will express the individual's voice.

All too often jazz music deals with its own codes and this is why it cyclically becomes boring. Jazz is a fantastic art form, perhaps the only one created and modified in terms of how the listener hears it and reacts. I mean the only one that can draw from the interaction between the musician and his public in that exact place and moment. And this is really fantastic! [213]

Bugge Wesseltoft, who often provoked with his perhaps too frequent use of the word "new" (new conception of jazz, nu jazz, etc.), contributed to the creation of this innovative movement, and also became one of its major promoters by founding Jazzland, a small label that played an important role in Norwegian jazz. Two decades after Jan Garbarek's instant success with his *Afric Pepperbird*, *New Conception of Jazz* opened the doors to a new musical aesthetic, and Jazzland became the new channel for its spread through Universal Records' powerful distribution network. Initially the label seemed to be closely tied to its founder's activities but soon revealed a much wider vision, releasing albums such as Eivind Aarset's *Electronique Noire*, Audun Kleive's *Generator X*, and Wibutee's *Newborn Thing*, as well as soul music with artists such as Beady Belle and Torun Eriksen, and more radical acts such as the super group Atomic, the trio of the pianist Håvard Wiik, and the young saxophonist Håkon Kornstad.

With Aarset's *Electronique Noire* and Kleive's *Generator X*, Wesseltoft introduced a highly original production style. While giving ample freedom to his friends and colleagues, he set down a few hard rules that were quite bizarre considering the world of jazz of the time: no typical jazz licks, no traditional solos, and total freedom to explore sounds and effects that drew the musician away from the canonical concentration on his instrument. These guidelines proved to be quite stimulating, and often prompted the acts recording with Jazzland to collaborate with new musicians.

Wesseltoft is an intriguing character, versatile and with an almost insatiable curiosity, who is also interested in folk traditions from all over the world. A member and leading composer of Talisman in 1988,[214] by the early 2000s he had become one of the most renowned musicians of the European scene, and in 2004 was awarded the prestigious Buddy Prize, after Molvær and before Arve Henriksen.

In the course of a few years, the movement initiated by Bugge Wesseltoft brought disruption into the programmes of European festivals, which started featuring, next to the usual American artists, a host of European and especially Norwegian acts: "You have no idea how many times I found myself in Schiphol [Amsterdam's airport, one of the main European hubs] catching a connecting flight, and each time I would run into some Norwegian musicians"[215] recalled Jan Granlie, *Jazznytt*'s editor until 2013, while talking about the early 2000s.

This new generation of Norwegian jazz musicians was undoubtedly inspired by the previous one, but shares neither its contemplative calm, nor the motto "the most beautiful sound next to silence" of Manfred Eicher's label. Wesseltoft and friends created a new musical genre and a small label that, with *New Conception of Jazz* sold over 40,000 copies in Europe. The numbers don't come close to those of ECM, but they opened up the opportunity for equally interesting and original new voices to attract attention outside Norway.

Nu jazz is certainly not the only offshoot of contemporary jazz, it could never replace the music of its origins and it makes no sense to draw a comparison between the two, and yet it embodies a vision that is quite consistent with those roots, although transformed according to the stylistic requirements of a new aesthetic. Faced with the inherent value of this movement and its deep and lasting influences on the European scene,[216] it is rather surprising and unsettling that nu jazz isn't even mentioned in jazz encyclopaedias. While this is understandable for Leonard Feather's and Ira Gitler's *The Biographical Encyclopaedia of Jazz*, or for Arrigo Polillo's 40 year old tome *Jazz*, it is not for the numerous more recent publications that completely ignore this scene, as though their editors hadn't been to festivals in years, or had only gone to the most formal and traditional events that, unsurprisingly, have never remotely considered inviting the musicians spoken about in this book.

17
Khmer
Nils Petter Molvær and Ulf W.Ø. Holand

"The first time I saw Nils Petter Molvær playing live I thought the world was coming to an end. It was at the Voss Jazz Festival in Norway, my first visit there in 2003. The members of his band were stretched across a huge stage in a sports hall, at the back of which ran black and white images which seared into my mind. The music was urgent, pulsing, unsettling. Cutting through it was the breath of an angel - not the gentle angels of Romantic paintings - but a powerful archangel brandishing a fiery sword - the sound of the trumpet.[217]

This is how Fiona Talkington of BBC Radio 3, one of the leading experts on the Norwegian contemporary music scene, describes being struck by Molvær's sound. How could you not agree? The release of *Khmer* in 1997 was a turning point not only in Nils Petter Molvær's career but also in Norwegian and European jazz history. After making a name for himself playing with Masqualero, Sidsel Endresen, Marilyn Mazur and Jon Balke, he finally recorded his own album for ECM. *Khmer* made him something of a celebrity, selling more than 150,000 copies, winning countless awards, and after its release Molvær performed all over the world. It's tempting to want to compare this album to some of the work of Miles Davis, but in fact what the two do have in common is the use of electronics, the instrument of course, and the fearless exploration of diverse musical genres. Not since *Afric Pepperbird* had a Norwegian artist achieved such international prominence and brought Norwegian music into the heart of Europe. Two decades after the glorious year of 1970, the miracle was repeated, again thanks to Manfred Eicher and ECM.

Born in Sula in 1960, Molvær was introduced to music by his father Jens Arne, a key figure in the local brass band. His first music related memory as he was growing up in a breathtakingly beautiful environment, is Billie Holiday singing "Summertime" on a scratched 78 rpm record, and his 4 year-old self learning to sing along with it without understanding a word. On the same record player that his parents had given him he became familiar with Louis Armstrong, and some time later when they asked him if there was an instrument he wanted to play, he answered without hesitation: the trumpet. It's strange that the small island of Sula, on the west coast between Bergen and Ålesund, is where so many important figures of Norwegian jazz are from: the Brazz Brothers,[218] Hild Sofje Tafjord,[219] the Sula Jazz Ensemble, the trumpeter Kåre Nymark, and the singer Lena Nymark for example. Once, speaking with Jan Granlie,[220] Lena Nymark told him that if you are born in Sula you can do only three things: play in a brass band, play football or drink.

The young Molvær was involved in the local brass band and joined the jazz summer camps led by Jon Eberson,[221] a guitarist who went on to play an important role in music education and became professor at Oslo's Norwegian Academy of Music. Molvær's growing interest in music led him to enrol with his friend and saxophonist Tore Brunborg in the Trondheim Conservatory, but he was already too busy playing to earn his final degree, and went to Oslo in the summer of 1982, at the invitation of Jon Balke.[222] Balke, who was a few years older than him, got him a 3-month job in a children's theatre. Molvær was grateful for the opportunity, and that was his first contact with the capital's music scene. In the autumn of the same year he saw a concert by Jon Balke, Arild Andersen and Jon Christensen in Kongsberg, and on that occasion Andersen asked him and Brunborg to form a new group with them. One of the greatest Norwegian bands ever was born: Masqualero.[223]

In the following years Molvær was a regular at Club 7 and played in other venues in Norway and abroad, and worked with the best players on the national scene: Audun Kleive (Oslo 13), Sidsel Endresen and Morten Halle (Chipahua), and Jon Eberson (Jazzpunkensemblet). With the Jazzpunkensemblet he recorded *Live At Rockefeller*, an album that didn't leave a great mark but had the merit of bringing together young emerging talents (Molvær, Tore Brunborg and Bugge Wesseltoft) and celebrated musicians such as the leader Eberson, Jon Christensen, Jon and Erik Balke, Torbjørn Sunde, and Bjørn Kjellemyr. Molvær recalls this period as "a golden period. In the same year I would play with ten different bands, and they were all terrific!".[224] Indeed, Masqualero was his main project but not the only one, as Molvær played regularly with many other bands, among these the soul orchestra Chipahua, developing a strong bond with the singer Sidsel Endresen.

In the late 1980s, after hearing Jon Hassell and Brian Eno, he took an interest in electronic music, buying his first Atari computer and becoming acquainted with the Tromsø dance floor and DJ scene. This shift led him to associate with the pianist Bugge Wesseltoft and the rhythm section of the trio Chaser,[225] Audun Kleive and Bjørn Kjellemyr, with whom he formed a new quartet. Of all the quartet members Wesseltoft was the one most involved in the DJ and techno scene, but all them started exploring regions of music quite distant from jazz and groove. The quartet began making a name for itself in and around Oslo, as Molvær continued working with other jazz related projects, for example with the Danish percussionist Marilyn Mazur and Oslo 13, but also with Olle Abstract and Pål Nyhus (DJ Strangefruit), whom he met when he was the supporting act for Howie B., a Scottish DJ and producer. Molvær immediately saw Nyhus's talent, developed a friendship with him and together they began experimenting with drums and DJ techniques. Just around that time Molvær was sorting out all the material and ideas he had recorded on tape since the mid 1980s, and the saxophonist Bendik Hofseth, a dear friend he had met when working with Chipahua, introduced him to Ulf W. Ø. Holand, an emerging sound engineer who invited him over to his studio.

A year younger than Molvær, Holand at the time was working at the Rainbow Studio,[226] where he rented one of the smaller studios that were always empty because musicians wanted to work with Jan Erik Kongshaug; after many ups and down in his career, it seemed like the ideal solution. In 1984 in Oslo, with a few friends, he had set up the studio Lydcompagniet,[227] but after a period of intense activity he went to university to study information technology and sold the studio and all the equipment. What he bought instead was a keyboard and a Mac computer, because as he recalls, being among the first interested in the world of digital sounds "I wanted to bring my background as sound engineer into a new adventure as IT graduate".[228]

After graduating Holand worked on many commercial pop music projects, where he applied his sound engineering skills while learning to master music sequencers. At some point, however, he longed to be involved with different musicians, who were freer and closer to the world of jazz, and Hofseth's suggestion that he work on Molvær's project came at just the right time. The recording sessions for what was to become *Khmer* were spread out over two years, using the studio when it was free. Working on the project at first were Holand and a trio made up by Molvær, Bugge Wesseltoft and the guitarist Eivind Aarset, but the chemistry wasn't right: there were too many strong personalities and constant disagreements. When Wesseltoft pulled out the project found a new balance and, while a few session musicians were called in from time to time, Holand, Molvær and Aarset did most of the work. The concept of *Khmer* really took shape when the trio performed it in public, beginning with the concert at Vossajazz 1996, the festival that had commissioned the project from Molvær.[229] Initially entitled *Labyrinter*, it was changed to *Khmer* by the time it was released on record. Three more concerts followed in Oslo, Bergen and London, while Molvær and Holand worked at the final mix. The work was ready.

Holand's role in the project was crucial because of his creative and technical input, and also because of the influence he had on Molvær and Aarset, introducing them to his more popular productions, especially those with Bendik Hofseth and with Bel Canto - a duo made up by Anneli Drecker and Geir Jenssen (aka Biosphere, see Box). Over the course of three years what came to life was a sort of collective that had the *Khmer* project as its focus, but remained open to anything that could bring in original insights and ideas.

Molvær had an interesting offer from Universal to release the album with them, but towards the end of the process decided to release it on ECM, consolidating a friendship he had developed with Manfred Eicher over many years of recordings with Masqualero and other groups. The record was finished and Manfred Eicher came to the studio as they were deciding on the track sequence. Everything was done, mixed and, apparently, definitive, but Eicher was eager to make the album as good as possible and wanted to come to the studio to check. As they were hearing the third track, "Access/Song of Sand I," Eicher asked Holand if he had a mix without the trumpet:

> I said yes, of course. Nils Petter looked at me and said "Without the trumpet?" But
> Manfred told him: "Relax, I just want to hear it without the trumpet". So we started
> listening to it, and at a certain point Nils Petter said, "The trumpet could come in
> here, couldn't it?" and Manfred told him, "Just relax". We heard a little more and
> Nils Petter went at it again: "How about here?". And Manfred responded: "Relax.
> I've just heard that trumpet scream for four minutes!".[230]

When the album came out, the third track had no trace of trumpet solos, and in the midst of a record in which the trumpet predominates it magically transformed the balance of the whole. It was a small but substantial change that struck Holand as a brilliant choice that only a producer with Eicher's expertise could make.[231]

Eicher is still as proud of *Khmer* today as he was then, even though it's still surprising that he accepted to take on a work that was so unlike the rest of the ECM catalogue. He had witnessed the project from the very beginning, being often downstairs at the main Rainbow Studio recording or mixing with Jan Erik Kongshaug. What was going on in the studio upstairs grabbed his interest day

Geir Jenssen aka Biosphere is one of the leading figures of the contemporary electronic music scene. Born in Tromsø, a city immersed in frozen silence 500 miles inside the Arctic Circle, he made a name for himself thanks to his very particular sound. Rising to fame in 1985 with the trio Bel Canto (see Chapter 14) along with Nils Johansen and the vocalist Anneli Drecker, he later chose the name Biosphere, inspired by the Biosphere 2 Space Station Project (a giant glass structure in the Arizona desert where entire families were made to live for years, experimenting with the possibility of recreating an artificial, self-sustaining ecosystem in outer space). For years Jenssen worked at developing an "Arctic" universe of sound, combining musique concrète, dance floor rhythms and ambient sounds. His most successful albums include *Patashnik* (1994) and *Substrata* (1997), which bring into focus the more astral aspect of his style, as well as *Microgravity* (1991), where techno rhythms predominate. His collaborations within the world of jazz haven't been so frequent, but his work on the DJ and electronic music scene has always been very influential. It doesn't come as a surprise then that Nils Petter Molvær, during his time as Artist in Residence at the Molde Jazz Festival in 2010, invited him to play along at 7 a.m. in one of the main events of the festival, "Break of day in Molde".
www.youtube.com/watch?v=LvJRRe8ijkl

after day, and Molvær increasingly reminded him of Don Cherry. Indeed, Cherry's influence on Molvær is pretty clear if you hear the work he was doing while living in Scandinavia, and especially the fifth track of the 10th October 1969 concert in Oslo (broadcast by NRK), in which the sidemen in Don Cherry's "Norwegian" sextet were Jan Garbarek, Sidsel Paaske, Terje Rypdal, Arild Andersen and Jon Christensen.[232]

Khmer, however, did something new, in a way that had never been heard before. Filled with Arabic and Asian colours, it followed a perfect narrative thread, without the slightest drop in tension. It was a masterpiece that stood on its own and that, after the magnificent 1970s of Garbarek, Andersen, Christensen and Rypdal, marked the beginning of a second golden age for Norway.

Molvaer's trumpet found its own voice inspired by instruments such as the North African ney, the Armenian duduk and the Indian flute where the breath, the movement of the air itself, dictates the sound.

Almost 20 years later, *Khmer* sounds as new today as when it was first released.

18
Club Blå
Martin Revheim
and the rise of one of the world's greatest jazz clubs

"What was important to me was that everybody would be interested in our programme, and that even the people working inside the music sector would be curious about acts that they'd never seen before, things that they would only see in our club. You know, if I go to a festival or a club, and looking at the list of events I realize that I know all the bands and musicians playing, I can have a good time because and can hear again stuff that I like, but what I really expect from a festival is that it's ahead of me. That's why I paid for a ticket. A festival as such has to offer propose new things not only to amateurs but also to people who work in the world of music and music organisation. Directing a club or a festival entails a great deal of responsibility: you need to reconcile between giving your clients what they expect and offering also something unexpected, that has never been hears before. This was the spirit that animated Blå during the years I directed it, and I think it still lives on today with the new owners, even though the music has shifted to electronica and the focus is more on the dance floor".[233]

This is the point of view of Martin Revheim, founder of the legendary Oslo club Blå. Looking at the club's programming history and comparing it to what Italian jazz clubs and festivals offer today, you would have to decide whether he was completely mad or absolutely brilliant, for the pioneering programmes he proposed to an increasingly qualified and selecting crowd, between 1998 and 2003.

It could be said that it all began on the crossroads between Kirkeveien and Ring2, Oslo's second ring road, when Martin was driving home from work and listening to Albert Ayler's *Spiritual Unity* on NRK. He was saddened by the fact that the historical Oslo Jazzhus, the venue he'd gone to for so many years as a jazz enthusiast, was about to close down. In its later years, the Oslo Jazzhus had failed to gather a crowd, with groups often playing to fewer people than there were on stage. It was then and there that Revheim decided to create his own club, revolutionising his own life and, in turn, the city's jazz scene. His intention was to create a club with a different DNA, one that would be open to all genres and reject any typecasting. He proposed the idea to his friend Kjell Einar Karlsen, who immediately accepted.

It was 1996, and the two started working assiduously on the project, although being trained as social workers they had no professional experience in the field of music. Revheim was only 23 years old, and threw himself wholeheartedly into this new enterprise. He began to deal directly with the musicians who until then had been his heroes and, with his partner, studied everything in detail, from the venue's interior design to general musical and entrepreneurial strategies, building up knowledge and expertise and, more importantly, generating a great deal of rumours and expectations. The club opened in February 1998, a few months later than announced, and it was immediately obvious that it was something completely new, something unique, perhaps comparable only to Club 7 in its golden period.[234] On the evening of the opening there were more than 1,200 people queueing all the way to the end of the road to get into a club that only seated 400. It was a truly extraordinary event, bordering on folly. The launch of Blå was the spark that set the wheel in motion. Martin Revheim made bold choices that spanned the whole spectrum, convinced that the only parameter that mattered in music was its quality. In doing so, he saved the Oslo scene from the decline it seemed destined to suffer.

Revheim was interviewed on the club's fifteenth anniversary by *Smug*'s Gaute Drevdal, and when asked what he was most proud of he answered: "Perhaps what I'm most proud of today is that we succeeded in creating a profile based on diversity. I think this is still true for the club today, the programming is defined by its diversity".[235] What amazed him and encouraged him was the interest and the support he received from musicians, even as the club was still in its early days. The artists who had always sought new collaborations and new avenues to explore, found in Blå an ideal partner to continue in their search.

It was such an honour that they were interested in what Kjell and I were doing. For me, being 23 years old, it was stimulating but also daunting, because we knew that without any financial backers we could rely only on our money. When I hadn't even spoken about it to anyone, in the autumn of 1997, I got a call from Paal Nilssen-Love, and when he told me he knew we wanted to open a club I had to sit and try to calm down. I was a great fan of his, and I just couldn't believe he wanted to play at our place, in a club that hadn't even opened yet![236]

The same happened later with Bugge Wesseltoft, Nils Petter Molvær and many others. It is awe-inspiring how a mere fan (although a dedicated one) of the Oslo Jazzhus and the festivals in Kongsberg and Voss could achieve such success, being completely new to the world of music on a professional level.

I believe that our luck was exactly the fact that we were outsiders. We had to take a lot of risks, take out a loan, and launch a club without having any training or receiving any public money. So before we began we were forced to assess every aspect of the matter, and since we didn't work in the field of music we interviewed more than 60 people who were very involved in it, with very diverse backgrounds. It was a long preparation that allowed us to have an instant success on opening night.[237]

Revheim found confirmation among musicians of his own dislike of labelling music, and out of this conviction came a club unlike any other in Norway and even abroad. These were years of feverish activity: Wesseltoft and Molvær were working on *New Conception of Jazz* and *Khmer*, a host of interesting projects were under way involving electronica and DJs, the trio Veslefrekk (Arve Henriksen, Ståle Storløkken and Jarle Vespestad) was teaming up with the rock musician Helge Sten (aka Deathprod), forming the band Supersilent, and the young Lars Horntveth had formed the collective Jaga Jazzist. It all happened in a very brief span of time, and Revheim decided to showcase all these new projects in his club. While they could not be strictly identified as jazz, he understood jazz as an open foundation from which suggestions could be offered, exchanged, and compared. The result was a real music laboratory, where ideas and suggestions came from Revheim himself or from people of his generation, which was the real driving force behind the club's project. Oslo was not New York, but what Revheim and Karlsen were looking for was a Knitting Factory vibe, so they searched for the location of their club in the rather rundown neighbourhood of Grünerløkka, among abandoned post-industrial buildings, next to the river, until they found one that had that special feeling.

Revheim thought that Jaga Jazzist reflected well the mood and atmosphere he wanted the club to convey, and asked them to play on the opening night. Wesseltoft was there that night, and after a while he joined Jaga Jazzist on stage in an unforgettable jam session. The club's second evening billed the band Element (which later became Atomic), featuring Javid Shankar on tabla, and on the following night the duo Per "Texas" Johansson and Paal Nilssen-Love took the stage. By the end of the first week, the club's profile was already unmistakable, as was its determination to give space to the up and coming and effervescent music scene. Supersilent played several times during Blå's first month of activity presenting their second album *4*, released by the recently born Rune Grammofon, which along with Smalltown Supersound was the label that supported the new scene. This was a new scene that also included the first examples of noise music, a brand new genre yet unseen on the international jazz scene that would go on to play an important role in the club.

In this exciting initial period Jaga were an integral part of the club, with half of the collective working at the bar, selling tickets and taking turns doing the cleaning. Revheim and Karlsen were surrounded by young and enthusiastic musicians, providing the ideal atmosphere for a club whose programming broke all the traditions, and featured for example Nils Petter Molvær in projects and contexts unheard of before. With such varied programming, it was normal to hear the most famous Norwegian classical music pianist Leif Ove Andsnes (a regular at the club for many years), as well as a lot of contemporary music with the Oslo Sinfonietta's director Christian Eggen, thanks to Blå's close collaboration with the Ultima Festival and NyMusikk.[238] It was also around this time that Paal Nilssen-Love and Maja Ratkje founded the All Ears festival, which was held at Blå for the first two years, and Ratkje was developing her concept of solo performance using electronics and voice which was soon documented on an album. Two other regulars at Blå were the founders of the new experimental label Sofa Music, Ingar Zach and Ivar Grydeland, who booked one night a week, bringing into the club the most representative musicians of the British improvisational scene, such as Derek Bailey and Evan Parker. It was at Blå that the founder of the label Smalltown Supersound, Joakim Haugland, developed a passion for free jazz and released some of the projects heard in the club's first months, such as Mats Gustafsson and Paal Nilssen-Love, following Revheim's suggestion.

In parallel, in 1999, Blå founded its own label BP Records, which released 14 albums in two years [see Box] and followed the club's same philosophy: open to all genres, no distinctions. A label's problems, however, are different from a club's, and records could not be sold relying solely on Blå's reputation. Revheim realized that while managing a club required openness, a label required very focussed work in that direction, and since the project was financially demanding decided to stop producing records. After all, Rune Grammofon and Smalltown Superjazz were already doing a great job of spreading the sound world and developed at Blå.

Between 1998 and 2003, under the management of Revheim and Karlsen, Blå

Martin Alexander Korsvik Revheim was born on 5 July 1973. After launching and directing the club Blå, he became director of the Kongsberg Jazzfestival (2002-05) and from 2006 orchestra manager of the Kringkastingsorkestret (KORK). In September 2009 he was appointed director of the Music Information Centre (MIC) and at that time was also a jury member of the Spellemann Prize. In addition he has been a member of the Arts Council, board director of the Oslo Philharmonic, and a member of the Ultima Festival, the Norwegian Academy for Music and By:Larm. He remained at the head of MIC until October 2011, when he accepted the offer from Sparebankstiftelsen DnB NOR to turn the bank headquarters building (12,000 sq m) into a new cultural centre in the heart of Oslo, an ambitious project that could open the doors to a future career in politics.

was open to all forms of music. The success of their approach was confirmed in many ways, for example by the evening that the Molde festival dedicated to the club; by broadcasts from there on the BBC Radio 1; by the frequent mention of the club in the British magazine Wire; and by the Sunday talk-show hosted in the club for television, presenting a long series of concerts for children, which received ample coverage on the international press. It was all thanks to the music, guiding Revheim and Karlsen on their mission to give space to all types of alternative musical culture. Supersilent, The Thing, Jaga Jazzist, Maja Ratkje, Lasse Marhaug, Nils Petter Molvær, Bugge Wesseltoft, Peter Brotzmann, just to name a few, were bands and artists that defied classification, and that would have normally played in very different contexts and for very different audiences. Instead they found a common home under the roof of Blå, in that industrial building in Grünerløkka on the Akerselva river, where Revheim and Karlsen redefined the borders and DNA of a new scene: with no boundaries, labels, or barriers of any kind. Revheim concludes:

Many of the things that put the Norwegian scene on the map in those years happened precisely because there was a place where people could experiment with music. It's a shame that there is a club in Oslo today called Nasjonal Jazzscene, because a name like that puts a limit to the music. If it didn't have that jazz label it could offer much more. To me it didn't matter if it was jazz or not. We had no restrictions, we just looked for artists that were doing something interesting, regardless of their genre. Nobody came there to play just as an ideal musician for a jazz club or any other kind of venue.[239]

BP RECORDS CATALOGUE

BP 99000 | *Cosmic Ballet* - Pocket Corner | 1998 (Didrik Ingvaldsen, Paal Nilssen-Love, Ståle Storløkken)

BP 99001 | *Shaman* - Element | 1998 (Ingebrigt Håker Flaten, Gisle Flute Johansen, Vidar Johansen, Paal Nilssen-Love, Petter Wettre, Håvard Wiik)

BP 99002 | *March 28th 1999* - The Quintet | 1999 (Bjørnar Andresen Ketil Gutvik, Carl Magnus Neumann, Paal Nilssen-Love, Eivind Opsvik)

BP 99003 | *Low* - Krøyt| 1998 (Kristin Asbjørnsen, Øyvind Brandtsegg, Thomas T. Dahl)

BP 99004 | *Tri dimprovisations* - Tri Dim | 1999 (Håkon Kornstad, David Stackenäs, Ingar Zach)

BP 99005 | *Blå Molde* - Jaga Jazzist, Krøyt, Phono, Spacebopcircus, Wibutee | 1999

BP 00006 | *Cloroform* - Do The Crawl | 1999 (Øyvind Storesund, Børge Fjordheim, Kaada)

BP 00007 | *The Only Way to Travel* - Per Oddvar Johansen, Petter Wettre | 2000

BP 00008 | *Egne Hoder* - Bjørnar Andresen, Svein Finnerud, Paal Nilssen-Love | 1999

BP 01009 | *The Mistery Unfolds* - Petter Wettre Trio | 2001

BP 01010 | *Dance this* - Close Erase | 2000 (Ingebrigt Håker Flaten, Per Oddvar Johansen, Christian Wallumrød)

BP 01011 | *Where the Ragged People Go* - Shining | 2001

BP 02012 | *Ten Songs and Hey Hey* - Jim Stärk | 2002

BP 02013 | *You're the One that I Want* - Jim Stärk | 2003 (Single)

In 2003 the young man who had taken his first steps inspired by the music of Element, Veslefrekk, and Airamero couldn't continue with the lifestyle that managing a club entailed, so often at odds with a family life. Revheim left Blå but he didn't leave music, going on to direct the Kongsberg Jazzfestival (the second most important in the country) and later being appointed to many important posts.

19
DJs and music in clubs
DJ Strangefruit, Disclab studio, and DJs from Tromsø and Bergen.
Italo disco and beyond.

"It all started when I got in touch with the Oslo disco club scene and became
interested in that kind of music and in the rituals connected with it, made of a lot
of house music, alcohol and drugs. Fortunately I didn't get involved in the
collateral aspects, because what really interested me was the music, the rhythm and
the extraordinary vibe in those clubs. In the early 1990s I started playing on that
scene and made friends with DJ Olle Abstract and DJ Strangefruit. One night I
heard Pål play as the opening act of a Howie B. concert, and it was then that I asked
him to join my band on the *Khmer* tour."[240]

The time recalled here by Nils Petter Molvær was a golden age for Oslo's
DJs. The clubs became bigger and bigger, welcoming crowds that shifted from
a few hundred to a few thousand, a young but rapidly growing scene in which
DJ Olle Abstract played a key role, along with his friend DJ Strangefruit (Pål
Nyhus). As the parties got bigger the music got more commercial, similar to
trance music, and so Abstract and Nyhus focused on the smaller clubs where the
music was more interesting to them, closer to funk which was what had brought
them together in the first place, as well as their friendship. Their preferred spot
was a small club called Skansen,[241] where Abstract used to invite fellow DJs and
musicians and give life to fully-fledged jam sessions. In this small club the two
DJs met the two rising stars of what would soon be the renaissance of
Norwegian jazz: Nils Petter Molvær and Bugge Wesseltoft. Although these two
came from the jazz scene, they were extremely open to all music, and they
approached the world of electronic music and techno and became part of this
new "partying" movement. At the time Molvær and Wesseltoft were playing in
a quartet with Audun Kleive and Bjørn Kjellemyr,[242] had just begun
experimenting with computers and electronics and, after a brief return to jazz
(especially by Wesseltoft, with Arild Andersen), tuned into this new trend that
was taking hold, seeing in this experience a turning point for their music, a new
path they had to explore.

The young Pål Nyhus came, like Jon Balke, from Hamar, where many aspiring musicians (including Molvær) had flocked to attend the prestigious Folkehøgskole. He grew up at the margins of the jazz scene, not particularly interested in that music or studying it in any way. His passion was for disco music and DJs, a passion that he cultivated in his room at home because Norway was not ready to embrace the phenomena that were going on in the rest of Europe. He both suffered and benefited from an isolation that, while keeping Norway behind, ensured that it would develop a uniqueness and originality quite uncommon in the era of globalisation. So in the 1980s, while disco music was all the rage in Europe, in Norway there were only a few figures (mostly from Tromsø, as we shall see) who quietly expressed their enthusiasm in private or domestic situations such as house parties and meetings with friends.

When Nyhus moved to Oslo in 1992 to do his national service, there was no scene to speak of but there was a buzz in the air, and the parties were starting to take hold. By 1993 he was already a key figure in this music, along with friends from Tromsø such as Bjørn Torske, Biosphere, and Bel Canto, but the real centre of attraction was Per Martinsen (aka Mental Overdrive), founder of Mental Overdrive Records. We often speak of a Tromsø "scene" of the late 1980s, but in reality it was more of a group of a dozen friends sharing their interest in a musical genre. In those early years there were no clubs and there was no public, and the country didn't seem ready to welcome this wave of novelty. The first real scene emerged in Oslo a few years later, thanks to Martinsen and the rest of the group. The first dedicated radio programmes were broadcast, the parties increased and over a few months the fever took hold.

A musician's and a DJ's point of view are quite different. The first tends to be slightly sceptical and displays a sense of superiority, the second is constantly claiming recognition for his role. Take for example what happened with the first samplers: only very few jazz musicians realised how those devices could be an innovative source with which to explore a new music, which didn't merely imitate existing instruments. In Oslo, Nyhus came into contact with several influential producers. In 1995, after getting to know Per Martinsen and Bjørn Torske, he also met Jan Bang, an emerging producer from Kristiansand who had worked on several pop projects with Hans Ole Gretheim and was a regular member of Oslo's Discolab studio. Nyhus and Bang immediately found themselves on the same wavelength, discovered they had a very similar background, and started collaborating. Just around that time, Molvær was working on *Khmer* with Ulf Holand and taking part in various projects, including *Future Song* with Marilyn Mazur. In addition, he and Wesseltoft were playing at Skansen, along with Nyhus and other DJs, creating a mix of musical genres and traditions that went to inform the masterpieces they were soon to release: *Khmer* and *New Conception of Jazz*.[243] Molvær and Wesseltoft actually articulated the influence and lessons of the DJs in very different ways, and although they were treading the same path they ended up creating very different albums. Wesseltoft took a more direct route, combining a strong thread of American jazz and techno rhythms, while Molvær took a more winding road, influenced by the Norwegian and African traditions as well as others; the first grafted onto his music techno beats and acoustic jazz instruments, the second integrated a mix of influences evoking folk music as well as Pink Floyd, the German Krautrock of Can, Neu and Kraftwerk, and much more.

Right after the release of *Khmer*, Pål Nyhus joined Molvær's band and went with them on a fantastic albeit exhausting tour. It was a great experience for him, that made him approach music in a completely different way. Being used to working in clubs, where his job at the turntables was apparently monotonous, in this new context he was forced to listen to the other members of the band and to interact with them, and in fact became a complete musician. Bringing his sound into a band made him change perspective and see things from a different angle. He paid more attention to his rhythmic input but at the same time shifted more and more toward atmospheres filled with voices and sophisticated timbres, avoiding the cliché of the DJ who with the turntable merely provides the rhythmic element over which the others play. Nyhus aka DJ Strangefruit created a perfect mix, a kind of floating island with which the other instrumentalists interacted. He stayed with Molvær's band for several years of touring and recording, and when he left began a project of his own, Mungolian Jetset. With this duo's first release, the 2006 *Beauty Came to Us as Stone* on Jazzland label, Nyhus did something completely new, much closer to jazz than before - not surprising, since over 250 concerts in the world's most important jazz festivals had to leave a mark! When the album was finished, Nyhus assimilated that influence and, never letting up, went on to change, exploring new paths.

While DJ Strangefruit was a regular in Molvær's band, an electronica scene emerged in Bergen that was quite unlike the one that had animated Oslo a few years before. In 1999 Annie (Anne Lilia Berge-Strand) and DJ Erot (Tore Andreas Kroknes)[244] released the single "The Greatest Hit" and it quickly sold out in the shops, a favourite in the clubs' underground circuit. What made this scene so different, however, was that it saw a renaissance of "Italo disco", an Italian phenomenon dating back to the mid-1980s. Behind this peculiar comeback was the young generation of Bergen musicians: Annie and DJ Erot,

Vegard Moberg and DJ Skatebård (still today among the leading experts of Italo disco in the world), as well as Röyksopp, Erlend Øye of Kings of Convenience, Sondre Lerche and Datarock. All these artists were inspired by the two Italian DJs Daniele Baldelli and Beppe Loda, who in the 1980s ushered a distinct genre, known as Italo disco or cosmic disco - featuring heavy use of studio effects as well as futuristic, outer space related sounds. While the drum-machine had kicked off the house and techno revolution in Chicago and Detroit, the DJs in Bergen, tired of techno's monotony and in search of a new melodic form, were taken by the smooth sounding neo-Romanticism of this 20 year old genre. This wave of novelty soon spread to Oslo and clubs such as Jazid and Head On, becoming a source of inspiration for future DJs and musicians including Lindstrøm, Prins Thomas, Rune Lindbæk, and the younger Todd Terje. More importantly, what the world came to know as space disco, nu disco, Scandinavian disco or Oslo disco, also inspired the genius of Jan Bang and Erik Honoré who, a few years later, veered Norwegian jazz along its most important path since Garbarek and nu jazz. This was the road to the Punkt Festival and Live Remix, to be explored further in the last chapters of this book.

Kongsberg Jazz Festival 2009 (All the photographs in this section are © Luca Vitali unless otherwise indicated)

"Break of Day in Molde," 2009 Molde Jazz Festival

Torunn Østrem Ossum and Linn Andrea Fuglseth (Trio Mediaeval), 2009 Molde Jazz Festival

Jon Balke, 2013 Le Torri dell'Acqua, Bologna, Italy

Arve Henriksen and Jan Ole Otnæs, 2009 Molde Jazz Festival

Per Jørgensen and Audun Kleive (JøKleBa), 2014 ParmaJazz Frontiere, Parma, Italy

Arild Andersen, 2009 Kongsberg Jazz Festival

Terje Isungset, 2011 Segni d'Infanzia, Mantova, Italy

Paolo Vinaccia, 2009 Kongsberg Jazz Festival

Nils Petter Molvær, 2012 Heineken Jazzaldia, San Sebastian, Spain

Sidsel Endresen, 2014 Molde Jazz Festival

Eivind Aarset, 2010 Nattjazz, Bergen

Stian Westerhus, 2012 Heineken Jazzaldia, San Sebastian, Spain

Audun Erlien, 2009 Molde Jazz Festival

Tore Brunborg, 2010 Vossajazz, Voss

Jan Erik Kongshaug, 2011 Rainbow Studio, Oslo

Ingebrigt Håker Flaten and Mats Gustafsson (The Thing), 2011 Ostinati, Padova, Italy

Helge Sten, 2011 Punkt Festival, Kristiansand

Håvard Wiik, 2009 Kongsberg Jazz Festival (left)
Morten Qvenild, 2012 Jazzahead!, Bremen, Germany (right)

Nils Økland, 2010 Mount Ulriken, Bergen

Per Oddvar Johansen and Jan Granlie, 2011 Jazz in a Nutshell, Bergen

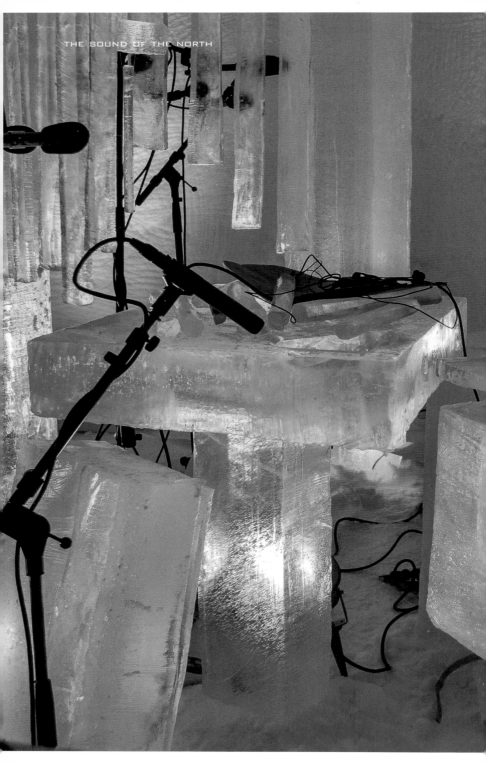

Terje Isungset, 2010 Ice Festival, Geilo

Jon Balke and Batagraf, 2013 ECCO-CAMP, N´Jawara, Gambia © Helge Norbakken

Eivind Lønning, 2014 Molde Jazz Festival (left)
Ivar Grydeland, 2011 Angelica Festival, Bologna, Italy (right)

Sofia Jernberg and Kim Myhr, 2012 Angelica Festival, Bologna, Italy

Supersilent & John Paul Jones, 2011 Punkt Festival, Kristiansand

Arve Henriksen and David Sylvian, 2011 Punkt Festival, Kristiansand

Jan Bang, 2010 Nasjonal Jazzscene, Oslo

Arve Henriksen and Evan Parker, 2011 Punkt Festival, Kristiansand

Bugge Wesseltoft, 2010 Dancity Festival - Foligno, Italy (left) - Audun Kleive, 2014 ParmaJazz Frontiere, Parma, Italy (right)

"Arctic Mood" (Brynjar Rasmussen), 2011 Polarjazz, Longyearbyen, Svalbard Islands

Trygve Seim and Andreas Utnem, 2011 Jazz in a Nutshell, Bergen

Vilde Sandve Alnæs, 2013 Angelica Festival, Bologna , Italy

Helge Norbakken, 2011 ParmaJazz Frontiere, Parma, Italy

Maja Ratkje, 2012 Ultima Festival, Oslo

Solveig Slettahjell, 2012 Jazzahead!, Bremen, Germany

Pantha du Prince & the Bell Laboratory, 2013 La Cigale, Paris, France

Jaga Jazzist and Britten Sinfonia, 2012 Ultima Festival, Oslo

Chick Corea and the Trondheim Jazz Orchestra, 2010 Oslo Konserthus, Oslo

Mathias Eick Quintet, 2010 ParmaJazz Frontiere, Parma, Italy

Ola Kvernberg, 2012 Jazzfest, Trondheim

Christian Wallumrød, 2013 Angelica Festival, Bologna, Italy

Ingar Zach, 2013 Amici della Musica, Modena, Italy

Hans Hulbækmo (Moskus), 2012 Jazzfest, Trondheim

Håkon Kornstad, 2010 Jazz Cocktail, Poggibonsi, Italy (left)
Jørgen Munkeby, 2009 Kongsberg Jazz Festival (right)

Torstein Lofthus, 2011 Jazzahead!, Bremen, Germany

Marius Neset, 2012 Jazzahead!, Bremen, Germany (left)
Lars Horntveth, 2012 Ultima Festival, Oslo (right)

Trond Bersu (Pelbo), 2012 Jazzfest, Trondheim

Paal Nilssen-Love, 2011 Ostinati, Padova, Italy

20
Jaga Jazzist
The jazztronic era: the meeting of pop, rock, jazz and electronica

"We started in 1994. We were all friends, 12 or 13 of us, and we began to rehearse
[…] I was 14 and my sister was 20, all the others were between those ages, mostly
16-17 years old. Our first concerts were like "rock against this or that": rock
against racism, rock against an environmental issue, etc. All the concerts were free.
The band went on for a couple of years until one day the keyboard player had to
leave. Most of us were finishing secondary school, and he was going to New York
to become a photographer. It's strange, because he's actually working for Magnum
now." [245]

The story of Jaga Jazzist is indeed a strange one, which seemed to end before
it really began, with the release of a "greatest hits" album, *Jævla Jazzist Grete
Stitz* (1996),[246] just two years after the band was born. The EP revealed only a
minimal part of these adolescents' potential, which exploded five years later in
A Livingroom Hush.[247] With this album Jaga Jazzist became instant celebrities,
and one of the most important bands on the Norwegian scene.[248]

Let's go back to the beginning. Lars Horntveth was only 14, and with his
brother Martin and sister Line he formed a band with Ivar Christian Johansen
aka Ravi (born in 1976) and a group of friends, all of them from Tønsberg. The
band called themselves Jaga Jazzist and were inspired by Jon Balke and Oslo
13. It was a kind of democratic collective, in typical Norwegian style, in which
all the members brought in their own material. Jaga's music had a jazz soul, and
while the other main influences were hip-hop and electronica, there were a host
of other influences as well, so many as to border on insanity... but in a context
of pure fun. When the keyboard player Jonas Bendiksen left for New York, the
rest of the band thought it was about time to document his departure with *Jævla
Jazzist Grete Stitz*.

The album received some acclaim and Jaga Jazzist began to get more and
more gigs, becoming the supporting act for one of the most famous Norwegian
rock bands ever: Motorpsycho. This led them to meet Helge Sten (aka
DeathProd) of Supersilent, who was also a producer and who later played a key

role in their EP *Magazine* (and whose contribution to the track "Plym," clearly inspired by Motorpsycho, is evident). This was happening in 1997, when Martin Revheim was making final preparations for what was to become the legendary club Blå, and hired Jaga Jazzist to play on the club's opening night.[249]

Jaga Jazzist was a real breeding ground for artists of the future music scene. Some members were too young to commit to music and took other roads, others instead stayed on and, when they left the band, continued their careers as professional musicians. Examples of the latter were the trumpeter Sjur Miljeteig (who was replaced by Mathias Eick in 1998), the saxophonist Jørgen Munkeby (2002), the pianist Morten Qvenild, and more recently the guitarist Stian Westerhus (2009). The band's greatest and most important turning point came in 2000, when they began working on *A Livingroom Hush* with the producer Jørgen Træen, from the Duper Studio. Once again, a pop-rock producer came into contact with a jazz act and with his input helped to produce a stunning success.

> It was in early 2000, we had some older songs, various compositions written over the previous months, and a few live versions. Everything seemed ready, but we weren't thrilled with it, and so we decided to get Jørgen involved. It was a radical choice but a brilliant one, because he did a sort of remix, something that was revolutionary for us at the time, since we didn't know about the editing work of Brian Eno and Holger Czukay, or about ProTools.[250]

The collaboration with Jørgen Træen marked a drastic break from the past. The sound image became larger, more powerful and consistent, the music was vivid and full of unexpected turns. Released in 2002 by Smalltown Supersound/Warner, *A Livingroom Hush* sold 20,000 copies in Norway, and became a great hit when it was licensed five or six months later by the prestigious Ninja Tune. The album's success exceeded all expectations, voted record of the year by the BBC in the UK, winning the Alarm Prize in Norway, and ushering in a long European tour. Until then known mostly through its collaborations with important rock bands (Motorpsycho, Bigbang, etc.), Jaga Jazzist were famous in their own right and made a name for themselves on the international scene. The following year they released *The Stix*, less revolutionary than the previous record but well balanced and skillfully constructed. Playing a key role in this album was the young pianist Morten Qvenild, who had only joined the band a few months before and who, despite his lack of experience, displayed remarkable talent in the use of the synthesizer. Jørgen Træen was once again producing, and brought quality and polish to an idea of music increasingly poised between jazz, electronica, pop-rock, improvisation and composition - a music that is well described by a term coined in those years: "jazztronica". Also noteworthy was the album's graphic design by Kim Hiorthøy, whom we'll meet again in the chapter about record labels.

Sometime after the release of *The Stix*, Morten Qvenild and alto saxophonist Jørgen Munkeby quit the band, no longer identifying with its schizophrenic soul, following its jazz roots on the one hand and tempted to continue collaborating with pop-rock groups on the other. Munkeby's new horizons were hardcore and John Coltrane's old school, and with Qvenild, Aslak Hartberg (double bass), and Torstein Lofthus (drums) he founded the acoustic quartet Shining, which released its first album *Where the Ragged People Go* on Martin Revheim's and Blå's label BP Records.

With *The Stix* Jaga Jazzist reached another performance high, and left for a 12-week tour of Europe and the United States. Meanwhile Lars Horntveth, who continued to be the mind and soul of Jaga Jazzist and who was always seeking new challenges, received a commission for a contemporary music work from Blå's new manager Erica Berthelsen and Smalltown Supersound founder Joakim Haugland, who were organising some events in collaboration with Ultima Festival (Oslo's contemporary music festival). The dream he had since he was 14 of focussing exclusively on writing and orchestrating music finally came true, even if it was just for a small orchestra section of 7 strings.

As a kid I wanted to become a jazz musician, and being a saxophonist and an improviser meant that Tore Brunborg was one of my heroes. But because of a medical condition I had to stop playing, and ever since then I delved into composing and orchestrating, trying to learn as much as possible about all the instruments, so that I could widen the colour palette of the band.[251]

Hearing Lars Horntveth's story, two other figures immediately come to mind by association. The first is Jon Balke who, like Horntveth, approached music at a very early age, was self-taught, and developed a passion for composing for large ensembles with Oslo 13; the second is George Russell, who approached composition because of an illness,[252] which in both cases transformed into new opportunities.

The work commissioned by Berthelsen and Haugland had its debut at the 2003 Ultima Festival and was recorded two weeks later in Bergen with the title *Pooka*. It was Horntveth's first album, and it won the 2004 Spellemann Prize for electronic and contemporary music and the 2005 Alarm Award for jazz. Just one week after the *Pooka* recording sessions, Horntveth returned to the studio to record *Come on over to the Other Side* with the band National Bank, a brand-new project commissioned by his native town of Tønsberg. Featuring Thomas Dybdahl (today one of Norway's best known pop singers), Morten Qvenild and Nikolai Hængsle Eilertsen, this entirely different project leaned toward pop and was extremely polished, much closer to the music of A-ha than to jazz, but it won similar acclaim: 50,000 copies sold in Norway and the Edvard Prize for pop music in 2005.

Horntveth has been involved in an increasing number of projects and is in demand for orchestral arrangements by the Norwegian Radio Orchestra (KORK). With Jaga Jazzist he has been concentrating more and more on composing, so much so that, in the last album *One Armed Bandit*, the improvisational element is reduced to a minimum, while there's a greater emphasis on multi-instrumental work - a strategy that provides Horntveth with enough variety in timbre and instrument choice that he no longer has to rely on effects or sampling. From this point of view it is remarkable how all the band members switch so easily between instruments without losing any of their quality on their main instrument. Perhaps the most eclectic is the brilliant trumpeter Mathias Eick who, during his years in Jaga (he left in 2014), played double bass, marimba, percussion and much more. As an outstanding sideman he appears of many ECM and ACT albums, and is also involved in projects in his own name also released on ECM.

Jaga Jazzist is a democratic project that feeds on grand ideals and who celebrated their 20th anniversary in 2014. Lars Horntveth is undoubtedly the leader, but the other members definitely play an active role in all of the band's projects. Jaga Jazzist is a constantly evolving collective whose income is entirely reinvested in music (studio recordings, equipment, tour bus, etc.), its members earning a living with other music projects or even with jobs outside the music industry.[253] It is an ongoing creative laboratory that has conceived some of the most exciting ideas in recent years and that has bred a few of the finest racehorses in today's Norwegian music scene. Among their many excellent performances, particularly worthy of note was the one on the closing night of the 2012 Ultima Festival, where they teamed up with the UK orchestra Britten Sinfonia, as part of the conexions concert series organised by Fiona Talkington.

21
The new independent labels
Rune Kristoffersen launches Rune Grammofon with Supersilent and Joakim Haugland creates Smalltown Supersound and Smalltown Superjazz

"Helge Sten worked a lot in the studio with me back then, mastering, mixing, and so on. He would often come into the office. It was a coincidence because I'd heard the Veslefrekk trio at the London Jazz Festival and I'd been very impressed. I'd never had any relation with totally improvised, free music before, in fact I probably thought it was just noise. I knew that Helge played with Motorpsycho and I knew about a few of his solo projects. But I'd particularly liked that Veslefrekk concert, and when Helge came into the office and told me he was forming a band with those three guys, I immediately thought that it would be a perfect project to launch the label I had in mind. Then, when it became clear that it was going to be a triple CD - a triple CD of impro-noise and hardcore music - we knew it was going to be special. And I thought, the best way to start is precisely with such a monumental work!"[254]

As Rune Kristoffersen explains, his experimental label Rune Grammofon was born in 1997 with the recording of the debut album of one of the most thrilling and provocative bands on the whole Norwegian scene: Supersilent, which took its name from a logo on the side of a truck spotted in Oslo. While still billed as Veslefrekk with Deathprod,[255] Supersilent played for the first time, without having rehearsed at all, at Bergen's Nattjazz Festival, and a few months later went into the studio to record *Supersilent 1-3*, released in 1998 on the new Rune Grammofon label.

Around that time, in September 1997, *Khmer*[256] had been released in Norway, and many in the press didn't know how to describe it, even though it was an ECM record. Some even chose not to review it because of that. So one can imagine the reception that awaited *Supersilent 1-3*! As something even more difficult and hard to digest, it was reviewed by Jørgen Schyberg on *Jazznytt* with these words:

"Let us now turn to the bloodbath: *Supersilent* is the most irreverent album I've heard in recent times, and as a consequence this review won't treat it with any courtesy [...] listening to this record induces something bordering on physical discomfort, and when it doesn't, it's simply boring. Noise can only be edifying in small doses, but if it persists, even the pain becomes boring."[257]

In other words, the album's music was totally new even to Norwegian ears. Revheim, on the other hand, was enthusiastic about it, and the band often played at Blå after that. People flocked to hear them at every concert, also attracted by the presence of Helge Sten, who had become famous through his collaboration with Motorpsycho. The work of Supersilent and Rune Kristoffersen also gained the respect of musicians, labels, and the music industry. This was a crucial moment for the small Norwegian scene which, 30 years after the rise of the first ECM generation, returned to the limelight with some of the most interesting and unique projects in the world: *Khmer*, *New Conception of Jazz*, Jaga Jazzist and Supersilent. What these very diverse projects had in common was that they were well supported by the two new independent labels Rune Grammofon and Smalltown Supersound,[258] by the young Jazzland (distributed by Universal), and of course by ECM.

To return to Supersilent, the band's way of making music made an impact inside and outside the country. The trio Veslefrekk, founded in Trondheim while its members were attending the conservatory and emerged in 1994 with their first eponymous album,[259] met Helge "Deathprod" Sten in 1997. The meeting also took place in Trondheim, where Sten was active as a musician and producer, and where he was studying graphic design. Sten had an impressive CV: from being a member of Motorpsycho in 1993, with which he released *Demon Box*, and later working on some solo productions.[260] When they met the chemistry between him and Veslefrekk was explosive, and as unpredictable as it was promising.

"We simply know that something will happen," says Storløkken. "It may sound a bit laissez faire or arrogant even, but the truth is that over the years we have reached a level of confidence in the format itself. Personally, it gives me a great sense of freedom; Supersilent is like coming home, it is where I have learnt about the aural realm and where I continue to feel most acutely present musically" [...] "Naturally this confidence rests on experience. It is not a matter of presuming success every time, but rather a certainty that the feeling of uninhibited freedom that we enjoy in Supersilent will put us on interesting paths. It is not like we go into this blindfolded; we build on what we have done before, but in an unpronounced, semi-subconscious way. Over the years a certain palette has developed of course, we know each other well and can sense directions that manifest themselves when we come together."[261]

To some, hearing the triple album was like a punch in the stomach. Most, however, noted a type of darker and sometimes schizoid sound that had never been heard before. The novelty was such that, as in the case of nu jazz, it needed a name that could define it. That name was impro-noise.

"I don't think darkness or obscurity is a function of Supersilent's modus operandi" says Storløkken. "In fact I don't think our music is obscure, certainly not in any conscious way. But the nature of experimentation indicates that one seeks to avoid falling into patterns and known structures. Instead, during our years of experimentation and exploring we have found new pathways to beauty and strong lyrical veins, which are both part of the Supersilent palette. What is fantastic is finding beauty when you aren't looking for it. In that sense it is perhaps true that our point of departure is a kind of sub stratum, a place where we can access things that are normally obscured by predetermined solutions and normative notions of music" [...] "We are very conscious about not departing from the outline that has disclosed itself over the years. Because the insistence on improvising and always looking for new paths - buried ones that lead to something without seeking it - is what makes Supersilent what it is. I also think the uncompromising nature of the band is what makes us interesting to others. We have managed to make it a tool of disclosure for ourselves, and maybe for the listener as well. It is about exploring the nature of the pure aural matter and all the ways of handling that matter without thinking ahead to overall form. Improvisation is a mode of being that forces you to relate to what is actually there and use it without preparation or plan." [262]

In synergy with Rune Kristoffersen and his label, the band set out on a course distinguished by independence and originality, with the austere album art by Kim Hiorthøy and progressively numbered albums: *1, 2, 3...* up to *11* (for now). The only exception was *Supersilent 100*, recorded live in 2000 at Paris's Batofar, which was part of the box set celebrating Rune Grammofon's hundredth release, *Twenty Centuries of Stony Sleep*. The band moved from jazz to electronica, in a (dis)organised sonic context of pure improvisation. The route they undertook at the Conservatory of Trondheim has objectives that go well beyond jazz:

Listening is the most important creative act in our music. When we started we didn't want to be bound by genre, we weren't interested in the jazz label. We began by playing entirely improvised music, in some ways freer than free jazz. Our aim is not to make jazz music but to make entirely improvised music.[263]

Having become an icon of impro-noise, Supersilent returned once again to the trio format in 2008, when Jarle Vespestad left and Arve Henriksen became the drummer as well as the trumpeter and singer of the band. The event was sealed by their ninth album, in which each one of them abandoned their usual instrument and played only the Hammond organ (something that was never repeated on stage). In their live performances, instead, they collaborated with Motorpsycho in 2009 on a 15-date tour, and invited special guests such as John Paul Jones (the first time at the 2010 Punkt Festival) and the young Stian Westerhus, whose fiery contribution to the band was immediately obvious.

The founder of Rune Grammofon, Rune Kristoffersen, had started as a bassist in the late 1970s, with the new wave band Fra Lippo Lippi. After a few albums released in Norway, the band signed with Virgin Records and flew to Los Angeles to record *Light and Shade*, under the supervision of Steely Dan's Walter Becker. Having come into contact with the world of record production, Kristoffersen decided to found his own company, Easter Productions to release their next album *Songs*, learning about all the aspects of the job, from the search for financing to promotion. After this experience and, having left Fra Lippo Lippi, Kristoffersen became label manager for ECM at Grappa Musikkforlag, a Norwegian record label directed by Helge Westbye. This was 1995, and although Kristoffersen was involved in the record industry, his desire was to found his own record label to produce experimental and avant-garde music. He talked about it to Helge Westbye, who liked his project and financed it, accepting the idea of starting with Supersilent and some Arne Nordheim compositions dating back to the late 1960s and early 1970s. This is how Rune Grammofon was born.

Kristoffersen had pretty clear ideas, and since his label was rather unclassifiable, refusing to be stereotyped by genre, he decided to adopt a very well defined image. Inspired by labels such as 4AD, Factory Records, ECM, Impulse, and Tzadik, through Helge Sten he contacted one of Sten's former fellow students at the graphic design department in Trondheim: Kim Hiorthøy, a talented graphic artist who had been attracting attention for his excellent work. Hiorthøy had already made the cover art for a few Motorpsycho albums, and Kristoffersen decided to put him in charge of the whole catalogue, giving him complete freedom. It was a rather bold move, which resulted in over a hundred records with a sometimes cryptic but unmistakable look, like small artworks to be cherished with the care of a collector.

The label's second release was *Electric*, featuring rich electronic music works that Arne Nordheim[264] had composed 30 years before, which had been ignored by academia and were no longer available on the market. Kristoffersen saw in Nordheim a sort of forefather of the 1990s electronic music scene, and in 1998 released an album in which Helge Sten and Geir Jenssen did remixes of the composer's pieces. This work was presented live at the Ultima Festival, inside the Domkirke (Oslo's cathedral) in front of the composer himself and a curious and ageless audience of a thousand people.

Rune Grammofon's adventurous trajectory has included in its course the rock of Chocolate Overdose with the album *Whatever*, the film music of former A-ha keyboard player Magne Furuholmen, and the experimental music of some of the leading figures of the future scene, such as Maja Ratkje, Alog (Espen Sommer Eide and Dag-Are Haugan) and others included in the compilation *Love Comes Shining over the Mountains*. The label's productions, however, slowly began to resemble too much those of the other very innovative and creative label of that period, Smalltown Supersound - or at least, this is the opinion of Smalltown founder Joakim Haugland.

Smalltown Supersound released Jaga Jazzist's albums and most of the acts of the electronica scene tending more toward the dance floor style, such as Per Martinsen aka Mental Overdrive,[265] Bjørn Torske, Annie, Arp, Kim Hiorthøy, and Lindstrøm. Unlike Kristoffersen, however, Haugland developed a close friendship and collaboration with Martin Revheim of club Blå, thanks to which he developed a passion for free jazz through Bruce Russell's record *The Dead C*,[266] as well as through the drummer Paal Nilssen-Love, the Swedish saxophonist Mats Gustafsson, and their respective connections with the Chicago and New York scenes (Ken Vandermark and Sonic Youth and their respective associated acts). The partnership Haugland/Revheim worked smoothly, the label and the club fuelling the fire of a lively Norwegian scene.

It is curious to note that in 1992, as a 17 year old fan of Sonic Youth, Haugland had skipped school to go and hear the band play at Oslo's club Alaska. Not too long after that, in 1999, he was in Sonic Youth's New York studio, with Thurston Moore and Jim O'Rourke, recording *SoWhat!* for his label. It was like a dream come true until 11 September 2001, when the attack on the World Trade Center involved the Murray Street studio and damaged irreparably all the tapes of the recording.

Being a restless character, never entirely satisfied with his work and always mindful of changes in the market, in 2006 Haugland decided to split his Smalltown in two labels, to differentiate them from Rune Grammofon and give them a more definite identity: on the one hand Smalltown Supersound, covering electronic music inspired by Rough Trade, Warp, XL Recordings, DFA,[267] and on the other Smalltown Superjazz, one of the most rigorous free jazz labels, inspired by BYG[268] and ESP-DISK.[269] The fan of Sonic Youth who had recorded Thurston Moore and Jim O'Rourke and unfortunately lost those recordings didn't lose his passion, and went on to release with Supersound all of Jaga Jazzist and a large part of the acts bridging electronica, pop and dance floor music, and with Superjazz the scenes revolving around Paal Nilssen-Love and Mats Gustafsson (who in 2012 with the trio The Thing released the masterpiece *The Cherry Thing* featuring the singer Neneh Cherry), and their already mentioned connections with Chicago and New York.

NOTES

1. Stuart Nicholson, *The New York Times*, June 3, 2001.
   http://www.nytimes.com/2001/06/03/arts/music-europeans-cut-in-with-a-new-jazz-sound-and-beat.html.
2. George Russell, *Lydian Chromatic Concept of Tonal Organization. The art and science of tonal gravity* (Brookline: Concept Publishing Co., 1953).
3. About George Russell, *http://www.georgerussell.com/gr.html*.
4. Stuart Nicholson, "In conversation with Jan Garbarek", January 18, 2010, available at *http://www.jazz.com/features-and-interviews/2010/1/18/in-conversation-with-jan-garbarek*
5. Author's interview with Jon Christensen, October 19, 2010.
6. Stuart Nicholson, "In conversation".
7. Gil Goldstein, *Jazz Composer's Companion* (Rottenburg: Advance, 1993).
8. George Russell, *Lydian Chromatic Concept*, Stefano Scippa, "Gravità Tonale e Lydian Chromatic Concept" (Thesis, Bologna: Conservatorio G.B. Martini, 2007-08).
9. Olav Angell, Jan Erik Vold and Einar Økland, *Jazz i Norge*, (Oslo: Gyldendal 1975), 122ß.
10. Michael Tucker, *Jan Garbarek. Deep Song* (Hull: University of Hull Press, 1998), 119.
11. He performed with Turkish drummer Okay Temiz, along with Rosengren and saxophonist Tommy Koverhult in Uppsala, and two years later with Sevda, a new band on the Swedish music scene led by Turkish trumpeter Maffy Falay, which Temiz later joined. Then in 1972 South Africans Mongezi Feza and Johnny Dyani joined this Turkish-Swedish band to record the album *Music for Xaba* (Sonet).
12. Tor Dybo, Jan Garbarek. *Det åpne rom estetikk* (Oslo: Pax, 1996).
13. J.W. Dickenson, "The impact of Norwegian folk music on Norwegian jazz, 1945-1995," (PhD thesis, University of Salford, UK, 2003). Dickenson's work was one of the main sources used for the historical reconstruction and the analysis of folk influences in this chapter and Chapters 9 and 13.
14. The events reconstructed in this chapter as well as Chapters 3 and 4 are mostly drawn from the following sources: Bjørn Stendahl, "Freebag? Jazz in Norway 1960-1970," Norsk JazzArkiv 2010; Steinar Kristiansen, "Jazz in Norway 1960-2000" (transl. and edited by Per Husby) *jazzbasen.no/jazz_eng.php?side=jazzhistorie_eng.html*; Bjørn Stendahl, "Turning pages. Jazz in Norway 1960-1970" *listento.no/mic.nsf/doc/art200312090959585894712*; "Under the Spell of Jazz" *jazzhouse.org/gone/lastpost2.php3?edit=955016324*.
15. The name of this concert/jam-session format, also called JATP, comes from the Philharmonic Auditorium in Los Angeles, where record producer and Verve Records founder Norman Granz organised the first show of this kind featuring Nat King Cole, Illinois Jacquet and J.J. Johnson, on 2 July 1944. The concert was recorded and became the first successful jazz record marketed to a large audience.
16. Randi Hultin, Sanctuary Publishing 1998.
17. The list of musicians who visited the house in Gartnerveien is stunning and includes, among many others, Eubie Blake, Dizzy Gillespie, Roy Eldridge, Count Basie, Clark Terry, Bud Powell, Dave Brubeck, Charles Mingus, Dexter Gordon, John Coltrane, Tommy Flanagan, Stan Getz, Bill Evans, Chet Baker and Keith Jarrett. All this is very well documented in the just cited *Born under the sign of jazz*, a book that includes a heartfelt preface by Sonny Rollins, a rich selection of rare period photographs and - in the 1998 English edition - a CD compiling some of the most significant jam sessions.
18. Bjørn Stendahl, "Turning pages. Jazz in Norway 1960-1970", Listen to Norway, *http://www.listento.no/mic.nsf/doc/art200312909595855894712*
19. Contemporary art-music composer Finn Mortensen (Oslo 1922-1983) studied with Torleif Eken and Klaus Egge (1942-43) and with the Danish pianist and composer Niels Viggo Bentzon (1956). He debuted with his first composition in 1954. Moderately modern at first, he came under the influence of the Viennese School and became interested in twelve-tone music, and from 1970 composed in what he called "neo-serial" style. From 1962 to 1967

he was active as a music critic, but his most lasting contribution is as a teacher and inspirer - a young Terje Rypdal was among his pupils. In addition, Mortensen had important institutional roles in various music organisations, acting as director of the Norwegian Society of Composers during the years 1958-60 and 1972-74 and of TONO in 1959-60, and as president of NyMusikk during the years 1961-64 and 1966-67.

20. The Norwegian Jazz Federation, an organisation promoting Norwegian jazz, was founded in 1953 in Oslo by a group of volunteers, and later fused with another organisation to become Norsk Jazzforum, a government agency under the Ministry of Foreign Affairs aiming to support and coordinate jazz musicians and music organizers.

21. In rare occasions the award is assigned to non-musicians. In 2003, for example, the winner was Petter Petterson, a key figure in the success of the Molde International Jazz Festival.

22. Steinar Kristiansen, "Jazz in Norway 1960-2000" (transl. and edited by Per Husby). *jazzbasen.no/jazz_eng.php?side=jazzhistorie_eng.html*

23. Karin Krog in Antibes in 1964; Bjørn Johansen in Zürich and Ole Jacob Hansen with Eric Dolphy in Paris in 1965; Karin Krog and Jan Garbarek in Warsaw and Prague in 1966, etc.

24. The Swedish association took its name from Dizzy Gillespie's piece released in 1947. Its aim was to present Swedish jazz in all its forms at its best. Emanon however was not a concert organising agency, acting simply as liaison between the musicians and various establishments, and remained active until 1966.

25. The role of leader of Jazzforum was subsequently taken up by Erik Amundsen in 1966-67, Josh Bergh in 1967-69, Vigdis Garbarek in 1969-70. This Jazzforum should not be mistaken with the offshoot of the Jazz Federation mentioned above.

26. Author's interview with Lars Mørch Finborud, 16 October 2010.

27. Ibid.

28. In Steinar Kristiansen, "Jazz in Norway 1960-2000" (transl. and edited by Per Husby). *jazzbasen.no/jazzhistorie_1960_2000_eng.html*

29. *Popofoni*, Aurora Records 1998. New edition Prisma Records 2012.

30. George Russell, *Electronic Sonata for Souls Loved by Nature*, Flying Dutchman 1971.

31. *www.nrk.no/kanal/nrk_jazz/1.7399198*

32. Stan Getz and Oscar Pettiford were among the first, followed by Dexter Gordon, Ben Webster, Horace Parlan, Thad Jones and many other Americans, who literally colonised the Danish jazz scene.

33. The low population number is mostly due to the harsh climate and environment, especially in the areas closest to the Arctic Circle. Today Norway has a population of almost five million, with an average density of 15 per square mile. Most of the population however is concentrated in the south and on the coast, where living conditions are more favourable. The Oslo metropolitan area is inhabited by 600,000 people, with a density of 1,178 per square km, while in the region of Finnmark to the north the density drops to 2 per square km.

34. Anders Heyerdahl was a relative of anthropologist and explorer Thor Heyerdahl (his great-grandfather was Thor's granduncle), one of the world's most famous Norwegians, who participated in the 1947 expedition on the *Kon-Tiki*, a raft (on display today in Oslo's Kon-Tiki Museum) on which the crew navigated the Pacific from South America to Polynesia for 4,300 miles. After that historical expedition, Heyerdahl undertook several more and was also active as a documentary filmmaker, spending the last years of his life in Colla Micheri, Italy, where he died in 2002.

35. Author's interview with Karin Krog, 31 October 2010.

36. Karin Krog, *By Myself*, Philips 1964.

37. Author's interview with Karin Krog, 31 October 2010.

38. Suzanne Lorge, interview with Karin Krog in *AllAboutJazz*, 13 October 2007.

39. Author's interview with Karin Krog, 31 October 2010.

40. "During the month I spent in America to record with the big band Don offered me a seven-year contract, but I couldn't accept - I had too much to do in Europe and I couldn't have recorded that much. I had a research project on electronics in Germany and several other projects coming up; and then I had two small children and I couldn't move to Los Angeles. For a moment I thought it might've been possible, but then I realized that there were too many other

things I cared about that I couldn't drop just to do that one thing." Author's interview with Karin Krog, 31 October 2010.

41. The album's title is from a phrase said at the table by pianist Dave Burrell during one of the already mentioned "free jazz meetings" in Baden Baden. The LP was released many years after it was recorded, and features tracks with Joachim Kuhn, Aldo Romano and Palle Danielsson, as well as examples of the use of the Oberheim modulator and of the work with John Cage begun at the Henie Onstad Art Centre and continued for several years afterwards.

42. The first issue of *Jazznytt* was published in 1957, but it was not so much a magazine as a simple leaflet with information to the members of the jazz federation. A more ambitious version appeared in February 1960 and only lasted until the summer of 1961. Then again a few issues came out in 1963, but the first, more "serious" magazine effort started in 1964, and the first issue in September of that year was labelled "no. 1" on the front cover.

43. Steinar Kristiansen, "Jazz in Norway 1960-2000" (translated and edited by Per Husby). *jazzbasen.no/jazz_eng.php?side=jazzhistorie_eng.html*

44. In 1970 the international anti-apartheid movement was growing, with an arms embargo imposed following a UN resolution, as well as several other embargo initiatives against South Africa by various organisations and associations. The international jazz community also participated, placing musicians who went to South Africa to play on a blacklist, a fact that could endanger their career in the rest of the world.

45. Kristiansen, "Jazz in Norway 1960-2000."

46. This is what happened for example to Pat Metheny on his return trip from Norway after the recording sessions of 80-81.

47. Kristiansen, "Jazz in Norway 1960-2000."

48. *Dansere*, ECM 2012.The box-set contains three previously released albums: *Sart* (1971), *Witchi-Tai-To* (1973) and *Dansere* (1975).

49. Keith Jarrett, *Sleeper*, ECM 2012.

50. Vold had been interested in jazz and writing about music in the newspaper *Dagbladet* since the late 1950s. Over the years his readings were featured on several recordings, including a session with Chet Baker in Paris in 1988. This material was brought to light by Lars Mørch Finborud's Plastic Strip Press in 2009 with the release of the box-set Jan Erik Vold, *Vokal - The Complete Recordings 1966-1977* (3 CDs+1 DVD/72-page booklet).

51. Kristiansen, "Jazz in Norway 1960-2000."

52. The term indicates a slight speeding up or slowing down of the tempo during the performance of a piece.

53. Well documented by the book *Horizons Touched. The Music of ECM* published in 2007 in collaboration with London's Granta Books.

54. Luca Vitali in *Allaboutjazz Italia*, 2 April 2008.

55. Author's interview with Jarle Førde, 7 August 2012.

56. The history of military marching bands of course goes back much further.

57. Tord Gustavsen, Luca Vitali in *Allaboutjazz Italia*, 6 May 2009. *italia.allaboutjazz.com/php/article.php?id=5188*

58. Author's interview with Martin Revheim, 1 November 2010.

59. The Norwegian Lutheran Inner Missionary Society founded a music department (LUMI), the Pentecostal church started a youth label Joy within the pre-existing Klango, and Forum Experimentale went on to become the record company Kirkelig Kulturverksted thanks to Erik Hillestad, son of the organisation's founder Olaf.

60. A compilation on Plastic Strip Press that documents the development of the Christian music scene of those years, and features a selection from the large number of records released on Christian labels. *www.plasticstrip.no/index.php?/cdvinyl/lukk-opp-kirkens-dorer*

61. Author's interview with Erik Hillestad, 30 October 2010.

62. Terje Mosnes (transl. by Virginia Siger), "Norwegian jazz. Something to do with mountains?, in *Listen to Norway, vol. 2*, n. 1, 1994.

63. "Hvilken by blir Nordens Newport?". The Newport Festival founded in 1954 in Newport, Rhode Island, was among the

first and was, during its time, the most important international jazz festival in the world. One of the main sources for the historical events recounted in this chapter is Ole Albrekt Nedrelid, Ballade, Moldejazz feirer femti med festbok, 2010. http://www.ballade.no/sak/moldejazz-feirer-femti-med-festbok/

64. Back then there wasn't even any television in Molde: too hard to get a signal in the middle of all those mountains! Once the festival started, however, a receiver was installed in what was deemed the best location, between Molde and Angvik.

65. "Det synes å være klart at Storyville Jazzklubb i Molde får et lite underskudd på den stort opplagte festivalen som ble avsluttet i går." One of the main sources for the historical events recounted in this chapter is Terje Mosnes, Jazz i Molde, Nordvest-informasjon 1980-1962: TV kommer.
http://www.moldejazz.no/2014/index.php?page_id=2105

66. During festival periods Molde is filled with feverish excitement as it welcomes a number of visitors more than three times its population (in 2002 there were 25,000 residents and 80,00 festival goers).

67. Terje Mosnes (transl. by Virginia Siger), in Listen to Norway, vol. 6, n. 3 1998.
http://www.listento.no/mic.nsf/00a622352d185c97c12576f900421dc9/6bf5a9b9939a0470c1256c3e002d93b3? OpenDocument

68. See Chapter 1.

69. See what the organisers had to say about this at the end of the 2012 festival in Ballade:
www.ballade.no/nmi.nsf/doc/art201207240923446167086

70. Terje Mosnes, Jazz i Molde, Nordvest-informasjon, 1980; Terje Mosnes-Vidar Ruud, 50 år med jazz i Molde, Ut av det blå, Kagge forlag, 2010.

71. Author's interview with Petter Petterson, 19 June 2011.

72. Author's interview with Martin Revheim, 23 September 2010.

73. His first explorations of African folk music go back to E'Olen (see Chapters 7, 9 and 11).

74. See Chapter 2.

75. The crisis must have started earlier in the south-east, considering that the famous Town Jazz in Hamar had already closed down in 1962.

76. An anti-American sentiment that is well represented in the famous essay We Who Loved America (Vi som elsket Amerika, Oslo, Pax 1970) by one of the most renowned Norwegian writers of the time, Jens Bjørneboe.

77. Author's interview with Jon Rognlien, 19 November 2010.

78. The Henie Onstad Art Centre opened only in 1968: see Chapter 2.

79. Line Alsaker, NRK, Frikeklubb fyller 50, historien om Club 7, 2013, http://www.nrk.no/fordypning/frikeklubb-fyller-50-1.11197428. This article was one of the main sources for the historical events recorded in this chapter.

80. See Chapter 4.

81. See Chapter 2.

82. Another source for the events reconstructed in this chapter is Steinar Kristiansen, "Jazz in Norway 1960-2000" (transl. and edited by Per Husby). jazzbasen.no/jazz_eng.php?side=jazzhistorie_eng.html

83. See Chapter 4.

84. Norwegian folk singer born on 23 November 1946 in the northern region of Telemark, who became internationally known with the release of the album Rosensfole (ECM 1989) with Jan Garbarek. In Norway the album was also released by the label Kirkelig Kulturverksted (1989).

85. Author's interview with Bjørg Eriksen, staff member from 1972 to 1983, 10 June 2011.

86. Author's interview with Miki N'Doye, 30 November 2010.

87. Ibid.

88. The concerts took place in 1984 and the recordings were released the following year on Jazzforum's label Odin as Tamma With Don Cherry & Ed Blackwell.

89. E'Olen, Mai 1979.

90. milestones, "Suono ECM, jazz, trombe e trombette," from the Hi-Fi/Hi-End video Hi-Fi forum. http://forum.videohifi.com/discussion/130601/suono-ecm-jazz-trombe-e-trombette/p1

91. In jargon the term is used to describe a sound image made larger than real through the use of artificial reverberation (such as the Lexicon's, which became a trademark of the Rainbow Studio and of a host of ECM productions).

92. See Chapter 4.

93. See Chapter 1.

94. Author's interview with Jan Erik Kongshaug, 15 October 2010.

95. And who would soon launch one of Norway's major folk music labels, Heilo Records.

96. See Chapter 4.

97. Keith Jarrett, ECM 1974.

98. Kongshaug recalls: "You played and recorded directly on vinyl, the sound quality was quite good, but you couldn't do any editing." With *Direct to Dis(h)c*, Frode Thingnæs won the Spellemann Prize in 1980.

99. Keith Jarrett, *Personal Mountains*, ECM 1979.

100. Author's interview with Jan Erik Kongshaug, 15 October 2010.

101. Ibid.

102. Author's interview with Sven Persson, 1 November 2010.

103. Ibid.

104. Including Stig Henriksen, Johnny Skalleberg, Geir Østensjø, David Solheim, and Anders Aasebøe.

105. Ole Mørk Sandvik, *Folkemusikk i Gudbrandsdalen*, Forlagt Av Johan Grundt Tanum, Oslo 1948.

106. Researcher, teacher and theologian, Sandvik (1875-1976) brought to light a large body of sacred music, religious folk melodies, wedding marches, and songs that constitute the largest part of Norwegian folk music known with *Gudbrandsdalen* (1919, 2nd revised edition 1948), followed by a thesis on music from eastern Norway (1921) and the collections *Østerdalsmusikken* (1943), *Setesdal's Melodies* (1952), *Norwegian Religious Folk Melodies 1-2* (1960-64) and *Springleiker i Norske Bygder* (1967).

107. See Chapter 1.

108. Jan Garbarek (saxophone), Morten Lassem (piano), Hans Marius Stormoen (double bass) and Torgrim Sollid (drums).

109. Helgesen was forgotten after his death, only to be rediscovered in the late 1970s thanks to Sandvik's publication of some of his recordings. In the 1980s these documents were in the possession of Helgesen's grand-nephew (see Chapter 15), and are currently kept at Oslo's National Library of Norway.

110. *Østerdalsmusikk*, Mai 1975 (personnel: Torgrim Sollid and Lars Martin Thomassen on trumpet and flugelhorn, Jan Garbarek on sax, Knut Riisnæs on flute and sax, Alf Erling Kjellmann on sax, Erling Aksdal Jr. on piano, Bjørn Alterhaug on double bass and voice, Ole Jacob Hansen on drums).

111. Author's interview with Torgrim Sollid, 24 June 2011.

112. Jan Johansson, *Jazz på svenska*, Megafon 1964.

113. Author's interview with Torgrim Sollid, 24 June 2011.

114. The phonograph cylinder was a medium for recording and reproducing sound invented by Thomas Edison in the United States in the late nineteenth century. Quite popular until the early 1900s, phonograph cylinders became obsolete with the advent of flat to disc records.

115. Helgesen's recordings date back to 1923.

116. Author's interview with Torgrim Sollid, 24 June 2011.

117. Tor Dybo, "Globalizing Perspectives on Norwegian Jazz History," paper for the 8th Nordic Jazz Conference, Aalborg, Denmark, 26 August 2009.

118. Frode Fjellheim Jazz Joik Ensemble, *Saajve Dans*, Idut 1994. Personnel: Snorre Bjerck (percussion), Tor Haugerud (drums and percussion), Torbjørn Hillersøy (bass), Nils-Olav Johansen (guitar and voice), Håvard Lund (soprano sax, clarinet, zampogna bulgara and voice), Frode Fjellheim (piano, synthesizer, percussion and voice).

119. Karl Tiréns, *Die lappische Volksmusik*, Stockholm, Hugo Gebers förlag 1942

120. Utla, *Brodd*, NORCD 1995. Personnel: Karl Seglem (tenor sax), Terje Isungset (percussion) and Håkon Høgemo (Hardanger fiddle).

121. Tor Dybo, "Cross-Cultural Forms of Improvisation in Norwegian Jazz Life," paper for the Ethno-musicological conference Music Grooves, Style and Aesthetics, Bergen, November 1999, and the Jyväskylä Summer Jazz Conference, June 2001.

122. See Chapter 7.

123. Born in the northern city of Norvik in 1945, Bjørklund was the pianist in Garbarek's quartet who let George Russell sit in for him during that legendary jam session in Molde (see Chapter 1).

124. Terje Bjørklund, *Moderne jazzimprovisasjon*, Norsk Musikkforlag 1983.

125. "Three little Chinese".

126. See Chapter 9.

127. Born in Los Angeles, the saxophonist Warne Marion Marsh (1927-1987) was, with Lee Konitz, one of the most eminent representatives of Lennie Tristano's "cool" school.

128. Author's interview with Torgrim Sollid, 24 June 2011.

129. Ibid.

130. In the Olavskvartalet of the Norwegian University of Science and Technology (NTNU, Norges Teknisk-Naturvitenskapelige Universitet).

131. See Chapter 4.

132. See Chapter 7.

133. See Chapter 7.

134. Although it might be unusual for a pianist, Balke was always deeply interested in percussion, and his joining Miki N'Doye with E'Olen was a symptom of that.

135. Author's interview with Audun Kleive, 17 October 2010.

136. Oslo 13, *Anti-therapy*, Odin 1983. Erik Balke, Odd Riisnæs (alto and soprano sax, flute), Nancy Sandvoll (baritone sax, flute), Carl Morten Iversen (double bass), Audun Kleive (drums), Stig Molvær (French horn), Jon Balke (piano, percussion), Rune Nicolaysen (tenor sax, flute), Thor Bjørn Neby and Torbjørn Sunde (trombone), Geir Hauger and Nils Petter Molvær (trumpet), and Geir Løvold (tuba).

137. Author's interview with Audun Kleive, 17 October 2010.

138. Jon Balke w/Oslo 13, *Nonsentration*, ECM 1992.

139. Author's interview with Audun Kleive, 17 October 2010.

140. Jon Eberson Group, *Jive Talking*, CBS 1981.

141. Chipahua, *The Soul Survivors*, Hit Records! 1984.

142. Bakken was among the first in Norway to use the Oberheim 4 polyphonic synthesizer (1979) and among the first, shortly later, to record with Synclavier digital system.

143. Author's interview with Audun Kleive, 17 October 2010.

144. Author's interview with Johan Hauknes, 1 September 2011.

145. Author's interview with Jon Christensen, 19 October 2010.

146. Masqualero, *Bande à part*, ECM 1985.

147. Author's interview with Jon Christensen, 19 October 2010.

148. Masqualero, *Aero*, ECM 1987.

149. Masqualero, *Re-Enter*, ECM 1991.

150. The name is an acronym of their surnames: JØrgensen, KLEive, BAlke.

151. Dag Arnesen, *NY Bris*, Odin 1982.

152. Jon Balke, Per Jørgensen, Audun Kleive, *On and On*, Odin 1991; Jon Balke, Per Jørgensen, Audun Kleive, *Jøkleba!*, Norsk Plateproduksjon 1992; Jøkleba, *Live*, Curling Legs 1994.
153. Jon Balke, liner notes to Jøkleba, *Jøkleba!/Nu Jøk?*, Universal Music Norway 2011.
154. Author's interview with Jon Balke, 26 September 2010.
155. Author's interview with Audun Kleive, 17 October 2010.
156. Jon Balke, Per Jørgensen, Audun Kleive, *Jøkleba!*, Norsk Plateproduksjon 1992.
157. Jon Balke, liner notes to *Jøkleba!/Nu Jøk?*, Universal Music Norway 2011.
158. Including the performance with Cikada, one of the foremost classical music ensembles, directed by Christian Eggen; with contemporary dance ensembles for the Norwegian royal family; the performance to an audience of just children, etc.
159. Author's interview with Jon Balke, 26 September 2010.
160. Understandably, since the first jazz course at a Conservatory was established only 1978 in Trondheim (see Chapter 10).
161. E'Olen, *E'Olen*, Mai 1979.
162. Considered to be among the most important Norwegian composers, Olav Anton Thommessen was born in 1946 in Oslo, the son of diplomats, and grew up largely abroad. He has received commissions from all the major Norwegian orchestras and festivals as well as from institutions abroad. His great knowledge of music history and film music has made him a much sought after teacher and lecturer. Thommessen holds a professorship in composition at the Norwegian Academy of Music. Among the numerous prizes he received, is the 1990 Nordic Council Music Prize for his composition *Gjennom Prisme* for cello, organ and orchestra.
www.mic.no/mic.nsf/doc/art2002100719321625537651
163. Author's interview with Jon Balke, 26 September 2010.
164. *Oo dja na* (1982), *Trojanerinnene* (1984), *Kvinner i Rød kveld* (1990), *Gå løs på vinteren med øks!* (1992), *Spinn* (1994) and *Come Nuvole* (1996).
165. Otnæs subsequently directed the Molde Festival until December 2012, and has been director of the Jazzscene (Jazzforum's club in Oslo) since January 2013.
166. Jon Balke, *Nonsentration*, ECM 1990.
167. Magnetic North Orchestra, *Solarized*, Sonet/EmArcy 1998.
168. Author's interview with Svante Henryson, 8 July 2011.
169. Author's interview with Jon Balke, 26 September 2010.
170. Author's interview with Bjarte Eike, 26 May 2009, published in *Mondomix*, 5/2009.
171. K. Olle Edström, "From Yoik to Music: Pop, Rock, World, Ambient, Techno, Electronica, Rap, and…", STM-Online, Vol. 13, 2010.
http://musikforskning.se/stmonline/vol_13/edstrom/index.php?menu=3
172. *Gula Gula* (*Hør stammødrenes stemme*), Idut and Real World 1990.
173. Author's interview with Mari Boine Persen, 19 October 2010. In the track she speaks about the male voice is provided by Ingor Ántte Áilu Gaup, another leading exponent of the yoik tradition.
174. Frode Fjellheim, *Saajve Dans*, Idut 1994.
175. Karl Tirén, "Die lappische Volksmusik," in *Acta Lapponica*, vol. 3, Stockholm 1942. The book, which includes over 550 tunes from Swedish Lapland, documents the yoik past back to the 1880s. According to Tirén, these are among the most ancient discoveries in the field.
176. See footnote 13, Chapter 1.
177. K. Olle Edström, "From Yoik to Music," see footnote 1.
178. Author's interview with Mari Boine Persen, 19 October 2010.
179. Author's interview with Terje Isungset, in "L'Ice Music mi ha insegnato a essere piccolo…," *Mondomix* no. 9/2010.
180. Ibid.
181. Ibid.

182. Ibid.

183. The performance is documented by two videos available on YouTube: one by the sound technician Asle Karstad (*www.youtube.com/watch?v=IqnuOtcQ2Uo*), and the other produced by Estonian national television (*www.youtube.com/watch?v= vc1WcTVYwQo*).

184. Isungset and Seglem worked together in Bergen, where they both went to live, forming some of the most interesting bands on that circuit, blending free jazz and folk music (the duo IsGlem, Utla trio with Håkon Høgemo, and the trio IsGleSen with Arve Henriksen).

185. Balke was talked about in Chapters 7 and 11.

186. Author's interview with Jon Balke, 27 March 2010.

187. Ibid. Balke is talking about percussion because the project took shape with the group of percussionists of the band Batagraf.

188. *Brudeferden i Hardanger* (1847) by Adolph Tidemand and Hans Gude.

189. On the occasion of a concert on the natural plateau on top Pulpit Rock, without any barriers, 600 meters above the Lysefjord.

190. See Chapter 2.

191. Christian Eggen, *Ufuge*, RCA 1974._

192. Jan Johansson, *Jazz på svenska*, Megafon 1964. See Chapter 9.

193. Author's interview with Christian Eggen, Oslo 1 November 2010.

194. See Chapter 4.

195. Vinko Globokar (1934) is a composer and trombonist of Slovenian origins, who became one of the leading figures of the French avant-garde in Paris. As a trombonist he has interpreted various works by Luciano Berio, Mauricio Kagel, René Leibowitz, Karlheinz Stockhausen and Tōru Takemitsu, and as a composer he is known for his use of non conventional techniques that highlight spontaneity and creativity, often integrating improvisation.

196. Terje Rypdal, *Q.E.D.*, ECM 1993.

197. Author's interview with Christian Eggen, Oslo 1 November 2010.

198. Terje Rypdal, *Skywards*, ECM 1997.

199. As a second trumpet and author of various compositions. For more on Oslo 13, see Chapter 11.

200. Author's interview with Rolf Wallin, Oslo 1 November 2010.

201. Author's interview with Christian Eggen, Oslo 1 November 2010.

202. Author's interview with Rolf Wallin, Oslo 1 November 2010.

203. A piano trio (Erlend Skomsvoll on piano, Håkon Mjåset Johansen on drums, Sondre Meisfjord on double bass) with Live Maria Roggen on voice, which had an instant success with its 2001 debut eponymous album.

204. *Come Shine - With the Norwegian Radio Orchestra in Concert* (2003).

205. Stuart Nicholson, *The New York Times*, June 3, 2001.
www.nytimes.com/2001/06/03/ arts/music-europeans-cut-in-with-a-new-jazz-sound-and-beat.html

206. See Chapter 2.

207. See Chapter 11.

208. During an informal chat I had with trumpeter Arve Henriksen, he said that Molvær is "a fantastic storyteller".

209. Author's interview with Jens Christian Bugge Wesseltoft, 2 July 2010.

210. Ibid.

211. Ibid.

212. Ibid.

213. Ibid.

214. In 1991 the band released *Dating* for the Odin label, an album with strong ethnic overtones, based on arrangements of ancient tunes and featuring Indian tablas and North African singing.

215. Author's interview with Jan Granlie, 15 October 2010.

216. These influences are quite obvious if only for how many Norwegian and European musicians have filled the

programmes of the most important jazz festivals in Europe and in the world over a five-year period.

217. Fiona Talkington in Nils Petter Molvær's website, Biography. *www.nilspettermolvaer.info*

218. See Chapter 5.

219. Daughter of Brazz Brothers member Stein Erik Tafjord. More about her will be said in Part II of this book relating to the impro-noise scene.

220. Editor of Jazzforum's magazine *Jazznytt* until 2013.

221. See Chapter 7, 11 and 15.

222. See Chapter 7.

223. See Chapter 13.

224. Author's interview with Nils Petter Molvær, 25 September 2010.

225. See Chapter 8.

226. At the height of its activity, between the late 1980s and early 1990s, Rainbow Studio leased two smaller control and live rooms upstairs to freelance sound engineers. See Chapter 8.

227. Recording *Panzer And Rabbits* by Holy Toy, a band where Rolf Wallin had played until 1982-83. See Chapter 15.

228. Author's interview with Ulf Holand, 28 June 2011.

229. See Chapter 6.

230. Author's interview with Ulf Holand, 28 June 2011.

231. To tone down this "censorship", the same piece was repeated at the end of the album in the version "Reprise/Song of Sand II" featuring the trumpet.

232. An unreleased recording just short of 40 minutes is available in the NRK archives: *web.comhem.se/kassman/doncherry.htm*

233. Author's interview with Martin Revheim, 1 November 2010.

234. See Chapter 7.

235. Gaute Drevdal, Smug, Blå 15 I En prat med far sjøl, 2012. *smug.no/post.aspx?ID=10569*

236. Author's interview with Martin Revheim.

237. Ibid.

238. The leading Norwegian contemporary music festival, and the government agency dedicated to contemporary music, respectively.

239. Author's interview with Martin Revheim.

240 Author's interview with Nils Petter Molvær, 25 September 2010.

241. In 2001, Glasgow Underground released a compilation that documents the club's aesthetics: G-Ha, *Skansen Music*, Glasgow Underground 2001. *www.allmusic.com/album/skansen-music-mw0000016005*

242. See Chapter 16.

243. See Chapters 16 and 17.

244. A talented DJ, who was affected by a degenerative heart condition and died in April 2001 when he was only 23.

245. Author's interview with Lars Horntveth, 25 September 2010.

246. Ibid.

247. Jaga Jazzist, *A Livingroom Hush*, Smalltown Supersound 2002.

248. All the more surprising if you consider that he grew up in a rural environment in Tønsberg, and old town of about 40,000 in the Vestfold region, one hour and a half south of Oslo.

249. See Chapter 18.

250. Author's interview with Lars Horntveth.

251. Ibid.

252. The illness that forced Lars Horntveth to abandon sax playing at a very young age is Chronic Fatigue Syndrome, the same ailment that affected pianist Keith Jarrett in 2000.

253. It's the case for example with Line Horntveth, Lars's sister, who works in health care.

254. Author's interview with Rune Kristoffersen, 19 October 2010.

255. See Chapter 10. Helge "Deathprod" Sten (electronics) joined the original members of the Veslefrekk trio (Ståle Storløkken, synthesizers; Jarle Vespestad, drums; Arve Henriksen, trumpet and live electronics) to form Supersilent. According to the unofficial website of Supersilent (*www.supersilence.net*), *Veslefrekk* means "'small spot".

256. See Chapter 17.

257. Jørgen Schyberg in *Jazznytt*, 01/1998.

258. The worthy successors of Odin (*english.jazzinorge.no/odin-records*) which, along with Curling Legs (*www.curlinglegs.no*) and of course ECM, had until then done most of the record production in Norway since the early 1970s.

259. Veslefrekk, *Veslefrekk*, NORCD 1994.

260. *Treetop Drive Part 1-3*, *Towboat*, Metal Art Disco 1994; *Imaginary Songs from Tristan da Cunha*, dBut 1996.

261. Christian Lysvåg, "Ståle Storløkken and Supersilent: The play of becoming," *Ballade*, 23 October 2009. *mic.no/mic.nsf/doc/art2009102311501020284733*

262. Ibid.

263. Author's interview with Arve Henriksen, 9 November 2010.

264. A celebrated Norwegian composer, since 1982 Nordheim (1931-2010) lived in the Norwegian State's honorary residence, Grotten, near Oslo's Royal Palace. In 1997 he was appointed honorary member of the International Society for Contemporary Music, and on 18 August 2006 he received a honorary degree from the Norwegian Academy of Music. When he died, he was given a State funeral.

265. See Chapter 19.

266. The Dead C, *The Dead C*, Language Recordings 2000.

267. For these British labels with very sharp connotations see:
www.roughtraderecords.com, *www.warp.net*, *www.xlrecordings.com*, *www.dfarecords.com*.

268. French jazz label founded in 1967 and then increasingly specializing in free jazz. Its production was celebrated by Thurston Moore of Sonic Youth and by critic Byron Coley, who in 2002 made a 3-CD compilation with Charly, and a 6-CD compilation with the Italian label Get Back Records.

269. Founded in New York in 1966, this label was very important for radical improvisation, releasing debut albums by artists such as Albert Ayler, Sun Ra, Gato Barbieri, Bob James, Marion Brown, Roswell Rudd, and more.

II

The Sound of Contemporary Jazz in Norway

22
Much more than "Nordic tone"...

Ever since Jan Garbarek rose on the European jazz scene, we have been nauseated by the way he's been presented. Whenever Norwegian jazz musicians are talked about in debates, interviews or reviews, foreigners always describe them in terms of the "Nordic tone", followed by inevitable images of mountains, fjords, plains and cold winters. The last time I heard something to this effect was during a workshop held by the German organisation Radio Research, where Norwegian jazz musicians were associated with snow! The British journalist and jazz professor Stuart Nicholson is one of these people who, in order to describe what Norwegian jazz musicians do, uses these metaphors *ad nauseam*. [...] As a general guideline, I would like to ban these descriptions of Norwegian jazz. Would our readers have understood what we meant to say about a jazz record if we'd written that a Düsseldorf group played Ruhr-jazz? Or a Danish group beer-jazz? A British one tea-jazz? A Spanish group torero-jazz and a Dutch one wooden clog-jazz? I don't think so. [...] For the coming year, however, we can lay down new rules in our editorial office, and say that these definitions are banned and will not be printed.[270]

Perhaps the *Jazznytt* editor will forgive me if I use the term in the very title of a chapter on contemporary Norwegian music, since I do it to concur with him. It's absolutely true: all too often you hear people talking about the Norwegian scene as interesting because it's exotic - the scene of the "Nordic tone". This doesn't do justice to the musical quality of the artists in this country, which has deep roots in the great tradition of the Hardanger fiddle. George Russell tuned into this great tradition and grafted his influence onto it, in turn stimulating Jan Garbarek's generation to rediscover their roots. This process was further consolidated as well thanks to the revolutionary influence that the Trondheim Conservatory had on jazz, with its two basic mottos: "don't learn the tradition, learn *from* the tradition" and "before you play, listen".

The Norwegian scene is a lively one, less preoccupied with technique than with putting out good ideas; it is a scene dominated by figures that don't care about stereotypes or trends; a scene that doesn't lose sight of its heritage and where an instrument like the Hardanger fiddle is used, for example, by Nils Økland to create a music poised between ancient and modern. It is a scene whose influences range from the folk of Mari Boine Persen, Terje Isungset and Karl Seglem, to the sophisticated pop of Susanna Wallumrød and Hanne Hukkelberg, via the modernity of Christian Wallumrød, the impro-noise of Supersilent and Puma, and the free jazz of Frode Gjerstad and Paal Nilssen-Love. As founding fathers the first ECM generation (Garbarek, Andersen, Rypdal, and Christensen and others such as Karin Krog) embodied a pioneering spirit that freed them from African-American jazz and helped to forge the identity of European jazz. The later Norwegian scene inherited this spirit but it didn't imitate those who came before. The drumming school that emerged after Jon Christensen is a case in point: Audun Kleive, Paal Nilssen-Love, Jarle Vespestad, Per Oddvar Johansen, Thomas Strønen, Torstein Lofthus and others - although very diverse - have all contributed to rewriting the instrument's stylistic articulation.

What is special about this scene is the search for an inner voice and a stylistic trademark that, mediated by a strong vocation for improvisation, translates into a musical universe blending influences that range from Ligeti to Björk, from Coltrane to King Crimson and Frank Zappa, without the reserves or the worries typical of our time, which can be summed up in a single question: is this jazz? The sound of contemporary Norwegian jazz is not necessarily based on typical jazz harmonies, it is extra-tonal, electronic, instrumental or vocal music strongly connected to nature and to the folk tradition, without ever being over-stylized but rather the expression of an inner process and of the artist's individual poetic.

There are various reasons for this. First of all, Norway is a young country that doesn't have to deal with the weight of history. It's a country characterized by a proud people, by the isolation from the rest of Europe (which has diminished only in recent years), and by an adventurous spirit, probably of Viking origin. Secondly, there's the tradition that started in 1961 with Molde, and which today sees more than twenty festivals scattered around a country of just five million people, (and in which the population often plays a very active role, not only as audience, but also as volunteers or as part of the organisation, all of which has contributed consistently to the musical education of Norwegians). There are courageous record labels such as Rune Grammofon, Sofa, Smalltown Supersound and Smalltown Superjazz. And finally, since the 1970s, the conservatories have provided aspiring musicians with the fundamentals while urging them to search for their individual voice, warning them against the risk of conforming to a standard musical aesthetic.

If you add all this up to the fact that Norway has a democratic type of society in which a sense of community plays an important role, and is a country blessed with oil reserves whose wealth is used proficiently by very efficient government agencies, it is understandable why today's music scene is so diverse, why its audience is so open and musically well educated, and why there are so many opportunities for musicians to play all year round, at home as well as abroad. The following pages explore this Norwegian reality, through a selection of some of the most active and representative figures in this ever-evolving context.

Garbarek's legacy

Håkon Kornstad is one of the Norwegian jazz musicians who've left the deepest mark both in his country and abroad. Through the Kornstad Trio, then Wibutee, and finally as a soloist, he showed how it's still possible to do very moving stuff on a saxophone. And as though that weren't enough, in 2009 he started developing an interest for opera singing, and by March of 2011 he was at the prestigious National Academy of Opera in Oslo as a tenor.[271]

The young drummer Øyvind Skarbø was right. It was 2012, and the musician he was talking about, Håkon Kornstad, is one of the most interesting saxophonists on the Norwegian scene. A musician allergic to clichés and repetition, Kornstad has always reacted to success by taking drastic changes in direction, an independent spirit just like his main inspirer, Garbarek. The two don't have that much in common, at least in terms of sound or phrasing; what they share instead is a thirst for exploration, and the pioneering approach that was the trademark of the early Garbarek. Trained at the conservatory in Trondheim, Kornstad is not heir to Garbarek as an instrumentalist, but as a musician who went against the grain in search of his own unmistakable voice.

While still a student, with the drummer Wetle Holte and the double bass player Per Zanussi, Kornstad formed one of the most interesting Norwegian bands of that period: Wibutee. In full Jazzland style, the band combined acoustic instruments and a substantial use of electronics, achieving acclaim with their debut album *Newborn Thing*, featuring Live Maria Roggen on vocals. In those years Kornstad had a passion for Björk's music and for the sound of bands like Massive Attack. Wibutee made a name for themselves at home and began to gather interest internationally releasing other albums,[272] but Kornstad went further, getting involved in a new trio that played post-bop and free jazz with the double bass player Mats Eilertsen and the drummer Paal Nilssen-Love. This new adventure put him in touch with the world of more radical improvisation and led him to collaborate with the trumpeter Axel Dörner and the pianist Håvard Wiik. Despite both projects going very well, in 2007 Kornstad made a clean break with what he had done until then and released a solo album, *Single Engine*, a work of great artistic depth in which he explored the nuances and the sonic possibilities of the saxophone. The record documented a remarkably mature voice, free from existing styles, rules and standards, and showed how he had reached a point in his creative experience where he could compose, play and produce in complete autonomy. Yet for Kornstad this was not an endpoint, it was a new beginning. In 2009 he released the more melodic and romantic *Dwell Time*,[273] stepping away from free jazz. As he was completing the recording in Oslo's Sofienberg Church however, he felt cornered, having the terrible sensation that he was merely repeating himself, and resolved to stop listening to jazz and to break from the past. In search for new inspiration he went to New York, and there one day a Norwegian friend took him to the Metropolitan Opera House, where he saw for the first time Mascagni's *Cavalleria Rusticana*. The experience blew him away. What particularly struck him was those voices, reaching the ears of an audience of 4,000 and making the whole place tremble with no amplification whatsoever. He began to sing as a hobby and then got more serious, enlisting the help of a private tutor. Having to start from scratch he faced quite a few difficulties, also because, unlike Italian, the Norwegian language seems to turn toward the "inside" of the body - something akin to ventriloquism. So Kornstad spent a month in Perugia learning Italian, and in 2011 decided to take the big step, taking part in the selections of the Operahøgskolen (the Oslo Opera Academy), where he was accepted as a tenor.

This is how Kornstad, at the age of 32 and in the middle of a successful career as a saxophonist, found himself debuting in February 2012 as tenor in Oslo's new Den Norske Opera in the role of the Podestà, in a student production of Mozart's opera *La finta giardiniera*. This new career path led in the same year to his new project *Tenor Battle*, in which he blended opera and jazz, and gave free rein to his twin tenor souls (voice and sax).

Norway boasts many other excellent saxophonists besides Kornstad. Among the older generation, deserving special mention is Masqualero's founding member Tore Brunborg (born 1960), who after the success of his debut solo album *Tid*[274] remained in the shadows for several years, to return to the scene only recently with a few collaborations on ECM projects (with Tord Gustavsen, Ketil Bjørnstad, Manu Katché) as a sideman. Another notable figure that in his early period was especially similar to Garbarek in his sound and phrasing (as Brunborg himself) is Bendik Hofseth (b. 1962). When he was 25 years old Hofseth moved to New York to replace Michael Brecker in Steps Ahead, staying until 1992. In 1996 he made waves with *Planets, Rivers and... IKEA*, released on his own label and pulled back from the market due to a legal dispute with the corporation. Regardless of the legal problems, the record won the NOPA Prize.[275] Today Hofseth is a key figure in the music industry as president of NOPA and by:Larm, as well as of the International Council of Authors and Composers of Music (CIAM), where he represents 2,600,000 thousand composers and lyricists in the whole world. For several years he was also the president of Phonofile and a board member of TONO (The Norwegian Performing Rights Society).

To return to Garbarek's legacy, the figure that carries on the originality of his sound better than any other is Trygve Seim, one of the most original voices both on tenor and soprano sax, and also one of the most consistent with the ECM sound. His debut dates back to 2001 with the project for large ensemble *Different Rivers*,[276] followed by *Sangam*.[277] In addition to working with a large ensemble, he has an ongoing duo project with accordionist Frode Haltli, whose releases include the fantastic album *Yeraz*.

Among other saxophonists, Karl Seglem is the most representative in the area influenced by folk music, Eirik Hegdal is the most versatile and eclectic (and leader of the Trondheim Jazz Orchestra), while André Roligheten, his fellow member in Team Hegdal and co-leader of the duo Albatrosh, is undoubtedly one of the most promising emerging talents of post-bop/free jazz.

Traditional jazz: the heirs to Bjarne Nerem and Knut Riisnæs

Can Norwegian tenor saxophonist Petter Wettre be called "the Branford Marsalis of Scandinavia"? Both saxophonists favour a big sound, steeped in tradition but not beholden to convention. Wettre was educated at Boston's Berklee College of Music before returning to his home and eventually founding Household Records, the primary vehicle for his output. His tastes run from post-bop to funk to free jazz. What is special about Wettre is his command of not only his saxophone, but each situation in which he applies his craft. Be it an improvised quartet or fronting an entire orchestra, his "sound" stands out with clarity and a sense of purpose that bespeaks his passion and leadership in jazz.[278]

Although Norway is not at the top of the list for bop players (be-bop, hard bop, etc.), there are a few of undoubted interest, and the leading one among these is Petter Wettre (b. 1967). Before Wettre, the outstanding figures of this American-born genre were, in the 1950s, Bjarne Nerem, and in the late 1970s Knut Riisnæs (b. 1945). A contemporary of Garbarek, Riisnæs was one of the most talented musicians of his time, who strangely chose to play the style that was least popular in that period. Despite winning the 1982 Spellemann Prize with the album *Flukt*[279] he was virtually unknown abroad, as in the early 1980s the spotlight was on players such as Garbarek and Andersen. It was only 10 years later (when Petter Wettre returned with a diploma from Berklee) that Riisnæs finally came into his own, winning the 1992 Gammleng Prize and once again the Spellemann.[280]

Petter Wettre was born in Sandefjord and grew up in a family of amateur musicians, and after starting off with the clarinet he moved on to the saxophone. As a young man, he seemed oblivious to the influence of Garbarek and other ECM artists, drawing inspiration instead from American acts such as Yellowjackets, Spyro Gyra, and David Sanborn.

After a year at Folkehøgskole he realised that music was not just a hobby for him. Jazz studies at the Trondheim conservatory were starting to gain a reputation (it was the years when Stian Carstensen and Arve Henriksen were students there), but Wettre saw in the Berklee School of Boston a better place to get his training. He was at a crossroads, but knew what he wanted:

> When I decided to play this American music I said to myself that I had to go study it where it was born, in the United States, where I could learn about Louis Armstrong. That's how it was, I just couldn't go to Trondheim, where nobody would've taught me that.[281]

He moved to Boston when his friend Ole Mathisen[282] had just finished his studies. Mathisen stayed on to study sax with Bob Mintzer and arranging with Maria Schneider in New York, Wettre instead returned home after finishing Berklee, in 1992. Once back in Oslo, he sent some tapes of his final exams to NRK, arousing great interest; as a result, he had a few radio programmes dedicated to him and started working with the orchestra of NRK. However, this was the period when Airamero was one the most popular bands, and it wasn't easy for Wettre to get gigs at clubs or festivals. He started playing with Jon Eberson and then met the drummer Per Oddvar Johansen, with whom he won the 2000 Spellemann Prize with *The Only Way to Travel*. Most importantly, Johansen put him in touch with Christian Wallumrød, with whom he debuted at the Kongsberg Festival in 1993 with his own quartet: "It wasn't easy for me to break into a scene that was monopolised by young people coming from Trondheim, and Christian Wallumrød accepted to play in my quartet to do me a favour. It was with that quartet that I started playing in the clubs".[283] Soon the quartet's personnel changed, with the arrival of Håvard Wiik on piano and Ingebrigt Håker Flaten on bass, who were both more in line with Wettre's aesthetics and members of the band Element.

Wettre's career finally took off in the period between 1995 to 1998, also thanks to a European tour of his quartet and the band Element (of which he was a member), two groups shortly afterwards were replaced by The Trio, with Håker Flaten and Jarle Vespestad, one of the most representative bands of Wettre's entire career.[284]

Wettre's idea of music making was not commonplace in Norway, where the mainstream style (with trios, quartets, etc. in one's name) found hardly any space in the cluster of bands out of Trondheim featuring collective names such as Wibutee, Supersilent, Farmers Market, etc. While Norwegian band members usually sought a collective form of music making, Wettre wanted to play as a leader and impart specific instructions to his musicians. It doesn't come as a surprise then that, for about 10 years, he relied on a Danish rhythm section (Jonas Westergaard on double bass, replaced by Anders Christensen, and Anders Mogensen on drums).

After the scene's renewal of the 1980s, the recognition that Petter Wettre finally garnered was a bit like "reinventing the wheel",[285] as he himself put it. At any rate, the bop scene in Norway was limited, including the saxophonist brothers Frode and Atle Nymo, the guitarist Staffan William-Olsson and the trumpeter Kåre Nymark - one of the rare Norwegian hard-bop trumpeters - with his Nymark Collective. Other names that deserve to be mentioned are those of John Pål Inderberg, among the founders of the Trondheim Conservatory, Bodil Niska, saxophonist and founder of Bare Jazz,[286] and Marius Neset, a rising star who at the 2011 Molde Jazz Festival received the prestigious JazZtipendiat, an endowment for the composition of a work for the Trondheim Jazz Orchestra (which was performed in 2012). Neset had made a name for himself in Denmark with JazzKamikazen, and that same year released the album *Golden Xplosion*,[287] which received five stars from the renowned British jazz critic John Fordham: "Marius Neset combines Brecker's power and Jan Garbarek's tonal delicacy, but has a vision that makes all 11 originals on this sensational album feel indispensable, and indispensably connected to each other. Neset is on his way to being one of the biggest new draws on the circuit." [288]

Finally, talking about swing and mainstream, two more names cannot be left out: that of the guitarist Jon Larsen, who keeps alive the tradition of Django Reinhardt and gypsy jazz with his quartet Hot Club De Norvège (inspired by Django's Hot Club France), and the label Hot Club Records, which celebrated its 30th anniversary in 2012.

Jon Christensen and the new drumming school

As Ken Micallef eloquently wrote in the American magazine *Modern Drummer*:

[Jon Christensen] has helped to forge a unique, original jazz imprint, which has only deepened over his 40 years as a musician. In Norway and abroad, his sprawling, elastic time interpretation and remarkable cymbal style have been elemental in defining the sound of music on ECM [...] Along with his contemporaries Tony Williams and Jack DeJohnette, Christensen changed the drummer's role in jazz from timekeeper to rhythmic/melodic inventor, colourist, and commentator. His ability to deconstruct jazz rhythms over the entire kit, while still swinging with ferocious energy, is equalled only by his crystalline cymbal work and unusual melding of loose rhythms within freely interpreted structures.[289]

A highly inspirational figure of the Norwegian scene (and not only for drummers) for his more than 50-year long career Jon Christensen has remained true to the few simple rules that he himself summed up in the liner notes of his album *Rarum XX*:

I. Band feeling is more important than bravura
II. Less is more.
III. How fast can you play slower
IV. A beat is not always what you think it is.
So good luck!
Jon Christensen.[290]

As a phenomenal artist who has never given in to the logic of imitation, like drummers of the calibre of Tony Williams and Roy Haynes he was also the initiator of a school: "I've always been hired to play like I play. I've been playing 'Jon Christensen' all the way",[291] he stated. Thanks to Christensen and the lessons of the Trondheim Jazz Conservatory, Norwegian drummers emerging in recent years are part of a phenomenon that is quite unique in the world.

It is no surprise that the first real "wonder" drummer to emerge after Christensen was Audun Kleive, who in 1985 recorded *Chaser* in a trio with Terje Rypdal and Bjørn Kjellemyr. Kleive's style, however, is completely different from that of Christensen. While Christensen has an unmistakable touch and *rubato*, Kleive's explosive drumming is more similar to a jazz version of Stewart Copeland. From the very start, Kleive wasn't interested in merely providing the standard rhythm section accompaniment and wanted to play an active role in shaping the music. What Kleive inherited from Christensen was a strong originality and an extremely flexible approach:

> If I think of Jon Balke, I can't avoid recognising that some things came out in me just listening to his piano. I know for certain that part of my music and my way of playing is also the result of the work I did with him. He's like a force that drives you [...] I also know that what I'm working on today [using exclusively electronic percussion] is just as strong and important as what I did before. It's the road I must follow. After many years of collective work, there comes a time when you no longer have to search for your own voice, you just know it's there somewhere: it's the synthesis of a life spent interacting and exploring with others.[292]

Two other drummers besides Christensen and Kleive have left an indelible mark: Paal Nilssen-Love and Torstein Lofthus, two earthy musicians with an impressive energy. Nilssen-Love is unbeatable in the contexts of noise and free jazz, and his technique is often compared to the multi-timbral technique of European drummers such as Tony Oxley, Paul Lytton, Paul Lovens and John Stevens. In addition to his technique, his muscular drumming and his way of always playing as though it were the last concert of his life make him a unique musician indeed. Torstein Lofthus, sometimes referred to as the John Bonham of jazz, has made frequent excursions into pop-rock, and especially into death metal, and jazz and prog, in an explosive mix that makes him one of the most influential drummers of the recent past. While he is a powerful driving force in Shining and in Elephant9 (where he plays with Ståle Storløkken, the keyboardist of Supersilent, and Nikolai Eilertsen, the bassist of National Bank), he is more restrained and measured when playing next to Gard Nilssen in Mathias Eick's quintet with two drummers.

Undoubtedly Christensen remains the most charismatic figure of the lot, the man who set the tone for a host of younger and extremely interesting musicians, of which the three drummers mentioned are the most representative but certainly not the only ones. It is impossible for example not to mention Per Oddvar Johansen (b. 1968), Grammy winner with Petter Wettre in 2000, whose lighter and poetic drumming is closer to Christensen's style, and is indispensable in any ensemble of Christian Wallumrød and Trygve Seim. Jarle Vespestad (b. 1966), on his part, is able to switch from the tense atmospheres of Supersilent to the soft ones of Tord Gustavsen and Silje Nergaard, and to the impossible rhythms of Farmers Market's Bulgarian music. Thomas Strønen (b. 1972), with his dense and hyperkinetic rhythmic textures, is ideal in solo contexts such as *Pohlitz*,[293] or in duo with the voice of Sidsel Endresen or Tone Åse, or with the British Iain Ballamy in Food, and in many other acts. Also worthy of a mention are Martin Horntveth, drummer and co-leader of Jaga Jazzist, the groovy Wetle Holte (with Wibutee and Eivind Aarset, but also with Luca Aquino), the earthy Gard Nilssen (Puma, Bushman's Revenge, and the Mathias Eick quintet), and the young Øyvind Skarbø, a master of the dialogue between traditional and contemporary with the trio 1982 (featuring Nils Økland and Sigbjørn Apeland).

With over 600 professional drummers in Norway, choosing between them isn't very easy. Of course these are not strictly jazz drummers, since as we said several times a clear-cut distinction between genres is not the standard in this country. Bearing witness to this fact is the *trommer julebord* (drummers' Christmas gathering),[294] organised for the first time in 2010 by Martin Horntveth, which saw the participation of musicians from all walks of life (death metal, jazz, pop, rock, symphony orchestra, etc.): about 160 participants in the first year and about 200 in the second, in an upward trend that bodes well for future years.[295]

Terje Rypdal's legacy

Like his Norwegian compatriot Jan Garbarek did on the saxophone, Rypdal managed to create one of the most recognizable sounds on his instrument: an icy, very expansive tone, full of reverb, in a way incredibly romantic because full of passion, but then of the kind that abhors intimacy but embraces distant horizons.[296]

The blogger Stef wrote these words in his review of Terje Rypdal's box set *Odyssey*, which documents the guitarist's mid-1970s work with his quartet Odyssey, and includes the 1975 double album *Odyssey* as well as the previously unreleased *Unfinished Highballs*, a 1976 recording for the radio with the

Swedish Radio Jazz Group. Rypdal was an innovator open to all explorations from the very beginning. After the rock experience of *Bleak House* and meeting George Russell, he worked increasingly with contemporary music and studied composition with Finn Mortensen. One of the results of this research was the album *Q.E.D.*, representing one of the high points in his career.

Rypdal was also the inspirer of that sound that audio engineer Sven Persson was looking for in the mid-1980s, and which found its clearest form in the *Chaser* trio/project. He also has been known to cause a stir, as when he passed on his project to drummer friend and fellow musician Paolo Vinaccia, since it was leaning too much towards rock and he couldn't release it with ECM, with whom he had signed an exclusive contract. It was a generous gesture that allowed Vinaccia, who was coming out of a difficult period because of health problems, to release in his own name a box set with the revealing title *Very Much Alive*.[297] It was a rich record, documenting the band Skywards at one of its heights and in its original form, and not the more palatable one of their ECM record,[298] guest starring Danish trumpeter Palle Mikkelborg.

Rypdal was never a point of reference strictly as an instrumentalist, and nobody even at home tried to imitate his sound or his phrasing. Rather, he inspired artists to make music in complete freedom. According to jazz historian Bjørn Stendahl, Rypdal "is not a jazz musician",[299] and yet he was the one to open the way for a musician such as Eivind Aarset, one of the leading figures of the European scene of the late 1990s also thanks to the release of *Electronique*

Paolo Vinaccia The descendant of a Neapolitan family of lute makers, Paolo Vinaccia (b. 1954) has lived in Norway since 1979. A drummer and percussionist, he started by playing in Jonas Fjeld's band for about three years, then moving on to Oslo Rhythm, Blues Ensemble and finally working with Jon Eberson in different contexts, both with Sidsel Endresen and in trio with the bassist Bjørn Kjellemyr. Gathering increasing acclaim, he began collaborating with Knut Reiersrud, Bendik Hofseth, Terje Rypdal, Frode Alnaes, Mikhail (Misha) Alperin, Arild Andersen and Bugge Wesseltoft. After several years of working with Nils Petter Molvær, Bugge Wesseltoft and Sidsel Endresen (before the era of nu jazz) he began collaborating with Terje Rypdal and Arild Andersen, becoming a regular member of most of their projects. His first recording was on *Sami Ædnan* by Mattis Hætta and Sverre Kjelsberg, a Sami song that won the 1980s Spellemann Prize (see Chapter 13), followed by a series of diverse recordings. In 1997 he finally released his own album *Mbara Boom*, in which Arild Andersen and Tore Brunborg interact with the Tenores di Neoneli, a Sardinian male choir following the ancient but lively *tenores* singing tradition.

Noire, a manifesto of that aesthetic along with *Khmer* and *New Conception of jazz*.

A musician with a very personal style, Aarset gathered increasing acclaim and found a new vein of creativity through his assiduous work with the remix wizard Jan Bang. After working with Bang on the ...*And Poppies from Kandahar* tour,[300] he made his debut on ECM with the album *Dream Logic*,[301] which turned away from the nu jazz brand, featuring a fresh and original sound with meditative atmospheres strongly inspired by Jan Bang.

Today's new star guitarist, however, is the dauntless Stian Westerhus (b. 1979), winner of the 2006 JazzIntro with the trio Puma. After the intriguing project with Indian singer Swati Natekar commissioned by BBC Radio, he released three albums in the span of three years, each more interesting and surprising than the last. When he replaced Aarset in Nils Petter Molvær's trio, Westerhus gave signs of embracing a more rock sound, but instead the release of *Pitch Black Star Spangled* was followed by *Didymoi Dreams*,[302] a live performance at Bergen's Nattjazz, where together with Sidsel Endresen he thrilled the audience like an acrobat without safety nets. Even more surprising was the next *The Matriarch and the Wrong Kind of Flowers*,[303] a little masterpiece recorded in the Vigeland Mausoleum in Oslo (where Arve Henriksen recorded his *Sakuteiki*). With its ghostly 20-second natural reverb (and the steady 5°C to preserve the paintings), the Vigeland Mausoleum is a unique place and gave Westerhus a further boost in creativity, bringing the exploration of the expressive potentials of his instruments to a new high. The result is a contemporary work that in some ways evokes the experimentations by Bjørn Fongaard [see Box], brought back to life thanks to the box set *Elektrofoni*[304] released by Lars Mørch Finborud (see Chapter 2). Winner of the Young Jazz Musician of the Year Award at the 50th Molde Jazz Festival, and of the BBC's Award for Innovation in Jazz in the UK,

---

Bjørn Fongaard (1919-1980), Norwegian experimental composer, guitarist and pioneer of micro-tonal music, is very well known at home because of his frequent appearances on radio and television as guitarist for famous singers-songwriters such as Alf Prøysen and Søstrene Bjørklund. He has taught guitar to Terje Rypdal and Egil Kapstad, among others. *Elektrofoni* is a very interesting documentation of his groundbreaking micro-tonal works, with the sound carefully restored and mastered by Helge Sten.

www.plasticstrip.no/index.php?/prisma-record/bjorn-f"ongaard/

Stian Westerhus is well on his way to becoming one of the brightest stars of Scandinavian jazz.

Arild Andersen's legacy

"[…] Arild Andersen gave life to extremely diverse situations, without ever worrying about how many records or tickets he sold. […] He is a great source of inspiration for me. He makes me think of how I'd like to be when I'm 65 years old!" [305] stated Martin Revheim.

Those who have been lucky enough to get to know Andersen have seen the stature and beauty of the person behind the sunny smile that he has always had in a career of over 40 years. He is a giant who, with Christensen, accompanied the best American musicians passing through Norway (Phil Woods, Dexter Gordon, Hampton Hawes, Johnny Griffin, Sonny Rollins and Chick Corea, just to mention a few), and who later forged his own path. An ideal fellow musician, he played in Garbarek's quartet, with Radka Toneff and then with Masqualero. Most of all Andersen has led unforgettable projects, sometimes more inspired by folk music (*Sagn*[306] and *Arv*[307]) and sometimes by jazz (the more recent *Live At Belleville*),[308] and has written some of the best pages in the ECM catalogue (with Ralph Towner, Nana Vasconcelos, Bill Frisell, etc.), becoming one of the key figures of the German label and highlighting a particular gift for melody.

As is usual with double bass players, Andersen has a fine ear, and was often called in by Eicher in Oslo's Rainbow Studio even if he wasn't the one recording:

"Manfred would call me and say he had Keith Jarrett or Chick Corea coming to town to record and ask if I'd like to come along to the studio to give my thoughts on how things were sounding", says Andersen. "When Keith Jarrett recorded *Facing You*, it was obvious that something really special was happening but nobody could have known then that this label was going to occupy such an important position in jazz all these years later." [309]

Andersen was an extraordinary mentor for Terje Gewelt (b. 1960), who took lessons from him in the late 1970s, made a name for himself on the scene, spent 7 years in the United States at the invitation of Michael Shrieve (Santana's drummer), recorded a couple of albums with Billy Cobham, and finally returned home. Gewelt debuted on ECM with Misha Alperin in *North Story* (1996), collaborated for several years with the pianist Dag Arnesen, and also recorded a few albums with the Italian pianist Enrico Pieranunzi (*Oslo* and *Azure*).

Another bassist of even greater acclaim is Mats Eilertsen (b. 1975), who made several recordings with ECM (Bobo Stenson, Tord Gustavsen, The Source, Jakob Young) and has a fine discography in his own name with the young label Hubro (jazz section of Grappa Musikkforlag, mentioned in Chapter 21). An eclectic musician and composer, Eilertsen shifted from experimental projects such as *Turanga* (with Ernst Reijseger, Fredrik Ljungkvist and Thomas Strønen) and *Food* (with Iain Ballamy, Arve Henriksen, and Thomas Strønen) to other softer and more polished projects.

Despite its population of 5 million, Norway boasts many talented double bass players. Ingebrigt Håker Flaten is the biggest name on the free jazz scene, but he also worked with Bugge Wesseltoft in *New Conception of Jazz*. After a stint in Wibutee, the Italo-Norwegian Per Zanussi seems to have settled into a post-Ornette aesthetic with Zanussi Five and Thirteen, while Ole Morten Vågan (b. 1979), winner of NOPA's Composer Prize in 2000 and of the DnB NOR Prize in Kongsberg in 2009, is highly focused on his band Motif.[310] Last but not least, Steinar Raknes (b. 1975) is an artist who was already mentioned in Chapter 13, younger brother of the singer Eldbjørg. Not only a brilliant instrumentalist in projects such as Ola Kvernberg's Folk trio, he often sings as well with excellent results, as in the album *Stillhouse* (2012),[311] in which he reinterprets songs by Prince, Bruce Springsteen and Joni Mitchell, among others.

Female vocalists

We are gathered here at the Victoria to celebrate Sidsel Endresen. We are not just celebrating her 60th birthday, we are also paying homage to one of our most representative singers, one of the undisputed queens of the voice, an artist who for years has had a key role in the Norwegian and international jazz scenes. A true pioneer of vocal improvisation and one of the leading exponents of the so-called extended vocal technique, Sidsel Endresen today is at the height of her musical career, and has taught for many years as a conservatory professor, inspiring singers such as Solveig Slettahjell, Live Maria Roggen, Kristin Asbjørnsen, Beate Lech and Lisa Dillan, just to name a few.[312]

On 8 and 9 November 2012, the jazz community gathered at the Nasjonal Jazzscene[313] to celebrate one of the most iconic singers of the Norwegian and European scenes, Sidsel Endresen. On the first day Endresen performed with the

Improensemble (Christian Wallumrød, Espen Reinertsen, Eivind Lønning, Vilde Sandve Alnæs, and Inga Margrete Aas) and on the second day other guests performed in her honour, with dedications, anecdotes, and touching testimonies, but also with a lot of joy and, of course, music. Fiona Talkington of BBC Radio 3 hosted the event.

Endresen, inspired by the star Radka Toneff (her contemporary and the real driving force in those early years), started her career with the soul band Chipahua and the Jon Eberson Group, achieving notoriety with *Jive Talking* (250,000 copies sold in 1981). She could have stayed on that road of success but, as resolute as her inspirer Toneff, took many other paths instead, moved by an increasing thirst for experimentation. After studying overseas with the vocalist and performer Meredith Monk and releasing two albums on ECM with Nils Petter Molvær, Django Bates and Jon Christensen, Endresen continued her successful career working in duo with Bugge Wesseltoft, releasing *Merriwinkle* with Christian Wallumrød and Helge Sten, becoming a member of the trio ESE (with Eldbjørg Raknes and Elin Rosseland), and releasing *Undertow* with Audun Kleive and Roger Ludvigsen. As an improviser it's very difficult to define her in just a few words, but her artistic quest has been unique, poised between sound abstraction and phonetic inquiry, and devoid of special effects and electronics. With her openness to the unexpected and to what the moment brings, Endresen always manages to touch the listener deeply, especially in live performances, which provide the ideal setting for her craft. Some of her best live performances have been with Jan Bang and Erik Honoré, Humcrush, Håkon Kornstad, Jim Black and Bram Stadthouder, and also with Stian Westerhus, with whom she recorded *Didymoi Dreams*, one of the most thrilling albums of 2012. Endresen's career has been showered with awards, including a Radka Toneff Minnepris (1993), four Spellemann Prizes (1981, 1985, 1998, 2002), a DnB NOR Prize in Kongsberg (1998), a Buddy Prize (2000), and two nominations at the Nordic Council Music Prize (2001 and 2011).

With the celebration at the Victoria theatre, friends, fellow musicians and writers (Norwegian and from abroad) wanted to pay homage to her but also to thank her for the deep inspiration and the teaching each of them received from this vocalist, who never worried about the microphone and who has always thought that "background noise doesn't exist".[314]

There were many singers who took part in the event, paying tribute to Endresen on MIC's magazine *Listen to Norway* and/or performing in the concert. Of particular significance was Eldbjørg Raknes, who trained at the Conservatory of Trondheim with Henriksen and Wallumrød, and formed the a cappella trio

ESE (1999) with Endresen and Elin Rosseland (another protagonist of the vocal scene). Also deserving a mention are Live Maria Roggen[315] and Tone Åse, who founded the ensemble Trondheim Voices in 2004 in the context of the city's Conservatory. Åse was artistic director of the ensemble from 2006 to 2011, when she was replaced by Siri Gjære and Live Maria Roggen. The ensemble features nine female voices strongly inspired by Endresen who, along with Maja Ratkje, Lisa Dillan, the emerging Mari Kvien Brunvoll and the already mentioned Raknes, Roggen and Rosseland, represent the cream of current vocal and experimental improvisation, not only in Scandinavia.

As we have seen, however, folk music continues to play a key role in Norway. While the great muses in this field are Agnes Buen Garnås and Mari Boine, one cannot leave out Berit Opheim Versto, nominated for the 1996 Spellemann with *Eitt Steg*, performing partner of Karl Seglem and member of the trio Utla, but also soloist in the contemporary ensemble BIT20. Another very representative voice of the Kirkelig Kulturverksted is Kari Bremnes,[316] vice-president of NOPA and winner of the Spellemann Prize in 1981 with *Mitt ville hjerte* (the album that launched the Kleive brothers) and again in 1991 with *Spor*.

Norway certainly has no lack of female voices, all diverse and each with her own style. Embracing a purer jazz aesthetic and adapting it to the surrounding music and culture is Solveig Slettahjell (b. 1971) who came into the limelight in 2003 with *Slow Motion Orchestra* featuring Sjur Miljeteig, Morten Qvenild, Per Oddvar Johansen and Mats Eilertsen. Standing out among the younger singers is the prodigy Åsne Valland Nordli (1975), who was already teaching at Voss's Ole Bull Academy at age 15, and who now frequently performs with Nils Økland and Sigbjørn Apeland.

In another of the lively areas of Norwegian music, the one inspired by the pop of Bel Canto and Röyksopp, a singer that shines particularly bright is Susanna Wallumrød (b. 1979), Christian's sister, who rose to fame in 2004 with her debut album *List of Lights and Buoys* in duo with the pianist Morten Qvenild (b. 1978), also known as the Magical Orchestra. In the same period, Hanne Hukkelberg released the small masterpiece *Little Things*, thanks to which she won the 2006 Spellemann Prize. Susanna Wallumrød and Hanne Hukkelberg opened the way for a generation of pop vocalists with close ties to the jazz scene. While Wallumrød began with Qvenild and then collaborated with Helge Sten and Pål Hausken, Hukkelberg has an important musical partner in Ivar Grydeland (Huntsville and Dans Les Arbres). Two very young singers also drew attention with their albums: *The Brothel* by Susanne Sundfør (produced by Lars Horntveth of Jaga Jazzist), and *Viscera* by Jenny Hval. Also deserving to be mentioned is

Beate S. Lech (aka Beady Belle), who after starting in jazz with bassist Marius Reksjø increasingly shifted to pop-soul, becoming one of the key figures of Jazzland (where she opened the way for the younger Torun Eriksen). Finally, Kristin Asbjørnsen (b. 1971) is the beautiful voice in Tord Gustavsen's *Restored, Returned*.[317] After several albums with the band Dadafon she launched her solo career in 2006 with *Wayfaring Stranger. A Spiritual Songbook*,[318] platinum disc in Norway. Her extraordinary voice was commended with the 2009 Spellemann Prize for her following album *The Night Shines like the Day*.[319]

Nordic exoticisms

The "Nordic tone", an overlooked feature of jazz for several decades, represents another way of hearing jazz, an ordered calm that can be mystically and aesthetically beckoning in the often frantic and occasionally rebarbative world of American jazz. "A little bit of a different angle" explains Arild Andersen, "the sound is very important, the space in the music is very important, the transparency is important, the dynamic is important, not how cleverly you can play your instrument, how fast you can play or how impressive you could be".[320]

However partial and applicable only to the visible part of the iceberg,[321] the definition of Nordic tone does belong to the Norwegian scene, and acquires meaning if applied to musicians whose music is chiefly based on melody and the folk tradition. It was an idea of music that emerged with Garbarek through his partnership with ECM, and that is best represented today by the pianist Tord Gustavsen, in whose music every note is essential and indispensable, nothing more and nothing less. Gustavsen's melodic research combines elements of Scandinavian folk and elements from the African and Caribbean musical traditions, and looks for inspiration not only in nature itself but also in the dialogue between nature and urban life. Gustavsen can be considered Garbarek's natural heir and it makes sense that, following the death of his trio member and double bass player Harald Johnsen, he introduced the sax of Tore Brunborg to the group, switching from a trio to a quartet. He is the kind of musician that a large part of the jazz audience expects when they think of the fjords, who corresponds to a specific idea of music in the collective imagination of ECM listeners, and whose role model is really Garbarek himself, rather than Keith Jarrett.

Unsurprisingly, Gustavsen is as successful abroad as Garbarek and friends were in the early 1970s, and is the Norwegian musician who has sold the most records after Garbarek.[322] Back in the 1970s, the dark side of the moon was represented by Svein Finnerud, Kalle Neumann and so on, while today it's represented by Helge Lien, Vigleik Storaas, Espen Eriksen and several other pianists who haven't been able to make a mark on the international market, despite their degree of success at home.

Born in 1970, winner of the 2010 Spellemann Prize for jazz, before starting his solo career, Gustavsen had already been an important part of the Norwegian jazz scene for several years. His playing has formed a cornerstone in projects featuring some of the finest Norwegian singers, including Solveig Slettahjell, Silje Nergaard, Siri Gjære, and Kristin Asbjørnsen. He launched his solo career in 2003 with his trio, rising to international fame thanks to *Changing Places*, his debut album with ECM and first in a trilogy including *The Ground* (2005) and *Being There* (2007), where he plays with the late bassist Harald Johnsen and Supersilent drummer Jarle Vespestad. Raised in the rural countryside near Oslo, Gustavsen trained at the Conservatory of Trondheim and then further studied theoretical aspects of music - psychology of improvisation, music theory and aesthetics - with a Ph.D in Musicology at the University of Oslo. The range of musicians and styles that influenced his music career is very broad:

I have been influenced by a very broad spectrum of musicians and styles over the years - naturally by Keith Jarrett and Bill Evans (like almost all the pianists in our generation), by James P. Johnson and other old jazz/stride/blues musicians, and by Scandinavian pianists Jan Johansson and Jon Balke. Also I have been strongly influenced by the lyricism and the interpretation of melody of the great singers of the jazz tradition, especially Bessie Smith and Billie Holiday. […] Then, there is the whole history of European classical music, especially the epochs of Baroque, Impressionism and Neo-Classicism, which have meant a lot to me. And folk music from many parts of the word, especially from West Africa and Scandinavia... […] The main challenge is always to make sense of all your inspirations and bring them into a field of personalized expression here and now, to combine post-modern openness with a romantic belief in the individual voice, in artistic honesty, in trying to say something that really matters instead of babbling along, in trying to get as close as possible to the feeling of sacredness in music. […] But I remain basically a songwriter rather than a composer. I'm still much more interested in exploring the small details and the finer nuances in interplay, and in building larger form on-the-spot with the ensemble, based on compositions that are small building blocks with good melodies, rather than composing with symphonic aspirations.[323]

Following Gustavsen's footsteps, the pianist Helge Lien attracted a great deal of interest with his trio, especially in Germany. Lien's pianism is filled with poetic sensibility and displays surprising improvisational power on entirely original material. The trio was formed in 1998, when the young Lien was attending the Norwegian Academy of Music in Oslo, studying improvisation with the Russian pianist Misha Alperin, who greatly influenced him and became his mentor. After releasing five albums and receiving the Hansa Award at Bergen's 2008 Nattjazz, Lien's career really took off with *Hello Troll*, which won the DnB NOR Prize for Best Musician of the Year as well as the Spellemann Prize and was, in Lien's own words, "a big step ahead". The trio's success grew beyond the borders of Norway, especially in Japan, Canada and Germany, with 15,000 copies sold and rave reviews in the most important international magazines. The daily *Dagbladet* defined it as "the best Norwegian piano trio in a long time", while according to Stuart Nicholson it was "one of the leading European jazz groups of the last few years to push the music out into new territory".[324] This is the success of an intimate type of piano playing that, after seeing Jon Balke and then Vigleik Storaas inspired by Jan Johansson and Bobo Stenson, today sees countless young talents emerging, and relying on the further legacy of the late Swedish pianist Esbjörn Svensson, a legacy that has been picked up in particular by Espen Eriksen's trio,[325] but also by Morten Qvenild with the trio In the Country and by Andreas Ulvo with the Eple Trio - all representing new sophisticated facets of a European style piano trio.

The Hardanger fiddle tradition

The Hardanger fiddle is more than just a violin: the tradition links its origins to the supernatural. Norwegian legends and fairytales are filled with references to otherworldly and subterranean creatures that carry a violin. This instrument is undoubtedly the symbol of Norway, a country that is politically young but culturally old and rich with folk traditions. When you speak of folk music you usually mean a music that is often anonymous, orally transmitted, and that has come to us through a centuries-long history.[326] The roots of the *hardingfele* are deep and go far back in time, and the values surrounding this instrument involve not only music but also symbolisms and emotional and existential realities that are anchored in the traditional Norwegian way of life, which is rural and deeply bound to a nature full of mystery and wonder.

The musician who today, more than any other, is able to transmit the essence of the instrument into a contemporary context is Nils Økland, who brings the Hardanger fiddle's sonic potential - heightened by its resonating understrings - to bear on current music and all the expectations surrounding it.

A musician with an unusual background, Nils Økland began playing violin and accordion (mostly dance music) with his uncle. He then continued with classical music studies first in Stavanger and then at the Music Academy in Oslo, where he came into contact with the jazz scene, and in particular met Calle Neumann and Bjørnar Andresen, who were very close to Svein Finnerud and Garbarek. In 1986 he released with Andresen his first album *Nils Økland & Bjørnar Andresen* (Hot Club Records, 1986), but shortly afterwards moved to Budapest, having become progressively involved in Balkan music. Økland concentrated solely on Gipsy music, and from 1984 to 1995 was active with the Balkansemblet. Upon his return to Norway he abandoned Balkan music and went back to what had fascinated him during his first years in Oslo: jazz and improvised music, and their connection to contemporary music. During this new phase in his career Økland met all the best Hardanger fiddle players and was invited by violinist Sigbjørn Bernhoft Osa to become director of Voss's Ole Bull Academy, encouraged to take the post also by the multidisciplinary artist Arvid Gangsøe, a former fellow student of his at the Musical Academy.

A unique fiddler, Nils Økland is an open and versatile artist. As director of Voss's Academy he got back in touch with his folk roots and, at the same time, became increasingly involved in contemporary music through his friendship and collaboration with Gangsøe and other art-music improvisers and performers. In 2000 he even performed on BBC Radio 3 with Supersilent, and host Fiona Talkington introduced him as a "virtuoso of the traditional Hardanger fiddle with a solo set that lights up the grey area separating folk forms from free improvisation and modern composition".[327] While he was a member of Christian Wallumrød's quartet with Arve Henriksen and Per Oddvar Johansen, he released two solo albums on Rune Grammofon documenting his artistic research, *Straum* (2000) and *Bris* (2004). Yet Økland is always bridging past and present, and so he also published the small masterpiece *Lysøen. Hommage à Ole Bull*, paying homage to one of the greatest Hardanger fiddle players of all times, Ole Bull.

Before the Oslo Academy took his name, Ole Bull had become something of a sensation in Paris in the period 1831-33 and in Italy (Bologna) in 1834. As is not unusual with Norwegian artists, he had brought along another of tradition's greats, Torgeir Augundsson, stage-name Myllarguten (1801-1872), sharing the success with him. Just as Ole Bull had found in Myllarguten the ideal fellow musician to help him bring the Hardanger fiddle out of the dance halls, a century later the great violinist Sigbjørn Bernhoft Osa transmitted his knowledge of their work to Økland, the inspiration of the current scene.

Outstanding in the current scene is the young Gjermund Larsen, the brightest element in Wallumrød's new ensemble. Larsen remains involved in folk music with his ensemble Majorstuen, and won the Spellemann Prize in the folk music section with his trio's album *Aurum*. Naturally the list of excellent Norwegian folk violinists is very long. Those mentioned here are just a few who have been most relevant to the jazz scene, and one could add to them Håkon Høgemo[328] and Ragnhild Furebotten, who like Larsen was also a member of Majorstuen. Although it might be more likely to hear Furebotten play at the Førde Festival (the most important folk festival) than at the one in Molde, in 2011 she came out with the very interesting *Never on a Sunday*, a reverse example of a project that started from folk music and went on to involve jazz musicians.[329]

Another name among Norwegian violinists that cannot be omitted is that of Ola Kvernberg (b. 1981). A true virtuoso of the instrument, he provides a clear example of how an artist can be original while playing every possible genre. The son of musicians and originally from Fræna, in the same region as Molde, he studied classical music from an early age and then attended the jazz programme at Trondheim's Music Conservatory. Kvernberg emerged in 2000 at the annual Django Festival, organised in Oslo by the label Hot Club de Norvège, where he performed with Toots Thielemans. After his classical music studies, he finished his music training in what can be considered the temple of innovative music, only to make a name for himself in a jazz festival dedicated to the tradition - as usual nothing is predictable in Norway! The turning point in Kvernberg's career, however, came in 2009 with the release on Jazzland label of his trio's album *Folk*, in which he gave a highly innovative rereading of the folk tradition, finally displaying all his virtuosity and originality. With his languid Scandinavian country-jazz atmospheres, Kvernberg is like a Bill Frisell of the violin. Among his other diverse collaborations, particularly worthy of note is the one with the Ingebrigt Håker Flaten Quintet and Sextet, closer to free jazz and inspired by some of the finest improvisers on the Chicago scene. In 2010 Kvernberg received an important commission from the Molde Festival, and the project he came up with was again different and unexpected, one in which the pop-rock atmospheres of Mathias Eick blended with Ravel-like rhapsodies and boleros. The project, guest-starring Joshua Redman and involving a sort of national under-40 team of Norwegian music, became the record *Liarbird*, which received the 2012 Spellemann Prize for Best Jazz Album, and thanks to which Kvernberg won the DnB NOR Award as best musician.

The bond with classical music

While there aren't many connections between classical music and jazz, the Norwegian classical composer par excellence, Edvard Grieg, was the one to discover in the obscure depths of Norwegian folk songs a treasure chest of previously uncharted harmonic possibilities. In doing so he opened a completely new perspective in the context of European art music, a perspective that remained unique for a long time and later became one of the fundamentals of Debussy's and Bartók's music worlds.

It was the just mentioned Ole Bull who discovered Grieg (1843-1907), recognised his talent and convinced his parents to let him continue his studies in Leipzig. Originally from Bergen, in Leipzig the diminutive Grieg soon emerged as one of the primary forces behind the ennobling of Norwegian folk music, which he considered to be a distinctive element of his country's culture and part of the national identity.

Grieg believed in the social importance of music and the educational role of art. A Romantic who was able to tune into the spirit of the new times, he had a naïve and innocent soul. He felt (like many jazz musicians today) like a rebellious student, and could not tolerate the obsession with technique that he felt would limit his imagination. Over time, this characteristic made him a composer more interested in lyric pieces than in large forms, and this is one of the reasons why he came to be one of the inspirations of the contemporary scene.

Among current jazz musicians, the one who best embodies Grieg's spirit is Dag Arnesen (1950), another pianist from Bergen. Starting in the mid-1970s he directed various jazz ensembles and won recognition with Per Jørgensen for the album *Ny Bris*. In 1982 he drew attention with his arrangement for saxophonist Knut Riisnæs's quartet[330] (of which he was a member together with Bjørn Kjellemyr on bass and Jon Christensen on drums) of some melodies by Grieg collected in 1896 by the composer's friend Frants Beyer.[331]

A few years later, Arnesen received a commission from Rikskonsertene (Concerts Norway)[332] for the 1993 Grieg Jubilee, and composed a work intended as a homage to the composer. His work was again inspired by the Hardanger fiddle and was titled *Wandering Around 152* (from the street number of the house where Grieg was born: 152 Strandgate, Bergen). Arnesen's successful career continued as he received the 1996 NOPA Work of the Year Award with *Rusler rundt Grieg*, released three albums in the series *Norwegian Song* (Resonant Music 2007, 2009, Losen Records, 2010), and received the prestigious Buddy Prize in 2009.

Different foreign traditions, through the Norwegian lens

Licensed to talk - When Stian Carstensen went to the Jazz Conservatory of Trondheim in 1991, he brought along his interest in musical forms that were foreign to the jazz community. Old Norwegian dance tunes, Gipsy music, hillbilly, Balkan, bluegrass! He wasn't sure whether he could bring this interest with him into the jazz world, and he was hoping that one of his professors would provide him with an answer to that. And the answer that came from Erling Aksdal was: "Follow your instinct!" [333]

That answer provided the young Carstensen with the confidence to believe in what he had to say, and at 20 years old, with a few fellow conservatory students (Nils-Olav Johansen, Jarle Vespestad who was also a member of Veslefrekk, Finn Guttormsen and Håvard Lund), he formed Farmers Market. The group began as a free jazz quintet, but soon set out along a very different direction, that of Bulgarian folk. At the 1994 Molde Festival they recorded a performance that was released the following year as *Speed/Balkan/Boogie*,[334] with four Bulgarian guests - two members of Les Mystère dés Voix Bulgares[335] and two folk musicians. Hearing their debut album, many realised that something new was happening, even though the purists didn't consider it jazz. Indeed, the music of Farmers Market was a mix of standard jazz, bluegrass, Bulgarian folk, and rock music, delivered along with a large dose of humour.

Farmers Market went on to play in all kinds of venues and festivals, becoming one of the most famous bands in the country and appreciated especially for their extraordinary live performances. Carstensen, who at the age of 11 had made his debut on television[336] and the previous year had gone on tour in North Dakota, was explosive, a real actor, a prodigy who could play any instrument. Or at least this is how the cellist Ernst Reijseger described him in 2004 when, during the rehearsals for *Backwards into the Backwoods*, Carstensen took his cello to show him something: "He wanted to play a particular passage for me, so he took my cello and started playing with techniques I'd never seen before. What an amazing guy!".[337]

Something similar happened in Molde, when Michael Brecker was Artist in Residence and Jan Ole Otnæs asked him who he wanted to play with. Brecker had been following Farmers Market for years, and had no doubt about his choice. He remembered having a blast playing with the band, saying about Carstensen that "he's one of the greatest musicians I've ever played with".[338]

That Stian Carstensen was dead serious about music was evident from the start. In the early days of Farmers Market for example, he went to Bulgaria to study the folk music and discover its roots directly from the source, going from village to village. He is a truly extraordinary musician, warm and funny with his audiences, a master of his instrument who combines his natural talent with discipline and dedication. When Oslo's Ultima Festival commissioned a contemporary music work from him, he created a masterpiece (which largely informed the album in *Backwards into the Backwoods*), showing that he could compose with great originality even for a symphony orchestra. It's not surprising then that over the years he frequently collaborated with Norway's most important orchestras (the Norwegian Radio Orchestra (KORK), the Stavanger Symphony Orchestra, the Trondheim Symphony Orchestra, the Kristiansand Symphony Orchestra). At the same time, however, he has continued to focus on folk and bluegrass with the same passion, with the fantastic trio Gammalgrass and with Ola Kvernberg.

Stavanger and the free jazz scene

The situation in Norway is and has been for a long time, that there is one major person and that person is Jan Garbarek. As we are such a small country, there seems to be little room for more than one trend. I feel though that the picture is slowly changing, but up until now, most musicians try to copy his music in a more or less successful way. Over the last few years I've met some younger musicians who want to move into free music. But very often, it is the *rubato*, dreamy kind of free music they go for. But again, that's what I call the "ECM school".[339]

This opinion expressed by Frode Gjerstad, the father of free jazz in Norway, is entirely understandable. In 1981, when Gjerstad, a self-taught musician who grew up in Stavanger playing in marching bands, decided to make music seriously, he signed up Eivin One Pedersen on piano and accordion but couldn't find a drummer even in Oslo, where people only seemed interested in Jan Garbarek and the ECM school. Back then, flying between Stavanger to Oslo cost as much as flying to London, and it was in London that Gjerstad finally met the drummer John Stevens, who enthusiastically accepted to come to Norway to play with him.

In the early days Gjerstad's trio was one of the very rare if not the only group doing free jazz in Norway, and there weren't many venues where they could play, barely putting together a week-long tour during the whole year. Gjerstad, who in

1966 had been dazzled by Ornette Coleman (seeing him on Swedish television, when he was playing in Stockholm around the time of *Golden Circle*) and then by an Albert Ayler interview (in a *Downbeat* issue that had Ayler on the cover), became a regular on the British scene, and welcomed in his trio guests such as Paul Rutherford, Barry Guy, Dudu Pukwana, Evan Parker and Harry Beckett. So finally, the following year, Gjerstad's trio debuted at the Molde Festival (with Johnny Dyani, Stevens's favourite bassist, replacing Pedersen).

The aspiring musician who had experimented with music in Stavanger in the 1970s and then had moved to Sweden to study economics, had the fortune upon his return to Stavanger to get to know Terrie and Lisbeth Nilssen-Love, the very open-minded and active managers (between 1979 and 1986) of the local jazz club. All the more reason, perhaps, for Gjerstad to settle back in Norway and try to make a living with music.

The Nilssen-Loves were the jazz club's managers and also the parents of Paal (b. 1974), a child prodigy who was already playing his father's drum set at the age of 5 - the same drum set he still uses today when he performs in Oslo or in the vicinity. Paal Nilssen-Love grew up listening to David Murray, Steve Lacy, Arthur Blythe, Don Pullen, Misha Mengelberg, Art Blakey, Tony Oxley and John Stevens, and by age 15 had an active role in the Stavanger free jazz scene, playing in trio with the trumpeter Didrik Ingvaldsen and - no surprise here - Frode Gjerstad. Soon afterwards he attended the Trondheim Conservatory for a few years, where he met the bassist Ingebrigt Håker Flaten. Finally he moved to Oslo, where he emerged as the natural heir to Gjerstad (with whom he continued the trio experience) and went on to bring Norwegian free jazz on to the international circuit and to be acclaimed as one of the best drummers in his field.

> The band Element was a sort of reaction to ECM and to saxophonists like Trygve Seim and Bendik Hofseth. I had nothing personal against them, but I felt that there was a need for something strong and fresh that would wake audiences up, and with Element we started on something based on Coltrane's tradition. We were looking for a specific type of energy and atmosphere, we wanted a more aggressive sound that should be played loud, but without any reverb or delay.[340]

In other words, he felt that something powerful and less toned down was needed. Twenty years after Gjerstad had looked for a drummer in Oslo in vain, his heir Paal Nilssen-Love - with a core of excellent musicians - still felt the need to go against that ECM aesthetic which according to many acted like an anaesthetic and a trap for the panorama of jazz. It's curious to consider that in the early days, after being inspired by Dexter Gordon for a time, Jan Garbarek had been blown away by Coltrane! Of course these were positions that were necessarily coloured by where one lived, since from a European point of view the ECM aesthetic was neither so in vogue nor so full of clichés.

Element, the band Nilssen-Love is talking about, was the precursor of one of the super groups of Norwegian free jazz, Atomic, and debuted in 1996 with the saxophonist Gisle Johansen as leader, releasing the eponymous *Element*.[341] The real soul of the band, however, was the earth-shaking trio made up by Nilssen-Love on drums, Håker Flaten on bass, and the extraordinary pianist Håvard Wiik. The band then went through a period of personnel change, with Vidar Johansen coming in on saxophone, followed by Petter Wettre. In 1999 the band released *Shaman*,[342] their first album on club Blå's label BP Records. Once again, Martin Revheim of Blå was a decisive element, since the core trio often played at the club and it was there that Nilssen-Love and Gjerstad came into contact with the noise scene (Lasse Marhaug, Maja Ratkje, etc.).

The shift from Element to Atomic was quite natural, with the core trio of Element being joined for a time by the very young saxophonist Håkon Kornstad, who also came from the Trondheim Conservatory and had made a name for himself with the band Wibutee. Soon after he was replaced by the Swedish musicians Fredrik Ljungkvist (sax) and Magnus Broo (trumpet), and it was with this personnel that Atomic released their debut album *Feet Music*[343] on Bugge Wesseltoft's Jazzland label. This recording was part of a niche of free jazz with which Wesseltoft launched the Jazzland Acoustic division.[344]

One of the crucial moments for Paal Nilssen-Love, Ingebrigt Håker Flaten and Håvard Wiik came towards the end of the millennium, when they met Mats Gustafsson and Ken Vandermark. Nilssen-Love and Håker Flaten joined Gustafsson forming the trio The Thing, which became one of the regular acts of Blå and Smalltown at a time when Martin Revheim's club and Johakim Haugland's label were in full swing. As far as Vandermark was concerned, his great merit was to open Scandinavia to one of the most relevant free jazz scenes in the world, that of Chicago, giving a great boost to the work that Gjerstad had begun. In the same period Nilssen-Love released *Sticks & Stones*, his first solo album for the newborn label SOFA, and decided to launch a festival in Oslo entirely focussed on radical improvisation, called All Ears. Initially he tried to involve SOFA founders Ivar Grydeland and Ingar Zach, but since they weren't interested he later found as partners in this project Lasse Marhaug, Maja Ratkje and Kjetil Møster.

The free jazz scene today is a small but excellent one, with musicians of the calibre of Paal Nilssen-Love, who is among the most active in Norway. With great focus and dedication, Nilssen-Love is able to create dynamically vibrant and rhythmically wide-open atmospheres, and expressing simultaneously a powerfulness and sensibility that makes him one of the best drummers in the world. Pat Metheny, who played with him when Nilssen-Love was Artist in Residence at the 2002 Molde Jazz Festival, said "He is simply one of the best new musicians I've heard during the latest years!".[345] while Dan Quelette of *Downbeat*, after having heard him during that same festival in nine different acts, wrote "His week at Molde proved a revelation: Nilssen-Love is one of the most innovative, dynamic and versatile drummers in jazz!".[346]

Impro-noise

2001 was a seminal year for Noise in Norway. The compilation *Le Jazz Non* got rave reviews and made the media aware of the fact that Norwegian Noise artists were having success abroad. And a lot of big names came to Norway: Masami Akita, Otomo Yoshihide, Tashimaru Nakamura, Francisco López. Suddenly "everybody" talked about Noise music. And I was in the middle of it all with a camera, asking every artist I met the same simple question: "What is Noise music?".[347]

Before 2001 no one except a few artists of the Norwegian underground scene had ever talked about noise music, but in 2001 Francisco López made a unique experiment in Trondheim with David Cotner, who ran around the small gallery that was the venue for the concert. The noise was so loud that some of the neighbours called the police. Those attending the concert were blindfolded and had the sensation of being led into the heart of darkness, into the bowels of the earth. On that same year, Otomo Yoshihide played in the context of the Kongsberg Jazz Festival for a few nights in the yard of the city's prison, and Masami Akita (aka Merzbow) played with the duo Jazzkammer (of which more later) at the jazz festival in Molde.

Something special was happening in Norway, and the British magazine *The Wire* hailed as one of the year's best releases the Smalltown Supersound compilation *Le Jazz Non*, which can be compared in terms of inspiration to what Bruce Russell did in April 1996 for the label Corpus Hermeticum. Trondheim[348] became the centre of this new scene which included noise musicians, visual artists, jazz experimenters and many more. Klubb Kanin became a reference point, where emerging artists could perform for a few minutes at a time with the gurus of this new musical frontier.

In 2001 Tom Hovinbøle, one of the organisers of an event that gathered together all the leading figures of the new music genre, made a documentary illustrating the entire phenomenon. Hovinbøle's initial intention was to focus on Lasse Marhaug (the other organiser of the event), but soon he realised that he had to document the whole pulsing situation revolving around the noise scene. The documentary was entitled *Nor Noise* and was released as a DVD on [OHM] Records in 2004, with an audio CD included.[349]

> I asked 12 very different artistes the simple question - What Is Noise? - and got 12 very different answers. To me that is still the best answer yet to this question. Because after all these years I still believe Noise to be more a matter of attitude and receptive listening than about types of sounds or form and structure or the instruments or the equipment used.[350]

According to Hovinbøle, a thin red line runs from Russolo and the Futurists, through Varèse and Cage, the avant-garde of the 1930s and 1940s, the modernism of the 1950s, the 1960s experimental electronic music of Pierre Henry, Stockhausen and the minimalist school of New York, to the industrial post-punk and the Japanese noise scene of the 1970s. Noise music is denoted by a physicality that links back to musique concrète, but it is mostly made with electronics, laptops and machines of all kinds.

The most interesting acts of the Norwegian noise scene emerged in those early 2000s, and it's not surprising that the impro-noise band par excellence, Supersilent, was born in Trondheim. Amongst the animators of the scene was Helge "Deathprod" Sten, Supersilent member and "noise soul" of the band. The pioneers of this new aesthetic included Lasse Marhaug, who with John Hegre founded the famous duo Jazzkammer, which many considered to be the Scandinavian equivalent of Merzbow, and Maja Ratkje, who studied contemporary composition at the Norwegian Academy of Music, and her friend Hild Sofie Tafjord (daughter of Stein Erik Tafjord of Brazz Brothers fame), with whom she formed the duo Fe-Mail.

All these musicians interacted heavily with the jazz scene. Lasse Marhaug, the most representative of this new wave, took on a key role in the interaction between noise and free jazz, collaborating regularly with the drummer Paal Nilssen-Love, the saxophonists Ken Vandermark and Mats Gustafsson, the trio The Thing, the saxophonist Kjetil Møster and the vocalist and composer Maja Ratkje. The collaboration among these musicians had resulted in the launching of the All Ears Festival in Oslo, and also led them to appear regularly at the Henie Onstad Art Centre,[351] thanks to Lars Mørch Finborud who, together with Marhaug, ran its music programme. (In those years Finborud released on his record label Plastic Strip little treasures such as *Popofoni*, *Fongaard* and others, which he had rediscovered while researching the archives of the Henie Onstad.)

Maja Ratkje is also a very interesting artist with an eclectic streak, who along with Jazzkammer, Alog, and Supersilent became an icon of the noise aesthetic of the label Rune Grammofon in those years, while releasing her debut album *River Mouth Echoes* on John Zorn's label Tzadik. She then collaborated on Frode Haltli's ECM debut album *Passing Images*, with Arve Henriksen and the Irish-born and Scottish-raised Garth Knox, and in 2012 was Artist in Residence at the important Huddersfield Contemporary Music Festival.

The scene didn't stop with musicians of that generation, finding new energy in the emergence of the trio Puma (Stian Westerhus, Gard Nilssen, and Øystein Moen), which debuted in 2007 with the album *Isolationism* (Bolage Records). This trio immediately appeared as the natural heir to Supersilent and was the perfect showcase for the extremely talented guitarist Stian Westerhus, who soon after released his debut solo album *Galore*.

Other names that should be mentioned next to Puma are Bushman's Revenge, a trio formed by Even Helte Hermansen, Rune Nergaard and Gard Nilssen (drummer of both Puma and Bushman's Revenge, as well as of the more pop-rock quintet of Mathias Eick and the decidedly more jazzy band Team). The young star Westerhus, on his part, became the guitarist of Molvær's new trio and co-produced the album *Baboon Moon*, formed a fantastic duo with Sidsel Endresen with a release on Rune Grammofon, and was also member of the duo Monolithic with Kenneth Kapstad, Motorpsycho drummer.

Jon Hassell's influence

It's a long story, but I could sum it up by telling you about what happened yesterday at the Art Museum. I was sitting with Jon Hassell and Nils Petter Molvær, and we were talking. It was fantastic to sit at the table with Nils Petter, my idol back at the time I was studying at the Conservatory, and with the musician who had in turn inspired him. I thought: it all started from here, from these two men. My music today owes a great deal to their music. It was almost touching to see the look on Jon's face when Nils Petter and I, hearing the notes of "The Flash of the Spirit" [a piece by Hassell dating back to his collaboration with Farafina], started singing and humming it. He said "It's too much for me!" Do you realize? It must've been strange for him, like finding himself before two pupils who know their teacher's work by heart. I also listened a lot to Don Cherry and Miles Davis, but Nils Petter and Jon are the ones who've inspired me the most. They had a very personal sound and I didn't, but one day Nils Petter turned me on to the Japanese shakuhachi, and that's when I realised what I had to do with my trumpet playing. It was a long and slow process of transformation, through hard work and many collaborations with artists such as Balke, Wallumrød, Jormin, and others, who've all helped me in these 25 years of growth.[352]

The long process that Arve Henriksen was a part of can be said to have begun with Miles Davis in the period of *On the Corner*, which American trumpeter Jon Hassell filtered with the further influences of the ideas and music of Terry Riley, La Monte Young, and Steve Reich. Hassell opened the doors to an even wider musical aesthetic, imbued in technology and rooted in Asian music, in minimalism, and in pure research. He mentored Nils Petter Molvær, and led him into the centre of a musical universe that seemed to abandon the jazz tradition. This influence extended not only to Molvær (who was in the audience with Garbarek at Oslo's Henie Onstad on 24 November 1985 for Jon Hassell's performance), but an entire generation of European musicians, mostly trumpeters (Arve Henriksen, Erik Truffaz, Paolo Fresu), who recognised the impact of Hassell while not forgetting the strong attraction of Miles Davis.

In Norway, however, the process was slightly different, since Don Cherry's presence in Scandinavia also left a very deep mark. It's striking, for example, to hear the similarity between the sound of the early Molvær and the one of Don Cherry in a few recordings with Garbarek's group, during the time that Cherry lived in Scandinavia.[353] Arve Henriksen instead seemed to be influenced more strongly by Cherry's use of the trumpet's voice, strongly inspired in this also by Per Jørgensen of the trio Jøkleba.

After a period of intense focus on free jazz next to Ornette Coleman and friends, Don Cherry plunged wholeheartedly into the discovery and assimilation of traditions from Africa and the Far East and, from *Eternal Rhythm* to *Brown Rice*, was a role model for many of the musicians who shared the stage with him in those years. As Maurizio Zerbo aptly writes:

> In addition to being aesthetically sublime, *Eternal Rhythm* provides a key to understand the close connection between cultural relativism and jazz aesthetics.
> It was a prophetic record, which anticipated the development of multi-ethnic

societies of the third millennium, and was informed by a far-sighted anti Eurocentric concept, elaborated by anthropologists and adopted by the counter-culture movements of the late 1960s.[354]

This doesn't mean that Cherry took an anti-European stance: on the contrary, like George Russell, he championed the rediscovery of European roots, perhaps boldly combined with other traditions. During the years of Ornette Coleman's revolution Cherry developed a technique of his own, which he perfected later thanks to his experiences in Africa and Asia. With his cornet he brought together the Indian singing of the teacher Pandith Pran Nath, free jazz, and Malian percussion, as can be heard perhaps more evidently in *Brown Rice*, a real precursor of Jon Hassell's world music. Molvær too, like Cherry and Hassell before him, felt similar attractions:

> Anyway, for me *The Pearl*[355] was a very important record. Also *Fourth World, Vol. 1: Possible Musics* by Jon Hassell.[356] When I listened to that one, I was very excited; suddenly it seemed possible to do the things I'd been dreaming about doing on trumpet. Besides that, I'd also been listening to a lot of world music - Middle Eastern music, North African music.[357]

Molvær was attracted in particular to African, Middle Eastern and Far Eastern instruments that had "that sound": the Armenian duduk, the Persian and Turkish ney flute, the Indian sarangi, the Japanese shakuhachi.

In the press notes to his album *Sakuteiki*, Arve Henriksen wrote "the trumpet has vast potential for tone and sound variations that we still have not heard. At one point, I think it was in 1988, Nils Petter Molvær lent me a cassette of shakuhachi playing. Then things changed". He started collecting records of Japanese music featuring koto, biwa, and shakuhachi: "I let the music ring and develop in my head. I was astonished by the sound of this flute".[358]

The sound of the shakuhachi was the spark that made him shift from the high-tension pulsing of Supersilent to a more meditative and minimalist form of expression. *Sakuteiki* was Henriksen's first solo album, released in 2001 on Rune Kristoffersen's label. The record made an impact, and marked the beginning of an important artistic course, whose next stop and first high point was the magical *Chiaroscuro*,[359] featuring Jan Bang's contribution.

Henriksen and Molvær are very strong personalities who represent well the Norwegian scene and whose approaches and tastes are similar and yet different, both influenced by Jon Hassell and sharing a way of playing so unlike that of

American boppers, as Hassell himself testifies:

> Musicians like me are usually poor, and when you hear that other musicians are trying to do something in the wake of what you've done, your first instinctive reaction is defensive: you want to protect your work from being copied. But in actual fact what these musicians have come to over time is a personal style, and perhaps they've opened a new perspective, which lays the ground for extending music in more directions.[360]

Molvær is at the height of fame despite his divorce from ECM after *Solid Ether* and the lack of a real producer in the studio. After the release of *Np3*, he has in fact revitalised his creative streak with *Streamer* and especially with *Er*, in which he collaborated with Jan Bang and DJ Strangefruit.

Henriksen undoubtedly became one of the role models among European trumpeters thanks to his lyrical sound, which enriched many ECM productions (Christian Wallumrød, Sinikka Langeland, Jon Balke, Arild Andersen, etc.), and also thanks to his release *Strjon*[361] and to his following ECM solo debut with *Cartography*.[362] Henriksen has alternated his solo career with collaborations with Supersilent and other important acts, which over time have made him a key figure of Punkt, the creation of Jan Bang and Erik Honoré explored in one of the next sub-chapters. Henriksen's projects have included a trio with Helge Norbakken and Audun Kleive on percussion, a strings-only project (Svante Henryson on cello, Gjermund Larsen and Nils Økland on violin and Hardanger fiddle, Anders Jormin on double bass) commissioned by Rikskonsertene (Concerts Norway), and in 2012 the release of the monumental *Solidification*,[363] a vinyl box set that highlights both sound quality and album art work, containing the first three albums released on Rune Grammofon and the new *Chron*.

Along with Molvær and Henriksen, there are at least 50 other professional trumpeters active in different musical areas. Standing out among these are some trumpet players with a smooth and melodic sound: Gunnar Halle, who emerged at home and then moved to Denmark where he joined the ILK collective;[364] Mathias Eick, who debuted with Jaga Jazzist and made a name for himself through ECM, first as a sideman (with Manu Katché, Iro Haarla, etc.) and then as leader (in 2008, with the album *The Door*); and finally Sjur Miljeteig, also a former Jaga member and musical partner of Solveig Slettahjell. Then there is Kåre Nymark, one of the few young trumpeters doing traditional bop, the emerging improviser Stian Omenås, who in parallel with the experience with the band Parallax in 2012 released two albums as leader,[365] and Gunhild Seim, one of the rare women trumpeters. Finally, the brightest emerging talent and the clearest heir to Arve Henriksen is Eivind Nordset Lønning. This young exploring musician, together with Espen Reinertsen (Streifenjunko), opened new perspectives in the music of Christian Wallumrød, and then became a regular member of Motif, replacing Eick.

Christian Wallumrød

I wanted improvisation to be a component, but not in the sense that there would have to be many solos like in good old jazz, because by that point I found this terribly boring, and not very interesting: I wanted to get a good mix.[366]

The pianist Christian Wallumrød (b. 1971) is undoubtedly one of the finest and most urbane figures of the Norwegian contemporary scene. Born and raised in Kongsberg, he started playing piano at the age of 12. His first musical influences came from pop and church music. He discovered jazz when he was around 15, thanks to his teacher Egil Kapstad, and got his jazz training at the Trondheim Conservatory. He started there in 1990 along with saxophonist Trygve Seim, and with him and two other musicians he met during his studies (the double bass player Johannes Eick and the drummer Per Oddvar Johansen) he founded Airamero,[367] a band that is by now legendary in Norway.

Airamero was one of the first young bands playing original compositions in ECM style to emerge in Norway after Garbarek's generation. Their 1993 eponymous album[368] put the four musicians, who were all just over 20 years old, at the centre of the national jazz scene. Influenced initially by Svein Finnerud and then by Paul Bley, Wallumrød continued to mature as a musician and in 1995 founded another formidable ensemble with Ingebrigt Håker Flaten (a bassist who had arrived in Trondheim in 1992) and his friend Per Oddvar Johansen: the trio Close Erase,[369] which released an eponymous album that same year.[370] In the liner notes to the box set that marked the dissolution of the band, *Close Erase - R.I.P Complete Recordings 1995-2007*, Martin Revheim wrote:

The influence that comes across with the most clarity is Paul Bley's trio around the *Barrage* and *Closer* albums. An edgy and stubborn touch with a heartfelt, contemplative impact. Svein Finnerud Trio is leaping at the water's edge. On the two electric records, *Dance This* and *Sport Rocks*, we hear Herbie Hancock's Sextant as well as Miles Davis's *Live Evil* and *Cellar Door*, where Miles combined the repetitive elements of both Karlheinz Stockhausen and James Brown, with stubbornness and love This, however, is overtly simplifying. Even though the musical shoulders on which Close Erase are standing are quite audible, the musicians themselves are always more present then their models.[371]

While studying jazz at the Conservatory, Wallumrød developed an increasing interest in improvisation, and realised how connected it was to composition. From there, he began composing more and more. In 1998 he released his first ECM album *No Birch*, in trio with trumpeter Arve Henriksen and the classical music percussionist Hans-Kristian Kjos Sørensen. In Wallumrød's words: "At a certain point Arve took the initiative. He decided to do something for trio, but with a classical music percussionist. We proposed the project to Manfred. It was something we thought was very in line with his label's aesthetic. This is how *No Birch* was born".[372]

Ivar Grydeland, Ingar Zach and Sofa Records Ivar Grydeland (1976) and Ingar Zach (1971) belong to a young generation of Norwegian jazz musicians who emerged in 2000. Ivar Grydeland is an experimental guitarist who studied at the Conservatory in Trondheim, his native city, where he met Paal Nilssen-Love, Ingebrigt Håker Flaten and a series of young musicians eager to take avant-garde jazz away from the serene ECM atmospheres. Ingar Zach is among the leading percussionists of the Norwegian scene in the context of both folk and avant-garde music, and has been living in Madrid for a few years. He began studying musicology in Oslo in 1993-94 and then went on to study jazz and composition at the Trondheim Conservatory, where he met Grydeland. In 1997 he took part in an exchange program at Stockholm's Royal Music Academy, and during his brief stay in the Swedish capital he met the drummer Raymond Strid and the guitarist David Stackenäs, who turned him on to improvisation. In 2000 Grydeland and Zach founded SOFA Records with Karl Seglem (who later left) and increasingly focussed on improvisation and experimentation - Grydeland with the drummer Tony Oxley and Zach with the guitarist Derek Bailey.

Getting involved in the No Spaghetti Edition collective, they met Christian Wallumrød and Xavier Charles, with whom they formed Dans Les Arbres, and Tonny Kluften, with whom they formed the trio Huntsville. In 12 years SOFA Records released many interesting and audacious records, promoting some of the brightest talents of the recent Norwegian avant-garde including Kim Myhr, Nils Henrik Asheim, and Martin Taxt, but also involving international celebrities such as Jim O'Rourke, Toshimaru Nakamura, Barry Guy and Axel Dörner.

Wallumrød's Trondheim based trio initially aimed at doing mostly improvisation and featured the fellow student and singer Eldbjørg Raknes. Once they were in the studio, however, they decided to record some compositions, and the percussionist Sørensen took Raknes's place. It was a debut album in which the trio left a lot of room for silence and which never really had a rhythmic pulse, unlike *Close Erase*, which gave ample space to electronics and in which the traditional jazz piano trio took on a decisively rock set-up, with synthesizer and electric bass taking precedence over their acoustic counterparts. *No Birch* presented a subtle music, with references to Bill Evans yet with very different results, and marked Wallumrød's first change in direction away from jazz, also thanks to the pure and refined tone colour of Henriksen's trumpet.

Some time later, Manfred Eicher introduced Wallumrød to Nils Økland, who joined him in what became a quartet with Henriksen and Per Oddvar Johansen. In this next phase, Wallumrød's work became increasingly creative in terms of timbre and closer to contemporary composers such as Cage and Kurtág. In the same period the guitarist Ivar Grydeland and the percussionist Ingar Zach, who felt a real affinity to this music, asked Wallumrød if he wanted to collaborate with them. He did so in No Spaghetti Edition,[373] an on-going project which also saw the participation of the French clarinettist Xavier Charles, and which sparked the birth of the quartet Dans Les Arbres (Charles, Grydeland, Wallumrød and Zach), in which they were refining their musical expression more and more towards the timbre of the instruments. While Dans Les Arbres started playing in 2004, it was only after a break that they resumed and released their first album *Dans Les Arbres* in 2006.[374]

Wallumrød had the possibility of simultaneously exploring improvisation with this new group, and composition with his ensemble, which in the meantime had enlarged from a quartet to a sextet (with Tanja Orning on cello, Gjermund Larsen replacing Nils Økland, who hadn't appreciated the increase in written music, and the Baroque harpist Giovanna Pessi). Right after *The Zoo Is Far*, however, Arve Henriksen left the ensemble, as he was concentrating on his solo career and on his work with Supersilent. What initially appeared as an irreparable loss turned out to provide a great opportunity, because just around that time the two young musicians Eivind Lønning and Espen Reinertsen, who were conducting an in-depth and radical research on their respective instrument's sound, asked Wallumrød to listen to their work (the duo Streifenjunko). As a result, Wallumrød decided to involve the young trumpeter Eivind Lønning in the recording of his ensemble's next album *Fabula Suite Lugano*, re-launching a project that appeared to be doomed after Henriksen's departure. Some time later, the process was completed with the exit of the harpist Giovanna Pessi and the entrance of the tenor saxophonist Espen Reinertsen, who integrated the on-going research done in duo with Lønning to the ensemble's evolution. The ensemble's new album *Outstairs*[375] was recorded in 2012 in the auditorium of RSI (Swiss-Italian public broadcasting corporation) in Lugano after a short tour in Italy, and featured Tove Törngren on cello. The sextet is a perfect example of how a chamber ensemble with relatively few elements can play like an organic whole, just as a large orchestra. Violin, cello, trumpet and saxophone blend into delicate melodic lines with ethnic connotations, sacred music and great modernity, developing juxtapositions of timbre of rare beauty. The ensemble creates an unusual musical universe made up of jazz, minimalism and Baroque music, without ever losing sight of its origins: pop, soul, and sacred music.

Christian Wallumrød's musical experience is anchored in great discipline and concentration, and he has been able to follow his own path without worrying about the opinion of others. His course has always been very consistent, particularly focussed on abstraction, following in the footsteps of John Cage.

After its participation at the 2011 Focus Norge, Bologna's Angelica Festival commissioned Wallumrød to write a composition for symphony orchestra for their 2013 festival. It was a first for him, and the project he produced was as original as always: he broke down the 68 elements of the orchestra into 7 sections, each executing different tempi, while maintaining a remarkable coherence of the whole. At the premiere of the piece "When celebrities dream of casual sleep (second try)" at Bologna's Auditorium Manzoni on 26 May 2013 Wallumrød's composition was performed next to music by two legends of contemporary music Giacinto Scelsi and Christian Wolff.

The Punkt Festival: from remixes to contemporary art music

Everything started when I began performing with Bugge Wesseltoft, I think it was 1996. He was beginning to lay down the ideas for *New Conception of Jazz*. Bugge asked me "I'm putting together a band and I'd like you to be part of it. What could you do live?" And I thought that I could use the Akai sampler that I had and could sample the sounds from the musicians on stage, instead of from records. So we decided to call this thing, which was totally new at the time, "live sampling", a definition that is still used today. This approach created a new opportunity for me to improvise with electronics, a difficult kind of work that requires great speed in order to keep up with the musicians - between present, past and future![376]

Jan Bang found a new way of improvising with a digital sampler, making it an instrument in its own right within the ensemble: he recorded fragments of the live performance, keeping them in his Akai sampler's memory for as long as the device allowed him, and played them in interaction with the musicians on stage. The bits were always fresh and original, small gems that he captured and inserted from a few seconds to a few minutes after they were originally played. It was a very quick process that required him to be constantly on the ball, "between present, past and future". He had to catch the right fragment, trying to follow the movement of the musicians who were performing in that moment (Jon Hassell, Arve Henriksen or Eivind Aarset) and as a result created a new group, cluster, or rhythmic pattern.

It was a completely new way of making music that he fully mastered in time and that required a kind of revolutionary interaction with the musicians. Although Bang expanded the way he worked and also began playing with non Norwegian musicians (for example Dave Douglas), the trust required by the presence of that "alien" instrument on stage made it so that, over the years, he built a regular body of musical partners whom he worked particularly well with. It was with these musicians that he and his friend Erik Honoré established a sort of collective called Punkt.

The young Jan Bang had arrived in Oslo from Kristiansand a few years before, in 1992, and as soon as he settled in the capital he became a member of a producers' collective, Disclab, founded by the king of Norwegian techno Per Martinesen. Martinesen, who was born in Tromsø but had matured artistically in Belgium through R&S Records,[377] had founded the collective with Hans Olav Grøttheim, who came from the London school and had produced artists such as Boy George and the Pet Shop Boys. In those years Disclab was under a strong influence from the Detroit techno scene, and was involved mostly in pop productions. Just a few years before, in 1987, an 18 year-old Bang had formed his first band with his friend Erik Honoré and released *Woodlands*, where he both sang and played keyboards, with lyrics and programming by Honoré. Included in the album was also the single "Merciful Waters", featuring Sidsel Endresen and A-Ha singer Morten Harket on vocals. It was his first experience as leader with which he made a name for himself in Norway. Thanks to this previous work and his involvement in Disclab, he had the opportunity of spending more and more time with Bjørn Torske, Röyksopp and Pål Nyhus. Slowly he entered the world of remix, until he received a call from an executive at Universal who had signed up Bugge Wesseltoft and who asked Bang to make a remix of Bugge's music. Bang didn't know Wesseltoft personally but had heard of him and had seen him perform in quartet with Molvær in Kristiansand. He made the remix under the pseudonym of Mother Nature's Cloud and Shower Show, and Wesseltoft liked it so much that he asked Bang to collaborate on the *New Conception of Jazz* tour. And so we come full circle, to when Wesseltoft asked Bang what he could do live on stage.

Their first performance was at Oslo's Head On. It was the very first time Jan Bang performed live sampling, and there was a big buzz in the air. The band made up of Anders Engen, Vidar Johansen, Ingebrigt Håker Flaten, Erlend Gjerde and Bugge Wesseltoft did the sound-check and Bang started sampling the live instruments: the spark was immediate. His contribution was a success, and with his live sampling Bang claimed his legitimate place in the Norwegian nu jazz scene.[378]

Through a collaboration with Bendik Hofseth, Bang met Eivind Aarset, and also got back in touch with Sidsel Endresen (he had sampled her voice for *Duplex Ride*, her album in duo with Wesseltoft released in Norway on Curling Legs and licensed abroad by the German label Act). In 1996 he did a few remixes for Nils Petter Molvær and then, through Wesseltoft and *Music for Science and Film*, he met GeneratorX leader Audun Kleive with whom he began collaborating. All these contacts formed the basis for what was to become a fully-fledged collective.

The network of Bang's collaborations continued to widen. Impressed by Christian Wallumrød and Arve Henriksen and their capacity to create interesting soundscapes, in 1999 Bang established Panavision in his home city of Kristiansand with his long-time friend Erik Honoré. They rented a studio and for a few days the four of them plunged head-on into a session of improvisation that became *Birth Wishes*, the first album of the newborn record label. It was in this session that Bang and Honoré, increasingly focussed on timbre and less on beat, realised how much there was to explore in that direction. In 2000 they arranged the Panavision Series of concerts at the Sørlandet Art Museum, where they live-remixed Molvær, Hofseth, etc. The next step was the Punkt Festival in Kristiansand. It was not too far off, since its embryonic idea took shape in 2002.

Punkt is the natural result, on a larger scale, of what I've been developing over the years, namely the concept of "live remix", in the broadest sense of the term. Rather than live sampling single musicians, at Punkt we sample entire concerts, and the multichannel sound of the main stage of the Agder Teater is transferred to a small stage/studio called Alpha room, open to the public only during the festival. In this intimate atmosphere the music from the live concert held a few minutes before on the main stage is remixed by musicians, producers and established remixers. The idea dates back to 2002, when Erik Honoré and I found ourselves sitting at the table of a café in Kristiansand and taking notes on paper napkins [...] It took another three years for the first Punkt Festival to happen. All of it is based on a network of people we've met over time and who, in our view, can bring something unique to the shows and to the event as a whole. So it's not just musicians but also visual artists, press agents, volunteers and all who revolve around the festival.[379] [380]

The first Punkt Festival took place in 2005. Taking part were just Bang, Honoré and their friends, and with them Fiona Talkington, BBC Radio 3 presenter who developed close ties with the festival from the very beginning, presenting the concerts and creating connections with the British scene. Talkington in fact was responsible for bringing the Norwegian scene to the 2008 London Jazz Festival, in a 10-day celebration of Norwegian culture that she curated.

In 2008 the festival developed a more international profile, featuring works and performances by Brian Eno and Jon Hassell, who was the mentor of many of the artists who gravitated towards Punkt. Hassell performed *Maarifa Street* with his group, made the installation Near Far (a sort of remix and re-harmonisation of the bells of Kristiansand's cathedral), and took part in a Conversational Remix with Brian Eno, who brought to the city the installation *77 Million Paintings for Punkt*.

"Hassell, yes!" - says Jan brightening up - "He is the master! I heard him for the first time when I listened to David Sylvian's album *Brilliant Trees*. It must've been 1985, I was 15. Usually the things you're exposed at that age determine your future taste. It's an age when you're very receptive and sensitive to impressions, so listening to Hassell then was fantastic. And in time I also got to know him personally.[381]

Hassell, who played such an important role in the musical growth of Henriksen and Molvær, soon became a point of reference for Punkt's collective. Bang became a regular in his band, and Eivind Aarset joined them for the tour of *Last Night the Moon Came Dropping Its Clothes in the Street*, released on ECM in 2009. "You know, they were sampling me and I was sampling them, and during the process you never really knew who sampled who. At my age, being next to people like them is a healthy hybridisation, a priceless reciprocal exchange."[382] What Hassell was describing was a sort of looped response, mirrors reflecting each other, a process of which he was the inspiring source while Bang and friends gave a concrete form to the extension of his sonic universe.

The evolution of Punkt didn't stop with Hassell however, since in 2010 the bassist of Led Zeppelin fame John Paul Jones came to Kristiansand, where he played with a legendary band of the Norwegian scene: Supersilent. The following year another British star came to the festival, David Sylvian, who had been in touch with Bang and Honoré for some time.

The first real contact between Sylvian and the Norwegian scene was in 2002, when he was making the instrumental album *Camphor*, and asked Molvær to make a remix of "Mother and Child" (from the album *Secrets of the Beehive*), a project in which Jan Bang and Erik Honoré also took part. When Bang sent Sylvian a copy of Henriksen's *Chiaroscuro*, Sylvian was so taken that he asked Henriksen to participate in the recording of some of his works (*Snow Borne Sorrow* and *When Loud Weather Buffeted Naoshima*). The two hadn't physically met but they started collaborating closely, emailing each other digital files, until Sylvian asked Henriksen to play some things on the trumpet for his poem *Before and Afterlife*, which he wanted to publish in an American art magazine. Henriksen in turn asked Sylvian if he could include that track in the new album he was working on. From that moment their collaboration intensified, and Sylvian took an increasingly active role in the making of the album, from suggesting its title *Cartography* to naming all of its tracks, to lending his voice for the poems used in the record.

The exchanges between Sylvian and the Punkt community grew, and in 2011 Sylvian released *Died in the Wool/Manafon Variations*[383] with Bang, Honoré and Henriksen, in the same year, was invited to the festival as curator and Artist in Residence. With the Punkt collective Sylvian performed live for the first time *Plight and Premonition*[384] and curated the programme of an entire day, from which Bang and Honoré extrapolated the album *Uncommon Deities*. For Sylvian this was a decisive moment, since after a couple of years of hesitation and difficulty in the preparation of a tour for *Died in the Wool*, he became convinced that Jan Bang was the right man to help him make it happen, along with that solid group of Norwegian musicians. Sylvian announced the European tour for spring of 2012:

> The notion of a tour has been floating in the ether for a couple of years but, when considering recent releases, I couldn't in my own mind and within seemingly tight restrictions make the transition from studio to stage. It's the smallest of gestures or coincidences that can take something that seems completely unlikely into the realm

of possibility. This is generally the coming together of one or two elements that act as catalysts for what will be. Working with Jan Bang might be considered one such catalyst. There's an ease and a trust that's growing between us that it'd be interesting to explore further in a live context which is where Jan appears to be very much at home. I've had notions in the back of my mind regarding the material, how it might be tackled. There are numerous possible permutations so it boils down to what appeals to me at any given point in time and what is a real possibility. It gets increasingly harder to put together the show one would like to take on the road so one tends to wait until the cards line up in one's favour. I think that's currently what's happening here.[385]

This tour, which Sylvian himself defined as a "personal milestone" and which would have involved himself, Jan Bang, Eivind Aarset, Gunnar Halle (replacing the unavailable Henriksen), the Icelandic cellist Hildur Gu_nadóttir and English pianist Sebastian Lexer, was unfortunately cancelled because of Sylvian's unexpected health problems. Meanwhile, since September 2012, the annual Punkt Festival changed venue, shifting from the Agder Teater (2005-2011), to the new auditorium of the Kilden Teater, under the artistic direction of Brian Eno.

Towards the future

In Norway young people are given great opportunities and support both during their time as students at the Conservatory and afterwards, and "the problem is rather when you get old, and they forget about you",[386] as the Russian-Norwegian filmmaker Pjotr Sapegin ironically stated in Bologna in 2011, at the Italian premiere of *Last Norwegian Troll* featuring live music by Karl Seglem.

The isolation from the rest of Europe that Norway experienced between the 1970s and the 1990s, the numerous inputs that the music scene received from the folk tradition as well as the jazz clubs, the pride of the people, and strong financial support for students - all these elements ensured that plenty of excellent and highly original musicians came out of Norway. It is what Stuart Nicholson defines as "glocalisation", a process that is the reverse of globalisation intended as American hegemony or Americanisation. There is another condition that is essential, however. "Norway is a country strongly projected towards the future, and makes important social and cultural investments", says Emilia Lodigiani of the Italian publishing house Iperborea.[387] "Norwegians know how to invest very well the money from their crude oil. Rather than spending it building skyscrapers like in the Middle East, they try to build a better society. They are almost obsessed by the idea of not taking any resources away from future generations.[388] This worry that Norwegians have is probably rooted in their still vivid memory of the difficulties in their past. Today, thanks to its crude oil reserves, Norway is experiencing a widespread wellbeing, but historically this was a land of poverty and emigration. The discovery of an enormous petroleum reserve in Ekofisk, in the North Sea, changed Norway's destiny whose economic growth had begun with the maritime industry after the second world war. In a few years Norwegians, who until then had been perceived by many as simple fishermen, farmers, Lutheran pastors and explorers, became "blue-eyed emirates".[389] Unlike other countries, however, Norway deposits the surplus wealth generated by its oil income in the Government Pension Fund Global (SPU), which no government policy can draw on. Remembering the great poverty of the past, and conscious that its land can be agriculturally exploited only for a few months in the year, Norway has a strict approach when taking any decision affecting its citizens' future.

Today Norway allocates about 1% of its national budget to cultural spending, wisely distributing it to all the forms of art present in the country. It's difficult to outline how the spending is allocated, since this is constantly evolving. However one can say that aspiring musicians have usually been to their first concert when they are toddlers (children's concerts are a source of national pride and one of the main activities for many professional musicians) thanks especially to Jazzforum's programme Barnejazz Fra A-Å (see Appendix for details on agencies, institutions, grants and initiatives mentioned here). Growing up with an interest in music, kids can join a local band, decide to go to Folkehøgskole for a year, and continue their studies in any Conservatory (the standards are extremely high and the choice is quite plentiful, from Kristiansand in the south, to Tromsø in the north, as well as in the capital). While they are attending the Conservatory, there are various initiatives aiming at identifying the most promising students and offering them, amongst other things, the possibility of performing in the local clubs. There are incentives from institutions at a national level (Jazzintro, Jazz Launch), as well as at an international level (Young Nordic Jazz Comets), the latter making it possible for very young musicians to play at important international festivals. In addition, there are private initiatives by record labels, for example the Grappa Record Company's Debut Artist Award, which in 2012 allowed the young pianist Anja Lauvdal to make her debut with the piano trio Moskus (Fredrik Luhr Dietrichson on double bass, Hans Hulbaekmo on drums) and pick up glowing reviews with Salmesykkel.[390]

"Moskus sound like Norway's latest young cult-status candidates,"[391] John Fordham wrote on the British daily *The Guardian*. This piano trio, clearly inspired by Close Erase (which we mentioned earlier), was not the only act among recent emerging talents. Jazzintro rewarded the quintet Mopti[392] with a grant of 150K Norwegian Kroner and concerts at the Oslo Jazz Festival, Sortland Jazzfestival, at Dølajazz and Barentsjazz, as well as a two-year promotional campaign that saw them playing in most of the national jazz clubs through Norsk jazzforum, and in jazz festivals abroad through the Rikskonsertene (Concerts Norway). The previous year, the Young Nordic Jazz Competition was won by the saxophonist Hanna Paulsberg and her band Concept:[393] the prize allowed her to record her debut album *Waltz for Lilli*[394] (which received international critical acclaim) and play at important festivals such as the Birmingham, London and Cheltenham jazz festivals, as well as taking part at Dublin's prestigious 12 Points Festival for new talents in 2013.

While these might not be future Garbareks, Molværs or Henriksens, they are young talents who have a potential they need to express and are duly supported in their effort of building their own future as professional musicians. In such contexts, the musicians rewarded are usually those who aren't satisfied with simply echoing the style of others, as was the case for Pelbo (Ine Kristine Hoem on vocals, Kristoffer Lo on tuba, and Trond Bersu on drums), a trio whose original style imbued with pop-rock influences has been appreciated all over the world and has revived young audiences' interest in jazz.

When these promising musicians give indications of having even greater talent, they can receive the JazZtipendiat, the most consistent grant assigned for jazz: 250K Norwegian Kroner to conceive and develop a new production with the Trondheim Jazz Orchestra, an award that is made during the festival in Molde. Every year at the festival the winner of the commission is announced just before the previous year's commission is performed. Jazz Launch, a Jazzforum programme in collaboration with Rikskonsertene and the Vestnorsk Jazzsenter, promotes the launch of an artist's career abroad with a significant sum (over 1 million Norwegian Kroner) over a three-year period.

"At the Ministry of Foreign Affairs, the impression is that this initiative has greatly helped the success of some of our most promising jazz musicians on the European jazz scene", says Sverre Lunde. "It's gratifying to see that it was a significant help for Arve Henriksen, who is among the most sought after trumpeters in Europe today. Kristin Asbjornsen, Paal Nilssen-Love, Eldbjørg Raknes and Morten Qvenild have all emerged in Europe thanks to Jazz Launch." [395]

The programme described here operates also thanks to the Europe Jazz Network (EJN), founded by the Italian Filippo Bianchi,[396] which celebrated 25 years of activity in 2012. It doesn't consist of a prize like the Buddy or the Spellemann, but in a range of opportunities with which to promote artists and make them known outside of Norway.

Although we have mentioned initiatives aiming to support young and emerging musicians, there are initiatives in place for musicians of all generations. Until December 2012[397] professional musicians and composers could rely on subsidies for travel expenses relating to concerts abroad, benefit from activities of support, etc., through the Ministry of Foreign Affairs and thanks to the MIC (merged into Music Norway since 2013), while through MEN (also merged into Music Norway since 2013) they could develop projects aimed at exporting their music. In addition to all this, there are the Arts Council Norway (Norsk kulturråd, the leading cultural organisation in the country whose remit also includes jazz), the Fund for Performing Arts (Fond for Utøvende Kunstnere, FFUK), and the Norwegian Composers Fund (Det norske komponistfond, DNKF), in other words a true paradise of incentives that would be unthinkable in many other countries.

Also worthy of mention is the support of the press: *Jazznytt* gives ample space to current music and young artists both in Norway and abroad, and both on paper (with a large magazine, very modern in both content and appearance, published on a bi-monthly basis until 2012 and trimestral since 2013) and on the web (with Jazzinorge.no, in cooperation with Jazzforum and the five regional Jazzsenters).

What Norway has been making available for years is actually an asset for all of Europe. Promoting its musicians abroad with tools unavailable to Italian, Greek or even Dutch musicians (who have recently seen drastic cuts in funds for music and culture) helps all of European jazz to thrive.

It doesn't come as a surprise then that the Norwegian scene still produces so many young talents, and it's reasonable to expect that it will continue doing so. The only worry derives from the process of internationalisation that Norway has undergone in recent years, but the fact that young protagonists of the last 20 years, for example Martin Revheim, have been rewarded and hold important posts at an institutional level is a source of great hope.

NOTES

270. *Jazznyttred*, 07 February 2011.
jazznytt.jazzinorge.no/leder/februar-2011-fjord-og-fjell-og%C2%ABthe-nordic-tone%C2%BB/
271. Øyvind Skarbø in *Jazznytt* 02/2012.
272. *Newborn Thing*, Jazzland Recordings 1998; *Eight Domestic Challenges*, Jazzland Recordings 2001; *Playmachine*, Jazzland Recordings 2004; *Sweet Mental*, Sonnedisk 2006.
273. *Dwell Time*, Jazzland Recordings 2009.
274. Curling Legs 1993, with Bugge Wesseltoft and Jon Christensen.
275. Norwegian association of writers and composers.
276. ECM Records 2001.
277. ECM Records 2004.
278. Mark Corroto, in *Allaboutjazz*, 16 September 2009. http://www.allaboutjazz.com/petter-wettres-a-music-supreme-by-mark-corroto.php?
279. Knut Riisnæs, *Flukt*, Odin 1982.
280. With the album *Knut Riisnæs - Jon Christensen Featuring John Scofield - Palle Danielsson*, Odin 1992.
281. Author's interview with Petter Wettre, 17 July 2012.
282. Born in Sandefjord in 1965, Mathisen played saxophone and clarinet. Once he finished his studies at Berklee in 1988, he decided to stay on in the United States and specifically in New York City, where he became very active, recording dozens of albums with some of the most acclaimed musicians on the circuit.
283. Author's interview with Petter Wettre, 17 July 2012.
284. The Norwegian scene was small and most of the best musicians not only were leaders of their own projects but also played in other groups. This is partly why so many bands folded only to be reborn in another form, with the exception of bands such as Supersilent or Farmers Market.
285. Author's interview with Petter Wettre, 17 July 2012.
286. "The record store I would've like to open when I grew up" according to Luigi Santosuosso, director of *Allaboutjazz Italia*. In *Allaboutjazz Italia*, "Things We Like," June 2012.
287. Marius Neset, *Golden Xplosion!*, Edition Records 2011.
288. John Fordham in *The Guardian*, 21 April 2011.
www.guardian.co.uk/music/2011/apr/21/marius-neset-golden-xplosion-review
289. Ken Micallef in *Modern Drummer*, August 1995.
290. Jon Christensen, *Recordings 1974-1997*, ECM 2004.
291. See www.drummerworld.com/drummers/Jon_Christensen.html
292. Author's interview with Audun Kleive, 17 October 2010
293. Thomas Strønen, *Pohlitz*, Rune Grammofon 2006.
294. www.trommer.no/nyheter-mainmenu-126/konserter/483-julebord-2011-surrealistisk
295. Most of the drummers mentioned participated in the first two events, along with rock legend Per Hillestad (A-Ha), Eyvind Olsen Wahlen (historical drummer of Egil Kapstad's trio), Ernst Wiggo Sandbakk (drum professor at the conservatory of Trondheim) and many others, including several students.
296. Stef in *Free Jazz Blog*, 20 July 2012. freejazz stef.blogspot.it/2012/07/terje-rypdal-odyssey-in-studio-in.html
297. Paolo Vinaccia featuring Terje Rypdal, Ståle Storløkken & Palle Mikkelborg, *Very Much Alive*, Jazzland Records 2010.
298. Terje Rypdal, *Skywards*, ECM 1996.
299. Author's interview with Bjørn Stendahl, 15 October 2010.
300. Jan Bang, ...*And Poppies From Kandahar*, Samadhisound 2010.
301. Eivind Aarset, *Dream Logic*, ECM 2012.
302. Sidsel Endresen & Stian Westerhus, *Didymoi Dreams*, Rune Grammofon 2012.

303. Stian Westerhus, *The Matriarch and the Wrong Kind of Flowers*, Rune Grammofon 2012.

304. Bjørn Fongaard, *Elektrofoni. Works for Micro Intervallic Guitar 1965-1978*, Prisma Records 2010.

305. Author's interview with Martin Revheim, 1 November 2010.

306. Arild Andersen, *Sagn*, Kirkelig Kulturverksted 1990 Norway/ECM 1991 Germany.

307. Arild Andersen, *Arv*, Kirkelig Kulturverksted 1994.

308. Arild Andersen, Paolo Vinaccia and Tommy Smith, *Live At Belleville*, ECM 2008.

309. Rob Adams's interview with Arild Andersen, *The Herald Scotland*, 14 October 2010 www.heraldscotland.com/arts-ents/music-features/meetings-made-in-jazz-heaven-1.1061355

310. Featuring Atle Nymo on sax and clarinets, Eivind Lønning on trumpet, Håvard Wiik on piano, and Håkon Mjåset Johansen on drums.

311. Steinar Raknes, *Stillhouse*, Reckless Records 2012.

312. Tomas Lauvland Pettersen, "Gratulerere Sidsel Endresen 60 år", *MIC Norsk musikkinformasjon*, November 2012.

313. Jazz club owned by the Jazzforum, in the former Victoria Teater on Karl Johans Gate, Oslo.

314. Author's interview with Sidsel Endresen, 31 October 2010.

315. Winner of two Spellemann Prize with the project *Come Shine* (2002, see Chapter 15), and with her own *Circuit Songs* (2007)

316. Born in 1956. See Chapter 5.

317. *Restored, Returned*, ECM Records 2009

318. *Wayfaring Stranger - A Spiritual Songbook*, Universal Music Norway 2006.

319. *The Night Shines Like The Day*, EmArcy, Universal 2009.

320. Stuart Nicholson, "The Nordic tone in jazz - does it really matter?", in *STIM* 26 September 2003 (*www.stim.se*).

321. How can you think of a "Nordic tone" when you listen to Supersilent, Atomic, The Thing or Lasse Marhaug?

322. As of 2012, both *The Ground* and *Changing Places* sold 100,000 copies, and *Being There* has sold 75,000.

323. Luca Vitali in *Allaboutjazz Italia*, 6 May 2010.

324. *Jazzwise* 152 (*www.jazzwisemagazine.com/feature-table-mainmenu-134/11888-helge-lien-trio-beyond-the-nordic-tone*).

325. With the two albums released on Rune Grammofon, *What Took You so Long* and *You Had Me at Goodbye*.

326. Similarly to very early jazz, which like folk music was mostly played to make people dance (as so-called Slått music).

327. Arvid Skancke-Knutsen, "Engelsk suksess for Nils Økland", in *Ballade* 23 November 2000. http://www.ballade.no/sak/engelsk-suksess-for-nils-okland/

328. Already mentioned in Chapter 14.

329. The project saw the collaboration of the two great big band arrangers Geir Lysne and Helge Sunde, and was performed by Ragnhild Furebotten and by jazz musicians of the calibre of Helge Sunde (trombone), Anders Eriksson and Marius Haltli (trumpet), Lars Andreas Haug (tuba), Frode Nymo and Torben Snekkestad (saxophones).

330. Knut Riisnæs, *Flukt*, Odin 1982, track 1 "I Ola Dalom."

331. *Fra 19 Norske Folkeviser* (19 Norwegian Folksongs), which later became Grieg's Op. 66.

332. Rikskonsertene (Concerts Norway) is an organisation established in 1967 by initiative of the Arts Council Norway (*Norsk kulturråd*), with the aim of making live music of high artistic quality accessible to all people in the country.

333. Johan Hauknes, "Interview with Stian Carstensen" in *Jazznytt*, no. 5, 2012.

334. Farmers Market, *Speed/Balkan/Boogie*, Kirkelig kulturverksted 1994.

335. The Bulgarian a cappella female choir known for its interpretation of Bulgarian folk music with modern arrangements, winner of a Grammy in 1990.

336. In 1983 he appeared in the programme "Halvsju," where he played "Dizzy Fingers" on the accordion.

337. Johan Hauknes, "Interview with Stian Carstensen" in *Jazznytt*, no. 5, 2012.

338. Ibid.

339. Vittorio LoConte, "Intervista a Frode Gjerstad" in *Allaboutjazz Italia* 2001-2003. frodegjerstad.com/?page_id=324

340. Author's interview with Paal Nilssen-Love, 31 October 2010.

341. Element, Element, Turn Left 1996.

342. Element, Shaman, BP 1998.

343. Atomic, Feet Music, Jazzland 2001.

344. Including the album that Håkon Kornstad, while involved with Wibutee and Element, released with Paal Nilssen-Love and Mats Eilertsen, Space Available (Jazzland Recordings 2000), as well as Shining's Sweet Shanghai Devil (Jazzland Recordings 2002), and Bjørnar Andresen's Samsa'ra (Jazzland Recordings 2002).

345. Author's interview with Jan Ole Otnæs, 15 October 2010.

346. Dan Quelette in Downbeat, 2002

347. Liner notes to the DVD Nor Noise by Tom Hovinbøle, July 2004.
http://pastichefilms.com/films/nor-noise/

348. The city which in the 1970s attracted listeners from all over Norway, who flocked in to hear performances by figures who had revolutionised contemporary music (La Monte Young, John Cale, Tony Conrad and Terry Riley), and in the late 1970s had seen the birth of the first jazz conservatory in the country.

349. The CD includes original material by Norwegian artists such as Duo Kanel, Domestic Purpose, Jazzkammer, Ryfylke, Fe-Mail, Tore Honoré Bøe, Crazy River, Kobi, Anders Gjerde, O. Melby and the Norwegian Noise Orchestra.

350. From the text of Tom Hovinbøle's lecture held at the Bergen Støyfest in Utmark/Landmark.
http://pastichefilms.com/films/nor-noise/nn-lecture/

351. See Chapters 3, 4 and 7.

352. Author's interview with Arve Henriksen, 27 October 2008.

353. See Chapter 17.

354. Maurizio Zerbo, "Eternal Rhythm e il '68 pan-etnico di Don Cherry", Allaboutjazz Italia, 6 June 2011.

355. Harold Budd and Brian Eno with Daniel Lanois, The Pearl, EG 1984.

356. Jon Hassell and Brian Eno, Fourth World, Vol. 1: Possible Musics, EG 1980.

357. Paul Olsonn, "Nils Petter Molvær: Skeletons, Samples and Fish Fillets", Allaboutjazz, 30 August 2010.
www.allaboutjazz.com/php/article.php?id=23039#.UDDW7N3N81k

358. Press notes for Arve Henriksen, Sakuteiki, Rune Grammofon 2001.

359. Arve Henriksen, Chiaroscuro, Rune Grammofon 2004.

360. Author's interview with Jon Hassell, 5 September 2010.

361. Arve Henriksen, Strjon, Rune Grammofon 2007.

362. Arve Henriksen, Cartography, ECM 2008.

363. Arve Henriksen, Solidification (7LP), Rune Grammofon 2012.

364. A Danish collective founded by the drummer Kresten Osgood and a few friends and colleagues. It includes the best musicians of the Danish free jazz scene, with a few notable exceptions like the Italian Francesco Bigoni and the Norwegian Gunnar Halle. www.ilkmusic.com

365. Stian Omenås, Klangkammer 1 (NORCD 2012), Stian Around a Hill, Alle Skal Få, (AIM Records 2011) and Parallax, Krutthuset (Pling Music 2012).

366. Author's interview with Christian Wallumrød, 16 November 2009.

367. Represented well in the documentary Ung norsk jazz (1991):
www.youtube.com/watch?v=I9EsTzBxITg&feature=share

368. Airamero, Airamero, Odin 1993 (Johannes Eick on double bass, Per Oddvar Johansen on drums, Trygve Seim on soprano and tenor sax, Christian Wallumrød on piano).

369. One of the leading bands of the club Blå. See Chapter 18.

370. Close Erase, Close Erase, NORCD 1995.

371. Plastic Strip Press CD720 2010, 5-CD box/20 pp. booklet.

372. Luca Vitali, "Intervista con Christian Wallumrød" in Allaboutjazz Italia, 16 November 2009.

373. A nucleus of artists who regularly play together and invite musicians from different genres, which over time has become a sort of platform for improvisation research.

374. Dans les arbres, *Dans les arbres*, ECM Records 2008.
375. Christian Wallumrød Ensemble, *Outstairs*, ECM 2013.
376. Author's interview with Jan Bang, in *InSound*, no. 51, 2010.
377. One of the most important labels of the techno scene, founded in Ghent, Belgium.
378. See Chapters 16 and 17.
379. Author's interview with Jan Bang, in *InSound*, no. 51, 2010.
380. As Erik Honoré specified in a conversation with the author in 2015: "For the rest of the 1990s Jan and I worked separately, apart from a few remixes. I was working more in the studio making records that were more and more based on 'deconstructing' the band and rebuilding a sound from my samples of them, rather than just recording and mixing a performance. That development reached its peak on the album *Lucia* by Velvet Belly which I co-wrote and produced (and won a Norwegian Grammy for) in 1997, where all the instruments had been through my sampler and treatment devices".
381. Jan Bang in *Jazznytt*, no. 4, 2010.
382. Author's interview with Jon Hassell, 5 September 2010.
383. *Died in The Wool/Manafon Variations*, Samadhisound 2011.
384. A classic ambient work by David Sylvian and Holger Czukay dating back to 1988.
385. David Sylvian, promotional note for the Implausible Beauty Tour 2012.
386. Author's interview with Pjotr Sapegin, 19 March 2011.
387. This Milan-based publishing house specialises in northern European literature.
388. Gabriele Catania, Linkiesta, 07/08/2011. *www.linkiesta.it/signore-e-signori-ecco-voi-la-norvegia*
389. Ibid.
390. Moskus, *Salmesikkel*, Hubro 2012.
391. *www.guardian.co.uk/music/2012/nov/08/moskus-salmesykkel-review*
392. Christian Meaas Svendsen on double bass, Andreas Wildhagen on drums, David Aleksander Sjølie on guitar, Kristoffer Eikrem on trumpet, and Harald Lassen on sax.
393. Trygve Fiske on double bass, Hans Hulbækmo on drums, Oscar Grönberg on piano.
394. Hanna Paulsberg Concept, *Waltz For Lilli*, Øra Fonogram 2012.
395. Interview with Senior Advisor of the Ministry of Foreign Affairs Sverre Lunde, on *Jazzinorge.no*.
396. Former director of the monthly *Musica Jazz*.
397. 1 January 2013, MIC (Music Information Centre) and MEN (Music Export Norway) were merged into Music Norway. Before the launch of Music Norway there was an institutional void that threatened the survival of the most important on-line music magazine, (*www.ballade.no*), until then under the direction of MIC. Fortunately the archives remained on line, and the website was rescued by the Ballade association (headed by Chairman of the Board Bente Leiknes Thorsen).

APPENDIX

NORSK JAZZFORUM - *jazzforum.jazzinorge.no*

Norsk jazzforum (the Norwegian jazz forum) is a non-profit organisation which aims at connecting the Norwegian jazz scene. It aims to work for the benefit of Norwegian jazz, culturally and artistically. It was founded in 1997 from the merger of the earlier Norsk Jazzforbund (established in 1953) and the Foreningen Norske Jazzmusikere (Association of Norwegian Jazz established 1979) and Den Norske jazzscene (The Norwegian jazzscene established 1991). Norsk jazzforum's primary aim is to spread jazz to the widest possible audience in Norway, speaking for Norwegian jazz nationally and internationally, as well as working for increased funding for Norwegian jazz. Its current (2014) membership consists of approximately 23 jazz festivals, 75 jazz clubs, 120 big bands, 590 professional musicians and 130 jazz students. In addition to the national organisation Norsk jazzforum in Oslo, there are 5 regional jazz centres in Norway: the Østnorsk jazzsenter (Oslo), Sørnorsk jazzsenter (Arendal), Vestnorsk jazzsenter (Bergen), Midtnorsk jazzsenter (Trondheim) and Nordnorsk jazzsenter (Bodø). The organisation operates on public funding, which goes straight to the Norwegian jazz scene in various forms of support for musicians, promoters and big bands. As well as extensive national touring, the new generation of Norwegian jazz musicians is increasingly in demand from international international clubs and festivals, and Norsk jazzforum funding is often vital for the realisation of a tour. Norsk jazzforum also arranges various projects for and with its members, on their own or in co-operation with other institutions. In addition, every two years the Norsk jazzforum, in collaboration with the Ministry of Foreign Affairs, makes a 3-CD compilation with a selection of the best music on the circuit, entitled *JazzCD.no*. The Norsk jazzforum organises three prizes: the Buddy Prize - best musician (as instrumentalist and/or innovator); Årets jazzklubb - jazz club of the year; and Storbandprisen, to the person, big band or venue that has made the greatest contribution to the Norwegian big band scene. The Norsk jazzforum also works actively to involve women musicians, and with jazzAKKS in collaboration with AKKSNorge it aims to stimulate the interest in jazz in children and adolescents. In 2006 a national jazz scene was finally established in Oslo on government funding. The National Jazz Scene is a place of meeting for the entire jazz milieu with extended effects not only in Oslo but nationwide. It aims at presenting the best jazz within all styles from both Norway and abroad.

JAZZNYTT - *jazznytt.jazzinorge.no*

The only Norwegian jazz magazine, it was founded by the Norwegian Jazz Federation in 1960. The current Editor is Rob Young who replaced Jan Granlie (2002-2013). Former Editors include Petter Pettersson, Olav Angell, Eivind Solberg, Bjørn Stendahl, Per Husby, Pål Gjersum, Lars Mossefinn, Geir Dahle, Rune Klakegg, Carl Morten Iversen, and Torstein Ellingsen.

JAZZ INTRO - *jazzforum.jazzinorge.no/jazzintro* - *jazzforum.jazzinorge.no/jazzintroturne*
2014 - Monkey Plot (Christian Skår Winther - guitar, Magnus Skavhaug Nergaard - double bass, and Jan Martin Gismervik - drums).

2012 - Mopti (Christian Meaas Svendsen on double bass, Andreas Wildhagen on drums, David Aleksander Sjølie on guitar, Kristoffer Eikrem on trumpet, and Harald Lassen on sax).

2010 - Ferner/Juliusson

2008 - Albatrosh

2006 - Puma

2004 - In the Country

2002 - Solid!

2000 - Ra 1998 - Urban Connection

JAZZ LAUNCH - *jazzforum.jazzinorge.no/norwegian-jazz-launch*
An annual grant for young composers and performers established in 2007 by Sparebank 1 SMN in cooperation with Midtnorsk jazzsenter and Molde International Jazz Festival for Trondheim Jazz Orchestra.The total value of the grant is around NOK 650.000. The musician/band who receives this grant can decide which musicians they want to be their version of Trondheim Jazz Orchestra (TJO) for the project. The project is overseen by Bjørn Willadsen, general manager of the Midtnorsk Jazzsenter and of the Trondheim Jazz Orchestra.The grant is awarded by a jury and announced during the Molde Jazz International Festival and the the jazZtipendiat concert is premiered at Moldejazz the following year. Recent recepients include:

2014 - Espen Reinertsen

2013 - Kristoffer Lo

2012 - Albatrosh(Eyolf Dale, André Roligheten)

2011 - Marius Neset

2010 - Stian Westerhus

2009 - Magic Pocket (Daniel Herskedal, Hayden Powell, Eirik Johannesen)

2008 - Kim Myhr

2007 - Kobert(Ingrid Lode, Daniel Formo, Erik Nylander).

YOUNG NORDIC JAZZ COMET - *www.ynjc.dk/taxonomy/term/28*
A competition from 2000 to 2011, since 2012 it has become a regular showcase for young Nordic jazz talent. The aim is to bring attention to these young musicians, giving them an opportunity to make a name for themselves abroad (members of the Young Nordic Jazz Comets are the jazz forums of Denmark, the Faroe Islands, Iceland, Norway, Sweden and the Åland Islands).

The winners of the competition:

2011 - Hanna Paulsberg Concept (Norway),

2010 - Isabel Sörling Group (Sweden),

2009 - The Ingimar Andersen Quartet (Iceland),

2009 - PELbO (Norway),

2008 - K Trio (Iceland)

2007 - Kristian Brink Quartet (Sweden), 2006 - Sun Trio (Finland),

2005 - JazzKamikaze (Denmark)

2004 - Kvalda (Finland),

2003 - Megatsunami (Norway),

2002 - Ilmiliekki Quartet (Finland),

2001 - Motif (Norway),

2000 - Fuchsia (Denmark),

2000 - Joona Toivanen Trio (Finland).

JAZZZTIPENDIAT

An annual grant for young composers and performers established in 2007 by Sparebank 1 SMN in cooperation with Midtnorsk jazzsenter and Molde International Jazz Festival for Trondheim Jazz Orchestra. The total value of the grant is around NOK 650.000. The musician/band who receives this grant can decide which musicians they want to be their version of Trondheim Jazz Orchestra (TJO) for the project. The project is overseen by Bjørn Willadsen, general manager of the Midtnorsk Jazzsenter and of the Trondheim Jazz Orchestra.The grant is awarded by a jury and announced during the Molde Jazz International Festival and the jazZtipendiat concert is premiered at Moldejazz the following year. Recent recepients include:

2014 - Espen Reinertsen

2013 - Kristoffer Lo

2012 - Albatrosh(Eyolf Dale, André Roligheten)

2011 - Marius Neset

2010 - Stian Westerhus

2009 - Magic Pocket (Daniel Herskedal, Hayden Powell, Eirik Johannesen)

2008 - Kim Myhr

2007 – Kobert (Ingrid Lode, Daniel Formo, Erik Nylander)

THE SPELLEMANN PRIZE - www.spellemann.no

The Spellemann is the Norwegian equivalent of the Grammy, which was established by the International Federation of the Phonographic Industry (IFPI) in 1973. The prizes have been assigned each year since. Currently there are 17 genre categories and 3 writer categories

(Contemporary Composer, Pop Composer, Lyricist), some of which have been added only recently. The Christiania Jazzband was the first to win in the Jazz category in 1973. A list of more recent winners includes:

2014 - Marius Neset and Trondheim Jazz Orchestra

2013 - Karin Krog & John Surman

2012 - Sidsel Endresen & Stian Westerhus

2011 - Ola Kvernberg

2010 - Elephant9

2009 - Tord Gustavsen Ensemble

2008 - Helge Lien Trio

2007 - Petter Wettre

2006 - Atomic

2005 - Hans Mathisen

2004 - Solveig Slettahjell

2003 - Atomic

2002 - Come Shine

2001 - Urban Connection

2000 - Petter Wettre & Per Oddvar Johansen

Many musicians mentioned in the text have won in the Open Class category: Nils Petter Molvær three times (1997, 2000, 2005), Bugge Wesseltoft once on his own in 1996 and twice with Sidsel Endresen (1998 and 2002), who had in turn been the recipient of it in 1981 and 1984 with Jon Eberson, while a special prize was given to Jan Garbarek in 1978.

MUSIC FUNDING

Norsk Komponistforening - *www.komponist.no/stotteordninger*

The Norsk Komponistforening (Norwegian Society of Composers) offers support to its members for equipment, concerts, recording and documentation of works, which can be obtained by submitting a request according to a schedule posted online.

Generelle støtteordninger (General Endowments).

Offers a long list of programmes for activities held in Norway on *www.legatsiden.no*

Fond for utøvende kunstnere (Fund for Performing Artists) - *www.ffuk.no*

It finances recordings in Norway by musicians residing and working in Norway.

Fond for lyd og bilde - *kulturradet.no/flb*

(The Fund for Sound and Visuals) promotes the production and distribution of audio and video recordings. Financed by the State, it compensates authors and copyright holders for lawful copies, use and private use of works.

Music Norway - *musicnorway.no*
Funded by the Norwegian Ministry of Culture, Music Norway became operational in January 2013, replacing MIC (Music Information Centre) and MEN (Music Export Norway). The core of the new organisation are 12 members of staff with long and distinguished careers at MIC and MEN. It receives an annual allocation of 17 million NOK from the Ministry, and administers an additional 10 million NOK of grants for the various support programmes. The organisation has headquarters in Oslo and branch offices in Berlin and London, and provides promotion and information to all Norwegian artists. It also offers support to Norwegian professional musicians for travel expenses relating to concerts, tours or festivals abroad.

The **Kulturrådets støtteordninger** (Arts Council) is the major government agency for the funding of all cultural projects, music included. *kulturradet.no*

The **Musikkfondene** includes the Norske Komponistfond (Norwegian Composers' Fund), Komponistenes Vederlagsfond (Composers' Compensation Fund), Norsk Musikkfond (Norwegian Music Fund) and Tekstforfatterfondet (Lyricists' Fund). It finances works by Norwegian composers and lyricists. *www.musikkfondene.no*

EUROPE JAZZ NETWORK (EJN) / 12POINTS!
The Europe Jazz Network (EJN) is a European network established in 1987. This organisation promotes the collaboration between festivals through the sharing of tours and projects. Established in Italy thanks to Filippo Bianchi (who was artistic director of the Ravenna Jazz Festival and the Reggio Emilia Jazz Festival for many years) and the support of the European Community, it has over a hundred members (festivals, promoters, jazz clubs, etc.) in 31 countries. In 2012, during the annual jazz showcase Jazzahead! in Bremen, to celebrate its 25th anniversary EJN awarded a prize to the Irish festival 12 points for its "adventurous programming." 12 Points is a project conceived and organised by the Dublin based company Improvised Music, currently directed by Kenneth Killeen, who replaced Gerry Godley in 2014. Following a unique and visionary concept, each year it selects and presents 12 young bands (or solo artists) from 12 different European countries who have not gained any visibility outside of their own country.
http://www.europejazz.net/
http://www.12points.ie/

Acknowledgments - I wish to thank: Claudio Chianura, for having set the wheel in motion by proposing that I write this text, and then seeing the Italian edition through with great dedication, honesty and competence, constantly raising the stakes despite the enormous difficulties in the publishing market; Fiona Talkington, for editing this English edition with passion, dedication and skill; Melinda Mele, for translating the text with care and expertise; Else L'Orange (Royal Norwegian Embassy in Rome) and Sverre Lunde (Norwegian Ministry of Foreign Affairs) for their friendship and for having believed in my work; the Royal Norwegian Embassy in Rome and all those who have made it possible for me to attend festivals all over Norway; the Norwegian Ministry of Foreign Affairs, Øyvind Skjerven Larsen and all of the Norsk jazzforum for having made this English edition possible; and Jan Granlie and Paolo Fresu for their beautiful and heartfelt words which introduce the book. Thank you to Daniele Franchi for his precious technical work on the colour photograph section.

Working on this book was an intense experience, which put me in touch with great musicians and, more importantly, extraordinary people. As I met the protagonists of this book in coffee shops, on Skype, in parks, or in their homes, I was always made to feel at ease, and never did I encounter any trace of reticence, disinterest, or conceit. On the contrary, I found generous and humble people, stars of Scandinavian and international jazz who opened up to me with enthusiasm and passion. I am very grateful to all those whose interviews and quotations appear in this book for sharing with me some truly wonderful and authentic moments.

A special thanks goes to Bo Gronningsaeter (and I wish he were still with us, so that I could do it in person), who with Lars Mossefinn gave me the opportunity to really get to know such a rich music scene. Thank you to Jazz in a Nutshell. I received precious and special help from Martin Revheim, Lars Mørch Finborud, Finn J. Kramer-Johansen and Tore Flesjø. I'm especially grateful to Per Husby for his photographs and his precious help in retrieving the historical images contained here. I would like to express my gratitude to all of the Norsk Jazzarkiv and to Wivi-Ann and Christina, Randi Hultin's daughters; to Terje Mosnes, Svein Christiansen, Roger Engvik, Rune Mortensen, Per Rønnevig, Knut Strand, Kaare Thomsen, Elmly Production, Gustav P. Jensen, CF-Wesenberg, Bjørn Gundersen, Arthur Sand, Arne Schanche Andresen, Arne Ove Bergo, Annette Jackbo, Anne Lise Flavik, Andrzej Tyszko, Pål Rødhal, Christian Eggen, Martin Horntveth, Paal Nilssen-Love, Helge Norbakken, Carsten Aniksdal, Jarle Førde, Karl Seglem, Jon Balke, Arve Henriksen, Per Oddvar Johansen, *Jazznytt*, *Dagbladet* and *Dagsavisen*, Gianni Gherardi, Jenny Servino and Bologna's Museo della Musica for having made the photographic sections of this book possible.

My gratitude goes to all the musicians, composers, colleagues and friends who, perhaps unwittingly, have helped me shed light on and make sense of the less obvious aspects of what I was writing about. To Raffaele Iaquinta and Enrico Merlin for their help on the section on the Lydian Chromatic Concept, to Roger Bergner for introducing me to Emanon, to Michael Dawson and Ken Micallef for the interview with Jon Christensen. To Melanie Arends, Andreas R. Meland, Marie Cécile Ferré and all those who kept on sending me music even if they knew I didn't have time to review it since I was so busy writing this book! I'm grateful to Jon Rognlien, Kristian Skarbrevik and all those whom I've talked to over these years about jazz and about the Norwegian people. I wish to thank Massimo Simonini, Gianni and Serena Baravelli, Marina Pugliano, Linda Skipnes Strand, Aslak Oppebøen, Tomas Lauvland Pettersen, Gabor Simon and Ernst Wiggo Sandbakk, all for different (but excellent) reasons. And Sidsel Endresen, Jon Balke, Christian Wallumrød, Jan Bang and Arve Henriksen for having welcomed me, taken me under their wing, and offered me friendship and respect, making it all simpler and even more stimulating, but also for their extraordinary musical vision, which has constantly fuelled my interest in the Norwegian scene. Finally, I'm especially grateful to Roberta for having been my third eye and my wise counsellor in times of uncertainty, and for having contributed, with the patience of a Zen monk, to the writing and double-checking of every single word and note in this book.

A mio padre

To my father

Printed in Italy
June 2015

da Rubbettino print
88049 Soveria Mannelli (Catanzaro)
www.rubbettinoprint.it